AF597839

TABLE OF CONTENTS

REINVENTING STRATEGIC INNOVATION

Create Deep Change

Kees Dorst
Rodger Watson
Barbara Doran
&
Contributing authors

BISPUBLISHERS

BIS Publishers
Timorplein 46
1094 CC Amsterdam
The Netherlands
bis@bispublishers.com
www.bispublishers.com

ISBN 978 90 636 9964 2
Copyright © 2025 Kees Dorst, Rodger Watson, Barbara Doran and contributing authors, and BIS Publishers.

Art: Cecilia Warren
Book design: Aphrodite Delaguiado
Editors: Rodger Watson, Kees Dorst, Barbara Doran

All rights reserved. No part of this publication may be reproduced or transmitted in any form or by any means, electronic or mechanical, including photocopy, recording or any information storage and retrieval system, without permission in writing from the copyright owners. Every reasonable attempt has been made to identify owners of copyright. Any errors or omissions brought to the publisher's attention will be corrected in subsequent editions.

PROLOGUE

STOP FIXING THINGS!

CLEANSING THE DOORS OF PERCEPTION

The writer and anthropologist Amitav Ghosh has famously said that the climate crisis is a 'crisis of imagination': if we can't imagine the impact of climate change there is no real incentive to act. That is what is holding us back.

These are wise words, but we would go a step further and say that this is not just a crisis of imagination, but a crisis of perception. The very world we see around us and take for real, isn't - what we see is just the surface. What is happening on the surface is the result of complex underlying processes. If we want to act wisely, we need to PUNCTURE the bubble of superficial 'reality', go beyond the symptoms and dig deeply to discover the underlying relationships and dynamics that actually matter. That is Reality with a big 'R'. (We will see later (in §4.1) that this a pragmatist definition of reality: 'real' is what you need to see and understand in order to engage with the world productively, to shape effective actions).

This means that a lot of what we see on the surface of the world is NOT REAL. How can that be?

This is a pattern that we will see time and time again, in this book. Examples will be drawn from right across society, from the private, not for profit and public services.

If we are not able to go beneath the surface to understand what a problem is actually about, we are powerless to resolve it. The underlying processes are undeniable and real, but we have the tendency to ignore them, and 'fix' the problem by reacting to whatever shows itself on the surface. In doing so we keep dealing with problems on a case-by-case basis, even against evidence that this strategy isn't working; the problem patterns keep repeating because the underlying causes are never touched. In this book we will map out a way to deal with the deeper reality, and how to create a space for deep change in our organizations and societies.

But first, we need to stop fixing things.

To quote William Blake (1790):

'If the doors of perception were cleansed every thing would appear to man as it is, Infinite. For man has closed himself up, till he sees all things thro' narrow chinks of his cavern.'

We have known this for a long time, but it is now more than ever the time to act on it. This book shows HOW.

An example:

A water company had an issue with people not paying their bills. It responded to this reality in the way all amenities companies do: if people don't pay their bills they get sent a reminder, and then another one. The scenario then escalates to sending letters with ever increasing fines, to the point of sending a debt collector - which almost never resulted in retrieving the money people owed. Ultimately, the customer would be disconnected from the water supply. On face value, this is a reasonable course of action.

That is, until the water company went deeper into the matter and realized that from the perspective of the customer, the water bill is probably the last one you don't pay: water is vital to life. So if you can't pay for water, you must be defaulting on lots of other bills too, and be in real trouble. This set them on the path of thinking from the lifeworld of the people and the communities they are servicing. They were shocked, and rightly so.

They also realized that the lifeworld problem was bigger than just the water company, and organized a 'vulnerability round-table' with other amenities companies (electricity, gas), banks, insurance companies and communication companies, about how people experiencing hardship can be supported rather than punished. The vulnerability round-table led to the founding of Thriving Communities Australia, a not for profit organization that enables collaboration across multiple sectors including business, academia, government, NGO's and people with lived experience of vulnerability. In the end, engaging with this deeper reality has not only helped these amenities to stop adding to the hardship of people, but it also resulted in more bills being paid. Being a good corporate citizen who seeks to understand the lifeworld of their customers, is not only good for their customers, it is good for business.

MOVING BEYOND INNOVATION THEATRE

One of the failure modes in efforts to tackle deep problems is that these problems tend to show up in the context of our organizations. So naturally, we try to create a response from the organization as it is, by innovating on that level, through a 're-organization'. But in this case, innovation as we know it falls short.

What do we mean by 'innovation' in an organization? The word is heavily overused, on the verge of meaninglessness. This leads a confusion between fundamentally different kinds of innovation. Innovation literature points to a golden ratio of innovation investment across a portfolio comprising of three distinct innovation modes; 70% towards optimizing, 20% towards expanding, and 10% towards transforming (Nagji & Tuff, 2012) (more in §2.7).

There is a fundamental difference between the practices, methods and tools needed for optimization, expansion and transforming, but often these three types of innovation are conflated. What we often see is that the language around innovation in an organization is couched in terms of missions, visions and radical shifts in thinking, but the tools and techniques applied are really the 'safe' ones that can only really be expected to lead to optimization.

Or, as the manager of the innovation unit at a major bank put it to us: *'what we are doing here is merely **'Innovation Theatre''***.

This pretense of transformational innovation without intending to actually change can become an obvious lie in an organization. This leads to cynicism, mistrust and 'innovation fatigue': people become despondent, they just lose faith that anything can ever change at all. This introduces significant risk to the organization.

In a complex and changing environment the organization will not last long if it is stuck like this, let alone be in a position to navigate complex environments and realize strategic innovation. The use of the wrong innovation strategies and tools can also be the result of an honest misdiagnosis of a problem situation – underestimating the depth of the issues at play, and therefore starting out with the wrong methods and practices. Any organization that finds itself desperately stretched in staff and finances might seek to 'fix' this by creating more efficiency in their processes. This will lead to much bigger problems down the line, as the fundamental issues are not touched.

In the case of the huge societal challenges ('transitions', see §4.4) we are talking about in this book, the problems have deep roots. As organizations, we need an extra shot of what Nagji and Tuff have characterized as their '10%' transformational innovation. In fact, that may need to be 20-30% or even more when a sector is to reach tipping point and actually on the verge of transitioning to a new way of working.

In this book we will see that in order to do this we require a different kind of logic than is often prevalent in organizations. Renowned strategic management scholar Gary Hamel (1998) points to what he calls *'strategy development's "dirty little secret"; that within strategy development, there actually is no articulation of a creative process that can lead to new strategies'*. These so-called innovation strategies claim to be grounded in solid analysis, every step of the way... but... how can that work? If organizations only use reductive and analytical ways of thinking, they are simply not capable of creating new responses to their challenges.

In Chapters 1-2 we will outline the type of thinking that is needed to move beyond innovation as we know it: the creative intelligence, logic, practices and structures to support this new type of Strategic Innovation.

In Chapter 3 we explore 21 case studies, drawn from our own community of practice, to illustrate the new strategic innovation in action. We will see in chapters 4 and 5 how we can move beyond the 'Innovation Theatre' that inhibits the real change from happening.

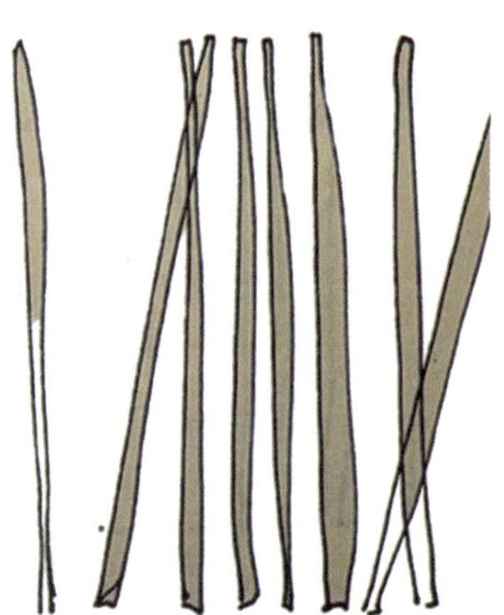

IT IS NOT WHAT YOU THINK, BUT HOW YOU THINK

We realize that the above may not paint a particularly cheerful picture of the situation we find ourselves in. We are trapped in a 'Comedy of Errors' and have to find a new way out... (or actually, perhaps not a Comedy of Errors but a Greek Tragedy, in which humans are whacked about by forces they cannot understand - and that they will only understand towards the end when, in the catharsis, it is all too late).

But why is it so hard to create progress in the face of the big challenges we face?

Our answer would be that the nature of the challenges we are dealing with has shifted, that there is fundamental mismatch between our normal ways of approaching problems and the new very open, complex, dynamic and networked challenges facing us today. What trips us up is that on the surface, the world looks pretty much the same, but the underlying dynamic has changed fundamentally. Problems are not what they used to be, and we are finding out the hard way that Business-As-Usual doesn't work anymore. Because the world has become more connected, it needs to be approached in a completely different way; Normal cause-and-effect reasoning (the idea that 'one thing' leads to 'another') that is the basis of normal problem solving goes out the window in this brave new networked world. Doing 'one thing' sets a network of reactions in motion that is hard to grasp and to predict. If you try to resolve such open, complex, dynamic and networked problems by normal everyday problem solving you end up confused, running around in circles, and just getting more and more stuck - as we see in the Care Futures example (§3.1).

When problems move from being very complicated to truly complex, our ways of addressing them should shift accordingly. In really complex systems newness comes from the emergence of order (rather than goal-directed creation), change is achieved through influencing the system (rather than implementation of a plan to 'solve the problem') and anew state of relative stability can be created through creating vitality (rather than striving for an immutable, stable structure).

There are no solutions.

A key misdiagnosis we should step away from is the idea that these problem situations can be resolved through acquiring more knowledge (and that when you know everything about a problem, it magically is 'solved'). In this case, more research is NOT needed. This may sound odd, coming from academics, but the big deep issues we are facing are problems of practice, of how we think and approach issues, not a knowledge problem. Looking at the Care Futures Lab (§3.1): we already know about the troubles that the Care sector is in. We need to find a way to shift the issues so that new paths to progress open up, and practices from many disciplines can be harnessed to move to impact. What we don't need is more research into the details of what is wrong with the current system. That is obvious; the current system was created in a completely different world, with different realities and assumptions. No one would create the Care sector as it is now. It is simply not fit-for-purpose and needs a complete re-imagining.

The good news is: this CAN be done, as we will demonstrate this time and time again in this book. We already have the practices we need, but they need to be freed up from their disciplinary silos and be used in a new transdisciplinary way (§1.2).

The bad news is: basically, we are the problem. We need to fundamentally change the way we think, and that is quite a journey. In this book we are taken along by remarkable people from across many sectors that have been on this journey with us. Central in this book are their stories, the case studies of their projects. What they show, as the next generation of strategic innovation leaders, adds up to the change we need.

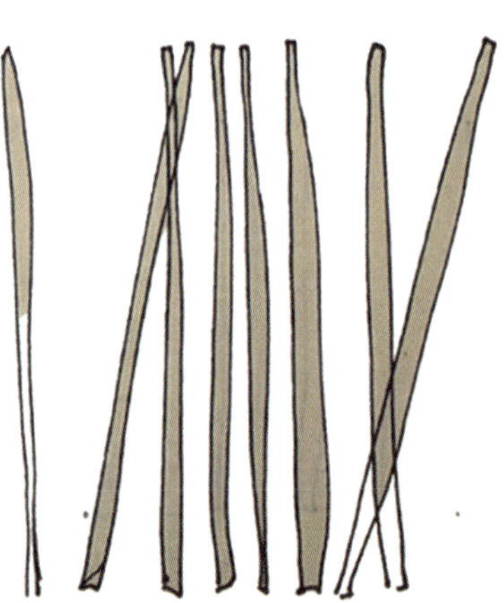

THE ANATOMY OF THIS BOOK.

This book is written for thoughtful, reflective practitioners that are ready for these big and deep challenges. We hope it can be the start of your journey towards new thinking and doing, or, if you count yourself as already part of the change we need, this can help you to also develop new practices as a Strategic Innovator and Game Changer.

This book presents the elements that we found useful, and shows some of the dynamics that need to be created to bring them together. Central in this book are cases by seasoned practitioners showing how this works, in a huge diversity of sectors right across society - we will see examples from (in alphabetical order): Advertising, Care, Corrective services, Education, Insurance, Leadership development, Regional transformation, Service design, Social enterprise, Strategic consultancy, Transport infrastructure, and much more sprinkled through the chapters. This is important, because practice leads at every step of the way. And real-life impact is the only thing that counts.

The structure of the book is quite open, to do justice to the fact that everybody will have to create their own journey through this space. We hope to mirror the complexity and show the richness of what becomes possible when you engage deeply with the challenge of deep change in this way. This book is not a cookbook centered around one model (it is more like a smorgasbord, or a tapas menu), and it is open-ended, propositional.

It is the culmination of an almost 20-year body of work. Some elements of his story have been published along the way by these authors in academic books (Design Expertise [2008], Frame Innovation [2015], Deep Change [2025]) and in practice-oriented books like Designing for the Common Good [2016], Notes on Design [2017] and Creative Reboot [2021]. The thinking has also been brought together in the curriculum of a transdisciplinary masters for innovative professionals (see §5.3).

As this is not an academic treatise, we have kept the theory elements short (but hopefully clear), taking just two pages per concept/ theory - for those who like to dig deeper, the references will lead to much more background on all of these, in books and papers. The Chapter 3 case studies that bring it all together are the absolute core of this book. They are a fountain of inspiration in themselves. But the models and theory are the vital connective tissue that empower the reader to create their own strategic innovation practice.

Seeing

Chapter 1: Embracing Creative Intelligence

Thinking

Chapter 2: Towards Next Generation Strategic Innovation

Doing

Chapter 3: Pioneers of a New Practice

Delivering

Chapter 4: Creating Deep Change; Strategic Innovation Journeys

Leading

Chapter 5: Next Generation Strategic Innovation Leaders

Figure 0.1 The anatomy of the book

To help with navigation, we have used different styles to highlight the different layers of text:

- The theory chapters are kept very brief; most concepts and models are introduced in just two pages, to allow the reader to navigate the book in their own way.
- The tools/exercises and workshops to explore and apply these concepts and models are given space at the end of their chapter.
- The theory, methods, tools and cases in this book are roughly structured along the categories in figure 0.1.

To return to the journey metaphor: through its open structure, the book furnishes a landscape of elements for the reader to make sense of, be attracted by, connect in new ways, make your own, and add to. In doing so, we are laying down a landscape while walking through it. Our motivation to publish this book now is because we see that this next generation of strategic innovation is urgently needed. Thank you for being on the journey with us.

Sydney, Eora Nation

Kees Dorst
Rodger Watson
Barbara Doran
& fellow travelers

CHAPTER 1

EMBRACING CREATIVE INTELLIGENCE

1.1

SEEING DIFFERENTLY

We are only human. We come to a new situation with what we have: our knowledge, skills, life experience and wisdom.

If a new situation is very different from what we know, we can use metaphorical thinking ('this is like that') to make sense of it, somehow. This means we are never a blank slate: we always perceive even a completely new situation in a particular way. In the terms that we will use in this book: we ALWAYS have a 'frame'.

That is a fact a life. This may get problematic when we are then using our thoughts to shape action in this new context. And a real problem, the kind of problematic situations we talk about here in this book, ALWAYS requires a shift away from the current way of thinking that led it to be formulated in a certain manner.

To move forward, we need to change the perception of the problem situation.

We will see that time and time again in this book; the case examples and the central case studies in chapter 3 and 4 can even be characterized in this manner:

People that did not pay their amenities bills in time were sent reminders for ever increasing amounts

... UNTIL...

the Water Company realized that if people in such financial strife cannot afford the basic amenities they need help, not prosecution (see the Prologue).

Alcohol-related violence in an entertainment district was suppressed through tough 'Law and Order' measures

... UNTIL...

seeing the situation through the lens of a 'music festival' led to the creation of an environment that supports a vibrant nightlife (see §4.2).

The professional systems to support health and wellbeing were struggling to cope with the demand for services

... UNTIL...

citizens organized themselves to support the people in need of care in their neighborhood (see §3.1).

We need to always and systematically question the assumptions behind the current ways of thinking that have led to the problem being formulated in the way that it is now. This may seem an extra and unnecessary step ('why don't we just get on with it?'), but it is crucial if we want to find new ways and create progress. Furthermore, if they remain unquestioned, these assumptions are the major source of risk for the intervention we come up with.

Much of this book will be dedicated to showing processes that help us delve under the surface of the problem-situation-as-it-presents-itself and rigorously question what we find there.

This is not easy, and also not always a very comfortable process: changing our way of seeing requires some force because we are creatures of habit. This personal reluctance seems to become amplified in organizations (this inability to shift, even if we want to, is called 'path dependence'). The current way of seeing the world and thinking about it is hardwired in our organizations, sectors and disciplines.

So, how can we shift from an old reality and truth to a new reality/truth? We basically have to throw everything at this that we have...

For example:

- We can set out to first puncture the current paradigm, calling the conventional wisdom into doubt. This is what we will see in the case study of §3.14, where Phil Hugill starts to make explicit what the 'cultural residue' is that keeps the prison system from innovating, even in the face of overwhelming evidence that a different approach would yield better results for society.
- Often, in this book, we will invite people to reconsider the current ways of doing things by reminding them of the core values that in the end drive everything that we do; the deep human values that we realize in our lifeworld. In §4.4, a deep understanding the lifeworld of the farmers shows how we can unlock the agricultural crisis in the Netherlands.
- This then leads us away from transactional ways of organizing ourselves to more informal, fluent, relational ones to create space for deep change.
- A key feature of these spaces is that it is better to have several frames operating in parallel.

This may seem very confusing at first, but it does make one so much more flexible and ready to take on any challenges the world might throw at us. In an open, complex, dynamic and networked world there are multiple essences that we need to keep our eye on, pragmatically choosing which ones should prevail in the current situation.

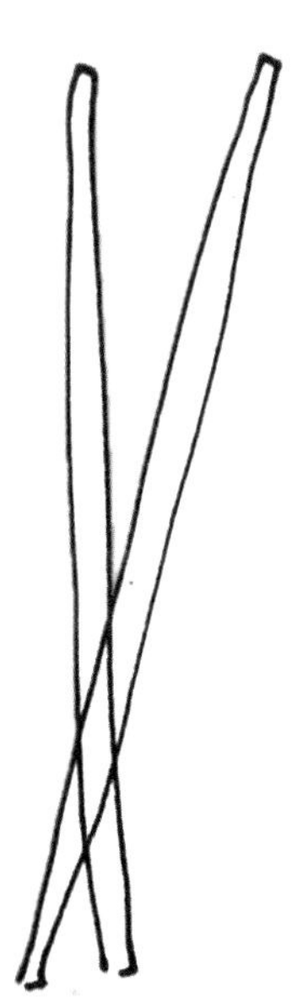

1.2

ON PRACTICES

One of the central concepts used in this book is 'practices'. Until now, we have leaned on the popular usage of the term, but we need to be more precise and specific because this concept is going to play a central role in the development of a new way of thinking in this book.

A practice is a deliberate and coherent set of activities intended to achieve something. It is a way of seeing, thinking and acting. We will here focus on the basic model of practices, that represents them as layered - see Figure 1.2.

actions
methods
principles
values

Figure 1.2 The layers of a practice

Looking at this from the top down: the first layer is that of the concrete Actions, the 'doing' of the practice. The second layer is more tactical and describes the Method(s) that underly the actions. Then there is a third layer that describes the Principles, the strategic approach to achieving the Values. The deepest layer describes the values that are embedded in the practice. In seeking to understand these values at the roots of people's practices, you dig for them by repeatedly asking 'What is this really about?'

Problems tend to present themselves on an action-level - something is not quite right, and we feel the pressure to act to change an unwanted situation into a better one. This means that more often than not, the first attempts to resolve a problematic situation will be based on the 'normal' repertoire of actions, drawn from the existing methods, principles, value set. This makes perfect sense as this the most efficient way to go about our business: expertise and resources are already available, and if these are at-hand the problem situation can be resolved with both efficiency and at speed. But when that fails to bring the desired results, we have to go back and rethink the approach itself, considering other methods. We seldom go back to the underlying principles and values - yet that is what is needed to deal with the complex problems of today's world! To create deep change we need to go to the level of values and principles and dwell there for a while, creatively reconsidering how they could be embodied differently through re-framing.

Practices that are often used successfully can become well entrenched and completely self-reinforcing. But although we might be unaware, they always contain choices about the values we find important, the principles we use to think about them, and the methods and actions we are going to apply.

The assumptions in practices are often most implicit and 'set in stone' around the level of principles. That is where the frames sit. The re-framing of a way of thinking happens when we are forced away from our normal actions, because they just don't work anymore. Then we have to go back to first principles, even reconsidering the values we are trying to achieve.

From this deep rethinking we can then access a very broad swarm of principles, methods and actions. This leads to the adoption of principles and practices that are new to the problem situation. And if this is done well, the new frame will be so compelling that it is impossible to wholeheartedly and completely go back to the old way of seeing. Because although that might have seemed inescapably logical and rational approach, it is just an approach: it ain't necessarily so...

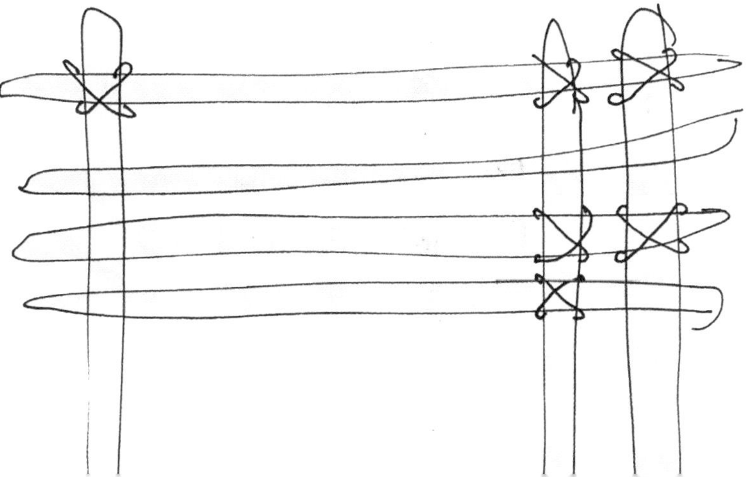

1.3

BEYOND DISCIPLINE

Practices don't come by themselves, they hunt in packs. These bundles of practices we call professions. The inner coherence of such a bundle gives professions their strength, and can make them hard to change. Undoing this bundle of practices within a discipline is crucial for real change to take root; later (in §4.4) we will see that the move towards a new agricultural system in the Netherlands inevitably means that it will be something else to be a farmer: the knowledge base, skills needed, the way of operating and sense of quality (what is a 'good' farmer?) will all have to shift. And not just for the current farmers: we will need to change the agricultural curriculum now, otherwise we will find ourselves educating 'old style' farmers for many years to come - effectively copying the old system into the new.

Every big shift we are looking for in practices, in society, will involve an educational change. Those tend to be incredibly slow. If we are not careful, education will be a laggard in developments it could and should be leading (see §4.6).

Yet disciplines are not as solid and immutable as they seem. Just think how your own profession has changed over the years. Or look at a field like Criminology...

THE DEATH OF THE CRIMINOLOGIST - PART 1

Rodger Watson

Having become a Criminologist and worked in crime prevention practice for some years, I had become a senior member of the government's crime prevention unit. While doing my masters of criminology, I had brought in many of the theoretical frameworks, tools and approaches into my professional work. I played a leading role in reforming the way the crime prevention unit operated. We moved from running as a bureaucratic, process driven unit that would provide funding to others to implement projects, to a proactive project-led unit that would develop interventions and oversee the implementation of portfolios of activities.

By any measure I was a leading practitioner in my field. I had the evidence of strict adherence to evidence based practice, and even demonstrated impact of successfully reducing crime. However, something didn't feel right. While we were successful in reducing some types of crime, there were others that didn't seem to fit the evidence- based approach that I had helped to develop.

We had operationalized a subset of a particular school of Criminology, Situational Crime Prevention, which aims to change or manage the proximal environment to reduce crime.

It is underpinned by two theories; Rational choice theory (Felson and Clarke, 1998) and Routine activities theory (Cohen and Felson, 1979).

Rational choice theory assumes that 'offenders' make rational decisions based on a risk and reward trade off. Routine activities theory poses that for a crime to occur there needs to be three elements in place; motivated offenders, desirable targets, and the absence of a 'capable guardian'.

Situational Crime Prevention then gives five principles to operationalize the underpinning theories; increase the effort to commit the crime, increase the risk of getting caught, reduce the end reward of the crime, reduce provocations to commit the crime, and remove excuses. These principles are then supported by practical examples of what might be done against certain types of crime (Cornish and Clarke, 2003).

The practice of situational crime prevention has been formalized in many jurisdictions across the world, and is supported by various sector awards (of which I am a recipient). It is a mature practice, and yet I could utilize the practice to good effect in some situations, and be completely ineffectual in others.

I didn't have the conceptual frameworks to identify why we were failing in some cases, and succeeding in others. Situational Crime Prevention was supposed to just work. When things didn't work, the establishment had ways of explaining it. "Implementation Failure" was one of the terms used to identify why the evidence-based approach hadn't had the desired outcome. Implementation Failure being an assessment that the intervention wasn't done properly.

There was nothing wrong with the theory, but it wasn't implemented appropriately. We were constrained to doing what the evidence said would be effective and had set up our unit to filter out any outlying ideas that didn't align with the evidence base.

My adopted discipline was bounded in a rationality that was resilient to variance and experimentation, and I had helped establish a practice that was rigid and not adaptive.

So what happens if there isn't an evidence base on what to do? What if the crime problem was unique? What if it was truly complex? I felt uneasy and I could find no answers. Until…I was given an opportunity to see how a different practice was taking on (literally) the same issues I had been struggling with.

Sent on secondment to work at the Designing Out Crime research center at the University of Technology Sydney, I saw how a design-led approach was being used to re-frame the very issues I was struggling to impact. This notion of re-framing the issue was so foreign to me as a criminologist, and yet so liberating. It gave me the permission to think outside of what situational criminology held as truth, and to draw on other evidence bases to create new approaches.

To be continued in §4.1...

By looking at disciplines as bundles of practices, we hope to spark exchanges of practices that will increase the speed of change. This is not as far-fetched as it may seem, because disciplines actually resemble each other in the sense that each discipline has to define its own way to deal with complexity, create newness, to learn, to judge quality, etc. We have found that talking with people about their own discipline in these terms, asking them to explain these practices, can be immensely empowering. And once you have defined how you see and deal with complexity, it becomes interesting to know how others are doing it. Suddenly, disciplines become treasure troves of practices.

For example: at some point in the development of the of a new transdisciplinary Bachelor degree (see §5.3), a staff member from Design came to discuss the exchange of practices with the Faculty of Law. The designer sought to learn how 'Law' deals with precedent - court cases are archived as situated knowledge, so that when the need arises, the earlier judgment can be retrieved and the old context and judgment be compared with the current one before the court. A subtle language game has been built up to guide the interpretation.

This is in marked contrast to the field of design, which has no systematic way of dealing with memory. As a designer you might be trying to use an earlier design for inspiration, but there is no way to identify the most appropriate one, and access the crucial contextual information to understand it.

The law representatives were interested in practices from design. They framed the question by explaining that currently, law is almost always 'too late' - when a new technical development emerges, the law profession only starts discussing it when the first court case happens. These early court cases tend to be long, expensive, and inadvertently hold up innovation. Yet design has sophisticated practices for 'looking ahead' (scenario methods, road maps, forecasting/back casting, etc.). This exchange sparked the creation of a 'future law center'.

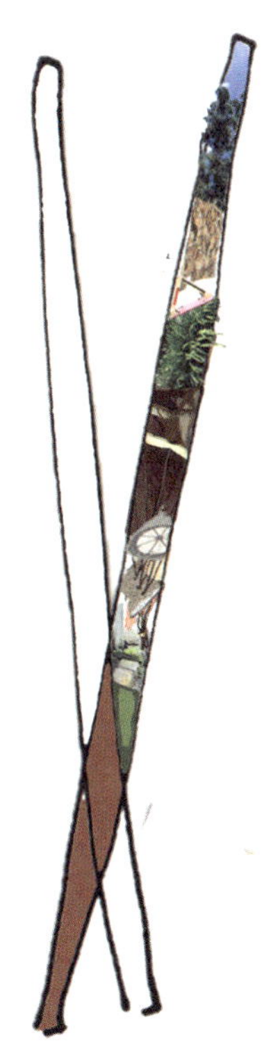

1.4

THE CREATIVE MENTALITY

The adoption of a method or practice doesn't mean a thing if it is not accompanied by the right mentality. Perfectly good tools (like the ones used in the business-school version of 'design thinking') inevitably fall flat if applied in a purely analytical context without a real understanding of the broader 'creative mentality' needed to make them a success.

But what is a 'creative mentality'? This quote of a lead creative practitioner, just to give an idea of how different the creative mentality is:

> "...I have perhaps one real talent. That is that I don't mind at all living in an area of total uncertainty..."
>
> **Ted Happold (Cross, 2006)**

You might be surprised to learn that Ted Happold is not an airy-fairy 'creative': he is a structural engineering designer, leader of an award-winning engineering firm creating huge structures (such as bridges) that we depend upon, on a daily basis. Yet in his creative process, he values the 'not knowing' over certainty. In approaching the design challenges and puzzles that make up his daily work, has a creative mentality.

The creative mentality is often ill-understood. The creative disciplines themselves are perhaps as guilty as anyone for this, because they like to present 'the creative touch' as some kind of wizardry that is out of reach for us mere mortals. The stories they tell are steeped in myth of 'the creative genius' achieving a 'light bulb moment'. But there is no reason to be mysterious about creative practice, we know how this works. There is an immense amount of literature that sets this out in great detail (see Doran, 2025).

The creative practice is the real driver of change, and needs to be taken very seriously.

People struggle to really take this creative mentality seriously because deep down, at the bottom of the misunderstandings between analytical thinkers and creative thinkers, is a structural difference in thinking patterns. Creative practice is based on a fundamentally different logic. Normally, a logical reasoning pattern is all about thinking forward; you move from causes (that which we know) to consequences (that which will then result/happen). Yet the logic behind creative practice works the other way: this thinking backwards, from consequences (that what we want to happen, the value we want to achieve) back to the causes (whatever we need to make this happen). This is a fundamentally open reasoning pattern: there are always several causes possible, so in a sense you never know whether you are right. There is no right or wrong. 'Truth' and 'being Right' just doesn't come into it. But this doesn't mean that this is sloppy thinking, or that 'anything goes'; Usefulness is all important, and Quality is a guiding light.

In saying this we are closely following the work of the pragmatist philosopher C.S. Peirce (1839-1914), who coined the word Retroduction for this 'art of thinking backwards' from consequences to causes - he later settled on the use of the word Abduction for this logic (for a much more extended comparison of logics, including a comparison between kinds of Abduction, see [Dorst, 2025]). In Abductive thinking, we need to work in a propositional manner; the only way to get from consequences to causes is to create something (a possible 'cause'), think it through, and analyze if it can be made to lead to the intended consequence. And - most importantly - you keep doing this, learning from the experience, creating better and better 'causes' over time.

We all know this dynamic from creative processes; you make a sketch, reflect and gradually learn your way towards a solution. From the outside, for someone who is only used to analytical thinking and linear problem-solving processes, this approach just looks playful and unserious. They can easily dismiss this as mere 'trial and error', completely missing the subtle creative learning process that it is. This is a terrible misunderstanding, that has caused us much harm.

If creative practices are not understood, respected and taken seriously - if they are forever in the 'nice to have' basket, not the 'need to have', then innovation will always struggle.

The creative mentality is the core of innovation and change.

1.5

TOOLS, TRICKS AND TIPS FOR SEEING DIFFERENTLY

THE LAYERS OF PRACTICE

As we will see in the case studies, the four-layer model of practices (§1.1) can be a powerful tool to look critically at the practices of an organization, and to inspire alternative ways of doing this.

Just listing out the stated values, principles, methods and actions often shows that there is misalignment, which is strange - if the values and actions don't align, we are doing the wrong things! Perhaps there has been a 'drift' over time, where originally they may have aligned. But often, we find that the deep human values just get out of sight completely: the structures and forms that make up the organization effectively become goals unto themselves. This is a serious problem because in the end, they can't be - all these structures and processes are just a means to an end.

The ability to analyze and see through the dominant practices in an organization gives great insight and is very empowering. And it can be used for inspiration; considering the themes that are at play in our field of operation, we can introduce other values that haven't been properly embodied in the organization to date. And to operationalize those values, we can look around to get inspired by practices from other disciplines that DO happen to be good at these.

This is the core of our model of transdisciplinarity; finding other principles, methods and actions to operationalize and realize the values.

METHOD CARDS

To play with practices, rethink and recombine them, it is necessary to have a succinct way of expressing them. We have found it useful to capture practices in 'method cards that can be arranged as necessary for the project at hand. These are loose cards that each describe a separate practice can be arranged as the project is being planned. The cards contain brief descriptions of the 'how, what, where and when' of a practice, in an accessible and straightforward style. Importantly: every card contains the name of the person that brought in the method, so this 'owner' can be contacted on details of the context in which the card can be used, and give tips how to use it.

Apart from allowing practices to be rearranged in the context of a project or challenge, and enabling practices from many different disciplines come together on an even footing, the working with method cards also helps ensuring that whatever you do, you are ALWAYS in a practice.

The cards provide a subtle reminder to not just sit around and be unstructured, but where possible work with intent and a method behind it.

Just having clarity within a team on 'what are we doing here?' and 'how are we going to do that?' is immensely helpful. At the same time, the format allows for a playful way of reaching alignment - and there can always be an unexpected card that pops up in your peripheral vision that just sparks a new direction.

In our own experience, the creation of these cards is a useful exercise in itself: it helped us to take stock of the various methods we used on projects, and discuss their merits (and pitfalls). Knowing what you can bring to the table from your own personal and professional background is very empowering.

The rich set of methods variously came from the discipline areas of the team members, or were newly developed in-house. Working with partner organizations we were often asked if we could share the method cards with them. In a way that is not too useful, because the exercise of mapping existing methods in a team is a powerful and bonding experience that you miss out on when you are just trying to use someone else's cards. So we strongly recommend you make your own - we will limit ourselves here to giving some examples, so you get a sense of what they are.

One of the disciplines that contributed greatly to a new transdisciplinary degree program was Midwifery. The card that was most picked up by people from other disciplines was on Triage:

TITLE Triage

WHY
Observing people interacting with their surroundings and other people to determine who is need of help/care/advice.

WHAT
Observe people- posture, expression, animation/dejection, movement, location in space etc. Listen to voice - tone, volume, speed, coherence of speech/sounds made. Observe environment: is it safe?

HOW
Use all your sense modalities; see, hear, touch, smell, taste, movement, intuition, and record what you find. Observe yourself in the moment and how you are reacting (e.g. calm, breathing rhythmically, pulse slow, or, sweaty palms, heart racing, hairs on arms standing up). Since your body will unconsciously be scanning moment to moment for safe/unsafe moments that also give you some indication of wellbeing in this situation.

One wished that many other disciplines would also do a Triage before they started meddling with a problem situation! Identifying this practice and making it explicit in a method card creates the opportunity to do so.

The faculty of Law was also involved, and opened up a whole world of understanding and valuing patterns of behavior:

TITLE Seeing the Rules

WHY
To gain insight into how law(s) regulate and influence activities/conduct/space.

WHAT
What is the reason people/actions/things/places the way they appear?
What are the rules?
Are the rules visible - e.g. as demonstrated by signs/notices?
Are the rules implicit - e.g. as indicated/suggested by structures/processes?

HOW
Observation and background research. Observe signs of order and ask yourself: Do you 'intuitively' know the rules? Are these the rules you would expect and/or consider would fit 'normally' in this setting? Then use background research to identify the rules. For example if you see a sign that prohibits an action, research to find out the 'rule' that is being addressed.

CREATIVE PRACTICE

These are some excerpts from books we have written about this, selected as the most useful by the professionals we have worked with as a quick but by no means exhaustive tour of creative practice selected by professionals:

ROAD BLOCKS TO CREATIVITY

I'm not creative – I can't draw

I was bad at art during school

I am creative – I know what creativity is and how to do it

I feel like I am being creative but am flying blind!?

There is no way I can do anything creative where I work

Creativity is for geniuses

Creativity is a transaction

People think I'm creative but actually I'm not... I am really insecure about it

People see my work as creative but I don't really think I am

COUNTER VIEWS

Every person is creative – it is intrinsic to living, responding and adapting

Creativity involves artification and that is different from social ideas of art

Being trained as a creative can limit wider improvisation

There are practices and methods that help us recognize creativity in motion

Context matters – there are always creative constraints and opportunities

Creativity as transformation – dual dance changing the self with others

CREATIVE CATALYST TOUCHSTONES

The exercises below have been used in a variety of contexts. This mix includes people working for large government and corporate organizations working with complex challenges like cancer, mental health, engineering and construction, homelessness, the education system, aged care and introducing sustainability practices into the business of building cities.

They equally work with people familiar with creative practices such as designers, film makers and creative writers, and planners. These situations come with serious issues to address, and institutional practices that more often than not dull out creativity. People from all walks of life have been attracted to them and find them easy to engage with.

More to the point, we recurrently hear how their creativity has been opened up and those elusive 'aha moments' have shown up either as shy, unexpected insights or brassy moments of shiny clarity.

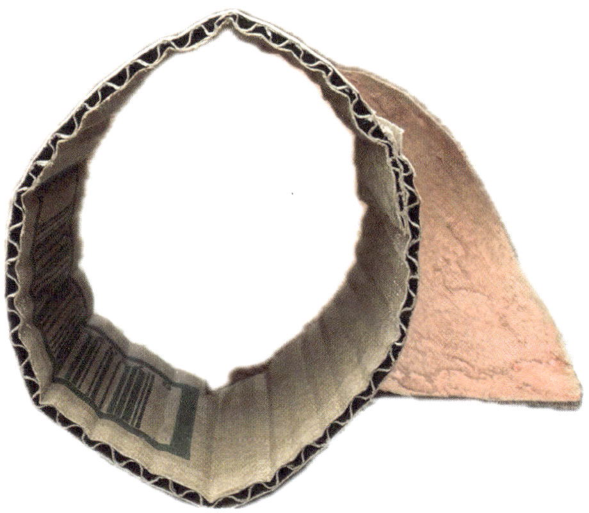

PLAY HISTORIES AND PLAYER TYPES

One powerful way to reconnect with a playful mindset is through exploring our play histories. These might stem from childhood or more recent memories. According to psychologist Stuart Brown, you can learn more about someone's motivation and personality through 20 minutes of play than hours of strategy meetings.

"The opposite of play is not work, it is depression."
- Stuart Brown

This simple exercise works beautifully across diverse groups. Recalling moments of joy and flow not only reignites personal memories but fosters empathy. People recognize the uniqueness of others' play styles and the creative value in that diversity. Talking about play gives permission for playfulness to re-enter spaces where it may have been squeezed out by formal expectations. It invites curiosity, collaboration, and the courage to drop unspoken rules that shut creativity down.

Reading the room is key. Performers or athletes may feel right at home in open, chair-less spaces. Others, more used to seated tasks or screens, may need gentler conditions to release their inner player.

Our play histories reveal where and how we've learned through play–and the roles we naturally take on alone or with others. These show up in adulthood, too, in how we work and relate. Psychometric tests can offer insights into these tendencies, as long as we don't let them box us in. After all, we're neuroplastic – change and growth are always possible.

Reflecting on our history with play helps us:

- To identify where we have experienced meaning and fun (flow) in our own lives
- Empathize with how others might be motivated
- Design engaging games
- Experiment and learn through feedback
- Learn to engage with open curiosity
- Figure out ways to collaborate with others who might play differently

Stuart Brown (2009) identified 8 types of player personalities. These personalities are useful in helping us to find the part of ourselves that steps into open mode. Equally so, it helps us to appreciate the diverse ways others play and how there are symbiotic relationships when we play together.

Each of us has a dominant play mode. This play mode can morph and change as context changes and as we age and grow, but in essence, it is the basis of how we are naturally drawn to interact with the world through play.

Take a moment to read the descriptions of each player personality on the following page and consider how closely you connect with each description.

There are also times where we may switch roles depending on the context. For instance, there is mutability in the role of storyteller, director and artist or competitor, director and kinesthete.

There is skill in reading the context and noticing play in motion.

These personalities are useful in helping us to find the part of ourselves that steps into open mode. Equally so, it helps us to appreciate the diverse ways others play and how there is a symbiotic relationship when we play together.

Part of this is developing a sense for when the time is right for 'open' mode/playful activity conditions

The Joker
Jokers love nonsense, silly sounds, being foolish and lightening the mood. They frequently connect with others through their jokes and love to make others laugh.

The Kinesthete
Kinesthetes love to engage in physical movement. Although they enjoy physical games, competition is not required; it is more about the movement. Play can range from clearing land to playing football, cooking, and sewing.

The Explorer
Explorers relish novel challenges. Whether visiting new places, researching new subjects or undergoing journeys where awareness is developed or deepened. Exploration is a tool for provoking imagination and remaining creative.

The Competitor
Competitors love specific rules and goals. They want to know how to win and who won - whether team sports or solo endeavors, physical or mental. They love score keeping and keeping track of progress.

The Director
Directors enjoy planning and executing. They frequently take the lead in teams, organize social occasions and coordinate events such as performances, festivals, parties and group gatherings.

The Collector
Collectors love to hunt for and gather objects; the best, the most interesting and unusual. They might also collect experiences, like visiting countries or seeing every show of a touring band. Collectors can play alone or as part of a social team or club. They also enjoy categorizing.

The Artist/Creator
The Artist/Creator loves to make things. They transform spaces into rooms with atmosphere and possibility. They often reside in workshops and studios overflowing with treasures and supplies. Some Artists/Creators like to make something brand new from a blank canvas, while others like to take things apart and reassemble. Regardless of whether they are recognized for their talents, the true Artist/Creator simply loves the process.

The Storyteller
Storytellers can make themselves part of any story. They take joy not only in telling stories but also in listening. They might relish in reading books, watching movies and making versions of their own. They love metaphor and symbolism and use them to make sense of the world. Storytellers are unique in that they can bring play to almost any activity or event.

QUICK TUNE UP

Portrait – no looking

This exercise has been used in all kinds of situations as a creative primer. It works a treat and is so simple and joyful to do. It's great for bringing in people who resist creativity; e.g. the audit, numbers-based people who have 'more serious and real stuff to do'. It can lift a room that has gotten heavy and bogged down in analytical and structural content or help people who don't know each other or might be concerned about how they will connect. It is agnostic and works with government, corporate and creative types. By drawing without looking at the paper, people are more or less on a level playing field. It's not about the drawing or how good you might be. Instead, people make eye contact, stop taking themselves seriously and let themselves play. Caricatures emerge and somehow point to a space where we are sensing each other in a way that still captures something essential but imprecise. Laughter fills the space, faces soften, people relax and engage at a more human level. Identities and professional utilities are set aside for a moment and the hive mind is primed for something else - a more porous, curious and open space. It is great way to recalibrate, revitalize or prime creative action. When dancers, stage and film directors have engaged in this exercise they have commented on how they use similar movement activities and games to prime performers in rehearsals, so they work as an attuned, creative organism. An organism that thrives through the interactions of curious responding individuals who feel safe to experiment together.

Visual stretch

For people who dub themselves as 'not creative', this activity works well after doing play histories and sensory tune ups.

This helps people recognize the links between play, creativity and how we lay down the basis of frames through poly-sensory connections.

Less than 30 seconds per exercise.

Sit with a partner.

Draw their face without looking at the page or taking your hand off the paper. Switch hands and repeat.

SENSING

This exercise has been used by all kinds of people - from CEOs looking to catalyze innovation through to social workers working on the ground in complex situations. They all comment on the profound ways separating the senses can reveal new perspective and expand experiences. Be it as mundane as writing a board paper or building a new product, it is an activity that starts out as a primer and ends up becoming a powerful way of reflecting.

A good way to warm up creativity and prime a flow state is to invite your senses in by taking them on a date. We often don't give much time to considering how our senses contribute to our experiences, yet we know they can significantly influence our perceptions.

For this task go on a date with each sense for an hour. You may wish to focus on a shared space, a smaller room or the whole environment.

SOUND

Yi-Fu Tuan observed that in an acoustic environment, our experience is always centered on our own position, the point from which the world's sounds reach us.

Our world is a rich, subtle assemblage of sounds that provide us with a 3D sense of place. Unlike other senses, our ears are always open. Listening is an act of finding our place in the world, primes us for action, helps invoke images and memories while expanding our spatial awareness. Sound also influences our moods (e.g. curiosity, frustration, anxiety, fear, boredom, and tranquility) though, what may be music to one may be noise to another.

Note the sounds:

- That give your environment personality
- Prime people to take actions
- Prompt memories
- Irritates or stimulates a feeling of space

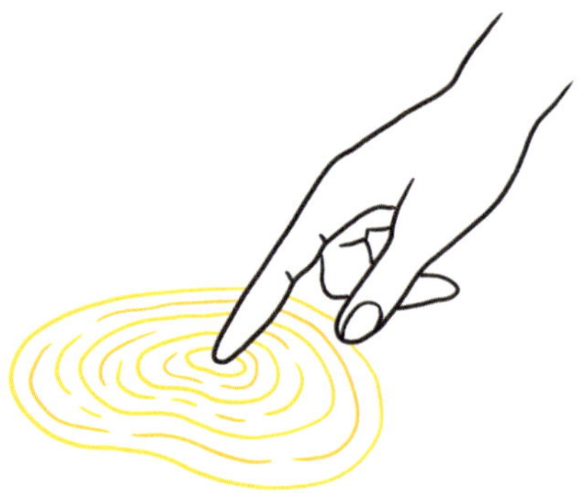

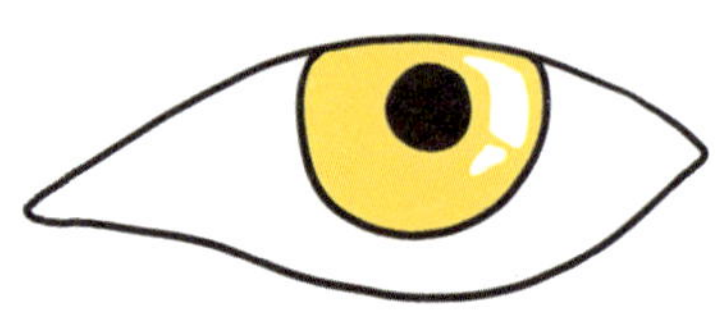

TOUCH

Our skin is our biggest organ. It provides us with data on texture, pressure, temperature and movement. Not only that, our skin gives off electro conductive signals that show we know something before our conscious brains do. Hold a warm drink for someone on a cold day and you will think they are a kinder, more generous and trustworthy person. Thick paper CVs are related to 'weight' of skills while hard textures (think your seat or footpaths) are equated with difficulty.

Spend an hour evaluating the touch of your environment.

Notice:

- Textures and your associations (clothes, surfaces, materials you handle)
- Temperatures
- What, how and who you touch
- How others respond to tactile
- Information

SIGHT

Sight is often regarded as the king of the senses but we rarely stop to consider how we see. Sight involves moving our heads and eyes which draws together information from our right and left visual fields. Sight involves responding to contrasts in texture, patterns of light and dark and noticing landmarks. Go on a date with a color per hour.

Date 5 colors. Pick a color (any color) and look for its presence.

Record the frequency, object/item and emotional timbre.

A note on color and emotion:

Some colors are culturally mediated but red is the only one found to elicit universal responses.

There are links between the color red and:

- Physical performance, verbal and mathematical performance
- Responses linked to danger and anxiety
- Sexual arousal

TASTE & SMELL

Though these senses have different pathways, we often experience them together partly because they have a direct line into the parts of our brain where non-verbal memory and emotion are housed. Both smell and taste can radically influence our reactions, associations and once fused in memory are difficult to untangle.

Note the smells in your environment:

- What associations or memories do they stimulate?
- Do they give you clues about materials, chemicals and aging processes?
- Do some smells trigger hunger or desire to eat?
- What are the kinds of food and drink smells?

SLOW PORTRAIT

This is a good one for people who say they can't draw. It is also resoundingly useful in stimulating experiences of flow. It is interesting to see how many people elect to do this exercise once they have moved past judgments about not being creative and/or their drawing skills. Many people report making the decision that they are not creative in early school years and often because they decided they were not good at drawing. Many people opt to use photographs, but photography is its own creative endeavor.

By drawing upside down, again the imperative to get it right, to work from a conceptual ideal is released.

By shifting focus to shadows, shapes, tones and colors people start to experience how imagery and perception come together as a gestalt. The shift in awareness can be quite significant and again, helps set up a space to question assumptions and look for wider patterns. People also recurrently comment on the calming flow space they enter by shading and surrendering to being deeply engaged in the moment.

Often people share how they notice their breathing, heart rate, and how time feels like it slows down even though the activity doesn't take as long as they thought it did. It does take time but for some, connecting to drawing and rhythmically slowing down spurs an ongoing commitment to reconnecting and growing a drawing as a practice. This activity also stimulates an attunement to the gestalt.

For a portrait to take on qualities of the whole it needs to tap into the relationships between relationships - those non linear qualities that bring parts into symphony. It involves drawing what you see, not what you remember. This is different from using symbols or rich pictures - it is about working with shadow, light, gradation, absences, looking for shapes and the way they connect or merge.

There are many ways in which portraits have been created throughout time and culture. Drawings and paintings of people tend to come to mind and they can be powerful ways of tapping into the wide range of phenomena at play - shifting light, emotional gestures, identity expressions - the worlds within and without. Landscapes, still lives, flora and fauna portraits are equally rich forms of portraiture. Portraits can be created through all kinds of media including pencil sketches, paintings, sculpture/3D, musical and textural. There are also a myriad of culturally specific practices such as dot painting, weaving, beading and dance.

For the purpose of this exercise choose a portrait subject and medium that you can visualize. Don't worry about your expertise, the real value is in the time you spend and the detail that emerges. You can do this in a single sitting or over a series of intervals though some elements will shift. An hour will provide a good degree of detail though portraits can be quite luring and may draw you in for a longer haul.

Here are some tips:

- Try drawing upside down
- Start with shadows and reflections and sketch softly
- Roughly block out the light and dark regions
- Look for the shape of dints, furrows, dips and raised section
- Sketch in angles and proportions
- Draw with different eyes
- Blur your eyes
- Use a mirror

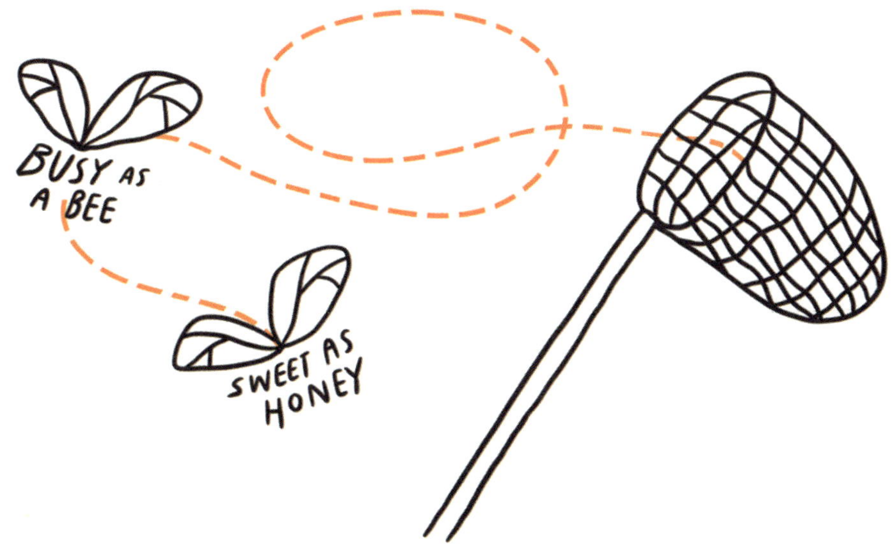

METAPHORS

Metaphors can reveal a lot about our assumptions and also act as portals for re-imagining them. What we choose to accept without reflection, how we might think of ourselves and our relationship to the world can be unconsciously revealed through the metaphors we choose. What makes metaphors particularly influential is their ability to seamlessly integrate fragmented and localized experiences with generalized understanding that we unconsciously mobilize in forming coherent meaning that shapes our perception of reality.

"If it is the case that our understanding is an effect of the metaphors we choose, it is also true that it is a cause, our understanding itself guides the choice of metaphor by which we understand...Thus, how we think of ourselves and our relationship to the world is unconsciously revealed through the metaphors we choose to talk about it"

(McGilchrist 2010, p97)

Metaphors are powerful short cuts to personal and collective ways of making sense of the world. Metaphors often embody cues to how we bind physical and emotional associations with shared cultural values.

Cognitive linguist George Lakoff claims that the use of metaphors is innate to our understanding of the world and we form deep neurological connections in childhood, such as the association between warmth and kindness or the notion that up means more. In this way, Lakoff suggests that we are always thinking in metaphor. Metaphors make use of contrasting associations: warm/cold, soft/hard, day/night. Contrasts help us create distinctions and they can form the basis of how we order and prioritize especially if we place them into fixed binary relationships. Equally so, they can reveal unquestioned biases and opportunities to re-imagine things. Many metaphors are also based in sensory experiences and can contain hidden associations between senses and thoughts that often go unnoticed.

Over the course of a week, notice the metaphors in your world. They are in conversations, emails, signage, lyrics, advertising, t-shirts - everywhere! Jot them down.

METAPHOR CATCHING

Use the metaphors you have found or if needed search for more on-line. Scan through and find a few that connect. Make notes:

- What are the key words - what are the physical and emotional associations?
- Are there implied hierarchies?
- Are there contrasts or binaries?
- Now spend some time playing with the metaphors:
- Try to change their meaning
- Can you turn a mechanical process or a living process?
- Replace or invert words and sensations - what happens?

What do you identify about power, hierarchy, assumptions? Find something you'd like to change in your world and make a metaphor that fits.

IGNORANCE MAPPING

The ignorance map was developed by researcher Ann Kerwin while Philosopher-in-Residence of the Curriculum on Medical Ignorance at the University of Arizona Medical School. Ignorance mapping aims to help you interrogate your knowledge, and assumptions about your knowledge.

Known Unknowns

Everything you know you don't know. These could include adjacent possibilities ('I know X but would like to know Y') or future scenarios ('Yesterday I did X, tomorrow I could do Y').

Unknown Unknowns

Everything you don't know you don't know. To explore these, ask yourself:

- If we'd known...
- We could never have known...
- What if...

Errors/Misknowns

Everything you think you know, but don't. One way to approach these is through writing down your assumptions and then challenging or reversing them.

Unknown Knowns

Everything you don't know you know. What's your gut instinct, your least 'engineered' response?

Taboos

Dangerous, polluting or forbidden knowledge. What is the most dangerous 'discovery' you could articulate? Who would be endangered and why?

Denials

All the things that are too painful to know, so you don't. Is there some knowledge that you really don't want to confront about yourself when tackling this challenge?

Try it yourself

Reflect on the zeitgeist - the sociocultural environment around you, what comes up for you might be influenced by the place you work, your habitat, social networks and the media you consume.

Jot down a few themes that seem persistent. Choose the one that invokes tension, paradox and emotional charge. Write responses to the theme using the ignorance map prompts. Imagine what some of the unknown unknowns might be.

Disliking uncertainty, we look for solid, stable items. Unless an image is truly ambiguous, its foreground catches the eye first.

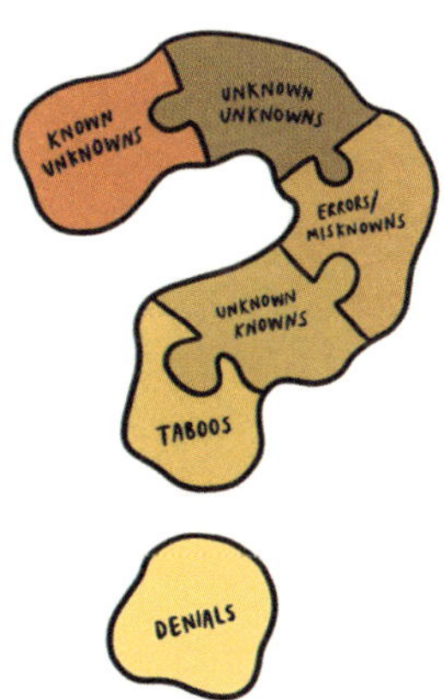

CREATE AN ALBUM OF MUSIC

Music is a wonderful medium to encounter and consider scale. Music channels our emotional spectrum and moves our bodies into moments of both solitary contemplation and impassioned shared activity. Music marries sound and creative expression, it can ground wavelengths and ranges of audible vibration. Music takes us through journeys of culture, history, and place while spanning technologies for creation, recording and performance. It takes us into relationships with all manner of other music makers in the biosphere - birds, crickets, whales, rock surfaces, forest floors and the sounds of the skies.

Brian Eno has been a long-term player in creating and reflecting on how music mediates our experiences of time and place. He as worked on all manner of projects which explore feelings and music, his work is a great source of creative stimulation. Scale and complexity in its multiple interpretations can be encountered through music, as David Byrne (2017) so neatly discusses in the first chapter of his book 'How Music Works'.

Thinking about the issue you are interested in, create a playlist of music (or if you are game, write your own). Then develop an artwork that visually expresses what the playlist is about.

Think about how to conjure a sense of scale. It is up to you how you interpret 'scale' but look to:

- Name your album
- Provide a one liner that helps listeners grasp your curatorial decisions. You can decide to make your work in multiple ways with various elements. It could either be a mood board for a production company rather than a finished graphic design or a single mock up of an album cover. In curating your album you may wish to consider:

  - The environment/ space/ room the music was made for
  - The instruments - materials, technologies and performance
  - Cultural context - collective, contemplative, for dance, for ceremony, power - for whom?
  - Era - when, where, historical influences
  - Inspiration - natural, emotional and mythical archetypes
  - Patterns, rhythms, shifts, surprises

SMALL TALK

Often dismissed as shallow and inconsequential, small talk is part of many meaningful exchanges and social rituals. Small talk sets the vibe, breaks the ice and creates a space for reading a range of subtle cues linked to mood, intention and personal or cultural predispositions. We tune in through posture, facial expression, vocal tone, gestures, body space, agreements on touch, symbolism (e.g. through clothing and furnished environments).

Small talk often joins us in the broad-brush stuff that connects as humans; food, weather, family, sleep. It is adaptive bonding, part of resilience, communal but individually negotiated. Dr. Justine Coupland is a sociolinguistic expert, in her book, 'Small Talk' (2014), she examines the powerful and affirming effects that small talk has in social interactions. She writes, "Small talk cannot be dismissed as peripheral, marginal or minor discourse. Small talk is a means by which we negotiate interpersonal relationships".

Create a coding system that records types of small talk in your world.

Things to look for:

- The number of conversations
- Themes of conversation: gossip, hobbies, interests
- Moments of kindness
- Tone of conversation (excited, blunt, instructive)
- Motivations for connection (formal and informal)
- Snippets of overheard or unseen conversation

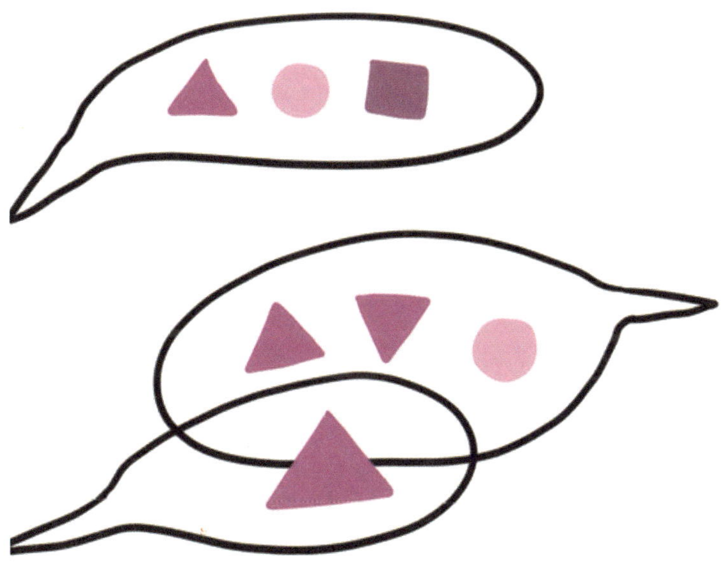

CREATE A CHARACTER

Stories are mobilized through characters. They might not be human, but making them human-like helps us switch on our mirror neurons and empathy pathways. This is one way we can find ourselves in the lives of others, allowing us to travel time and space by suspending our disbelief. But, in order to do so we need to feel characters are relatable. This means bringing in quirks, inconsistencies and flaws. There are many disciplines that use scenarios but they often don't account for the way that behavior can be inconsistent; personas can shift depending on the situation at hand or in response to unexpected curve balls. Building a multidimensional, character with quirks and inconsistencies sets the space for real world story building.

Animators, theatre and film makers, game builders, and increasingly the full spectrum of design practices, all work with character creation. For director Julie Taymor, a key part of any dramatic process is to find the 'ideograph of a moment', the scene where a character is reduced to its essence 'like a Japanese brush painting'. Animation studio Pixar are renowned for innovating in graphics technology, often spending months of research and development to accurately render character details like the folds of clothes and hair, or the way gestures convey a character's personality.

Create a character based on a personality or occupational role you would like in your world. You could do this on paper, digitally or bring to life with your body by dressing up.

Build a character and give them:

- A name
- A history and family life
- Some individual quirks e.g. lovable to some more annoying to others, 'details' oriented, a social connector
- A rebellious tweak and a more traditional or conservative trait
- Dress your character. Think about these elements: color, style, influences, context/situation, group membership

STORY MAKING

The art and value of story has also been explored extensively by Joseph Campbell (2003) who uses the hero's journey as a narrative framework. Though there are many ways to tell stories, we have become comfortable with the linear Three Act structure; the Setup, the Confrontation and the Resolution.

In recent times, non-linear and divergent story telling has gained traction particularly through gaming and interactive technologies. It can be useful to notice the differences between linear and non-linear story lines.

Make a short story that shows tension, surprise, and creative hope. Aim to impart your message story within five minutes or less. Take it a step further - do this is a group and find ways to connect stories. What happens afterwards - do things evolve in predictable and connected ways or float off into different realities?

There's lots of options in how you convey your story such as:

- A short script for film, TV or theatre (here movement, action and props are also important)
- A poem, song/ballad or segment of a saga
- A cartoon or zine
- An aural account (recorded)
- A sequence of music
- A children's picture book
- A game

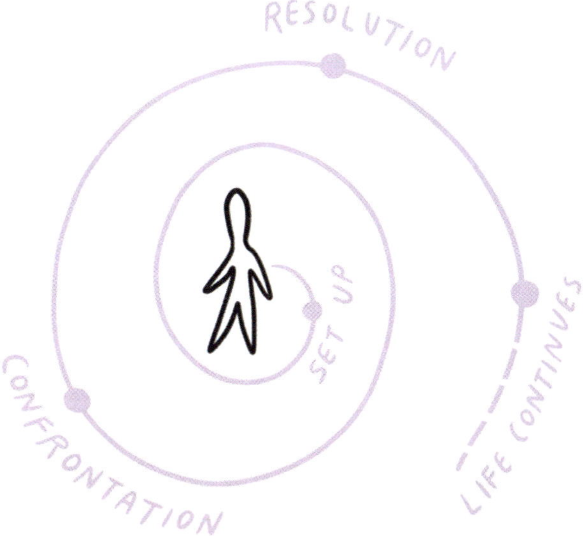

CHAPTER 2

TOWARDS NEXT GENERATION STRATEGIC INNOVATION

2.1

ELEMENTS OF A NEW STRATEGIC INNOVATION PRACTICE

Chapter 1 is an invitation to embrace your own creative intelligence. The creative intelligence tools at the end of the chapter help to build new creative strengths, and develop creative muscle memory. We need to build this capacity to re-wire our own thinking to create deep change. In this chapter we introduce the key strategic innovation models, tools and methods that provide the conceptual and structural scaffold for the innovation journeys that are the core of this new strategic innovation practice.

We will then go on and see in the case studies of Chapters 3 and 4 how the contributors from many different professional fields and organizations have used these methods and tools to achieve deep change; how they use Frame Creation (§2.2 and §2.3) to unlock the complex situations, how they use the Game Changers model (§2.4) to make bottom-up meet top-down in a dance that can reshape an organizations' approach to innovation.

They use the Changing Minds (§2.5) methodology to inspire their colleagues to join the innovation journey. The Colors of Change model (§2.6) helps navigating the complex structures and human interactions within a changing environment, while the Studio Model (§2.7) gives us an infrastructure that can be built within organizations to deliver strategic innovation as an ongoing practice.

To create this Studio is a bit of a journey in itself; in §2.8 we will share the step-by-step process that the Pioneers in the next chapter have used on their journey to create their own Strategic Innovation Studio.

2.2

FRAME CREATION

FRAMING AND RE-FRAMING

To create progress in a complex world, we need to move away from purely analytical ways of thinking. In the face of true complexity, we need to embrace it by dynamically interacting with the whole system through a process of framing (deframing and re-framing). This is a playful, designerly process. The innovator does not attack an open, complex problem head-on, they will dance around it to find a new way in.

In creating new frames we develop new ways of seeing the world, new ways of thinking about it, and new ways of acting upon it. But how can frames be created? How does the innovator manage to do this?

In the Frame Creation process the innovator embraces the complexity of a situation, and then gets back to first principles, the deep human values to re-anchor their thinking.

Starting with these values allows them to think about the problem in a different way, propose new frames, playfully suggest new ways forward, test them, and loop back to re-frame when the proposed direction doesn't quite work out.

This is basically a learning process; you are learning your way towards a new frame.

This starts with the acknowledgment that a problem has its roots in a specific context. To create a new frame that context needs to be critically looked at, and changed. This is how we move beyond the simplifications and assumptions that underlie conventional views of the problem.

The creation of new frames in design can be modeled as a process of nine simple steps (figure 2.2a). The most important step of the process is built on the fifth step, which is the deep exploration of the underlying values of the stakeholders and broader field. In this step the innovator is preparing for the cognitive shift from inquiry and analysis to abductive creativity.

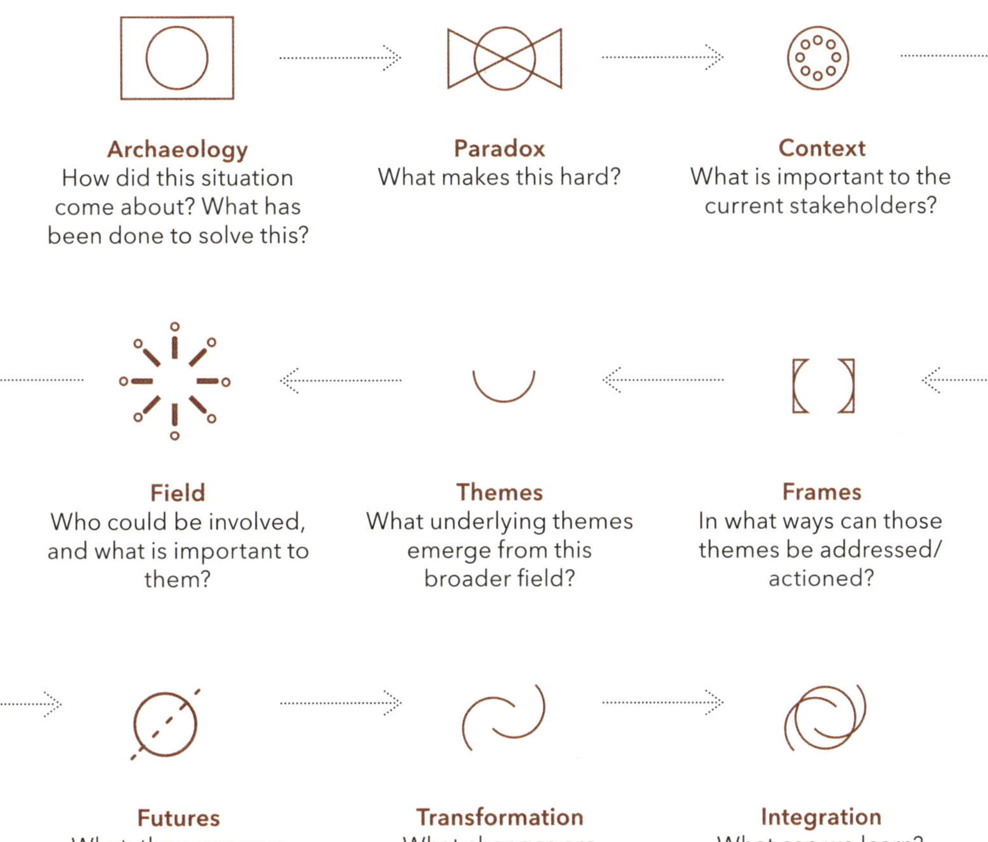

Figure 2.2a Frame Creation from Dorst, Klippan, Kaldor, Watson (2016).

See Appendix 1 for a step by step example of the use of Frame Creation in a workshop setting.

2.3

FRAME CREATION IN PRACTICE

Frame Creation gives the innovator a process of thinking that takes them away from how the issue they are confronting is currently framed. It is a process of zooming out, expanding, and concentrating again as new frames come into view. The expansion of the problem space allows new patterns to emerge. At this point the innovator must be quite disciplined in setting aside how the issue is currently framed. In that sense the problem is the problem, and if the experts haven't been able to solve the problem, then what hope does the innovator have?

This deframing liberates the innovator to concentrate on understanding the underlying values of the broader field, and to deepen the Themes. Building a deep understanding of the Themes helps to create a picture of 'what is really at stake'. This is also an opportunity to bring the core stakeholders into the thinking, having them share in the efforts of understanding what is truly important creates a bridge for them to cross into exploring new frames. Then we need to deepen the Themes - the depth and richness of understanding of the Themes really determines the quality of the end result of the whole process - and makes sure that the Frames are strong enough to evoke a very clear picture in the mind of all the stakeholders. The core of the Frame Creation process can be compressed in a workshop that itself can be done in two to three hours, or over a week-long deep dive. These are quite a magical sessions: at the end of the workshop your thinking has actually shifted, and moved away from old patterns.

But this sudden change can be a bit misleading: in a complex problem situation such a workshop takes months of preparation. And afterwards it takes months to rework the session more thoroughly, check assumptions that have entered the discussion, dig to achieve depth and thoughtfulness in the Themes, sharpen the Frames, make an exhaustive exploration of possible interventions and map these against the original problem, etc. After the adoption of one or more frames, the path to action can still be hard and long. New frames invariably disturb organizational cultures, processes, and structures that have been set up to support the conventional problem-solving in an organization. Moreover, in a networked world, these frames invariably cut through organizational boundaries in unexpected ways. It is crucial that the innovator support the problem owner in the hard task of following through on the path to action toward real-world, on-the-ground results.

Confronted by a world that has become more open, complex, dynamic and networked, we need to reinvent all disciplines. These new problems and opportunities can only be tackled by embracing complexity, bringing together viewpoints and creating new perspectives through deframing and re-framing.

We can use the design practices as a starting point, but in the end the way forward will arise from the development of creative practices within the disciplines themselves - to be effective, creative practices need to be integrated in the disciplinary practices, knowledge and skills. This is not something that design alone can do.

This is not the kind of problem area where a professional can come in from the outside and create a clever solution: the answer to this complex issue lies within the deep knowledge and expertise of the professionals in the field, and the challenge is to see how the innovator can help these people develop their own creative practice.

Kees Dorst:

In the course of a project on the radicalization of urban youth, I met a youth worker who has become my absolute hero. His approach to helping youth at risk of becoming radicalized is basically perfect: he is personable, knowledgeable, experienced, sophisticated in his approach and above all authentic. He went through a lot himself and can talk with the authority of first-hand experience. Wherever these kids might be going, he has been there. He connects very deeply with this group, and can support them in just the way they need. He is the solution to the huge societal problem of radicalization - the only thing is, we need a thousand of him. How can we scale? What can we scale? Together we are now carefully tracing his practices, to find out which ones could be 'formalized' in such a way that others could learn how to do them. He, in turn, has become inspired by the re-framing approach and is setting up his own experiments to extend his repertoire of interventions.

2.4

GAME CHANGERS

A compelling new frame, once seen, cannot be unseen. But seeing potential and realizing potential are two very different things.

A new frame sitting on paper is vulnerable and sometimes leads to an allergic reaction by the organization. The organization is structured in a certain way, engineered to achieve the outcomes it is achieving. A new frame can trigger the immune system of the organization and become isolated or flatly rejected. So, if an organization is good at staying resilient to the adoption of good ideas, what can be done?

For a new frame to 'change the game' it needs to engage strategically with the organization and the learning loops that themselves might be quite implicit in the organization. Through making the implicit explicit, the frame can then set the conditions for experimentation. We don't know if a compelling new frame will actually 'work' until we try it, and in trying it we are testing the underlying assumptions as well as observing the impacts (intended, and unintended). This deliberate experimentation means that we are open minded about the frame and can adjust actions based on reflections in action (see Figure 2.3a).

At this level we are moving from operational thinking to tactical thinking and establishing what Charles Leadbeater calls a "washing machine". The activities go around in circles, with local project level impact, and can be seen to fit with the organization's strategy because the impact is measurable against the current metrics. Innovation teams nest well in this space because they are contained, understandable and sadly ineffective at realizing the innovation ambition behind them. For real change to happen in the organization these projects and the lessons learned need to impact the practices of the organization.

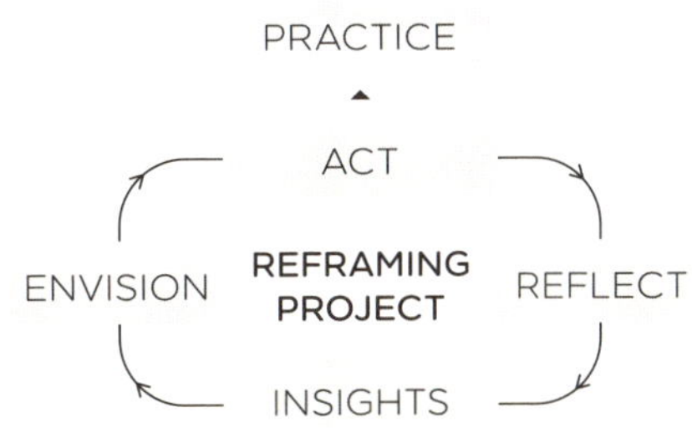

Figure 2.3a The 'washing machine'.

The next move is to go beyond tactics and to engage with the organization at a strategic level as it is the organization's strategy that should determine its form and operational function (see Figure 2.3b).

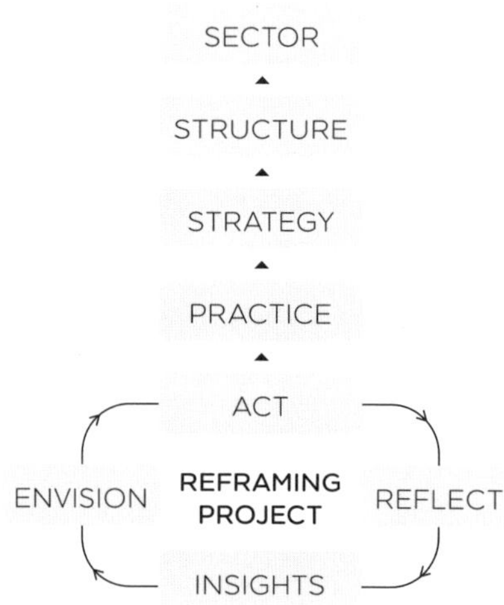

Figure 2.3b The path to change.

This move is an effort to create bottom-up impact, where the insights coming from the projects inform the organization how it needs to adjust and change in order to realize the impact it is seeking. At this point the innovator often bears a resemblance to Sisyphus, struggling to push the boulder up the hill (Figure 2.3c).

The problem is that the innovator attempting this move is working against the natural flow of the organization. Strategy is normally determined top-down, not bottom up. This is a moment of extreme vulnerability for the innovator, their passion to achieve the values of their organization can be seen as insurrection. At this point it is crucial to level up again and become a 'game changer'. The organization is part of a broader sector that has its own orthodoxy and there us another layer of influence even above that. It is what Bourdieu (1999) calls a 'Field', and it sets the norms of the sector, which then influences how organizations' strategize and set structure, see (Figure 2.3c). The Field consists of the prevalent paradigm(s), the infrastructure and disciplines that support the business-as-usual, as well as the narratives about its role in the world and relationships with other sectors and the lifeworld of people. It holds 'the rules of the game' in place (Dorst, 2025).

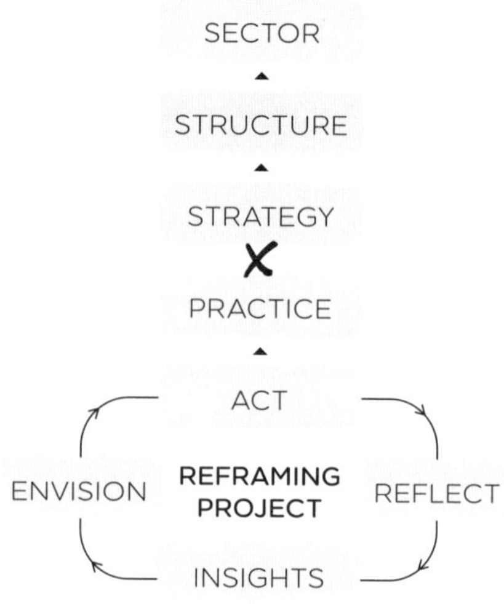

Figure 2.3c The blockage.

What we call 'the blockage' is the collision point between the top-down structure and strategy and the bottom-up practices that have adjusted and developed relative to the lessons learned from the experiments at the operational level. Failing to navigate this conflict point leads to frustration, resignations, and unrealized potential. It is a real problem, and yet it is unintended.

The 'game changer' will navigate this complexity by engaging with the Field. By feeding the insights from the project level directly into the narrative of the Field, the 'game changer' is changing the perception that an organization has (Figure 2.3d).

This creates a new dynamic, combining the two movements: as the insights that come from the projects are used to create a new Field, the organization adapts to this new Field by using its normal top-down adaptive processes, and meets the bottom-up movement halfway (Dorst, 2025). Organizations are adaptive, striving to mirror the developments in their relevant environment, the 'Game Changer' sees this and gives the organization what it needs to make decisions that support 'bottom-up' innovation.

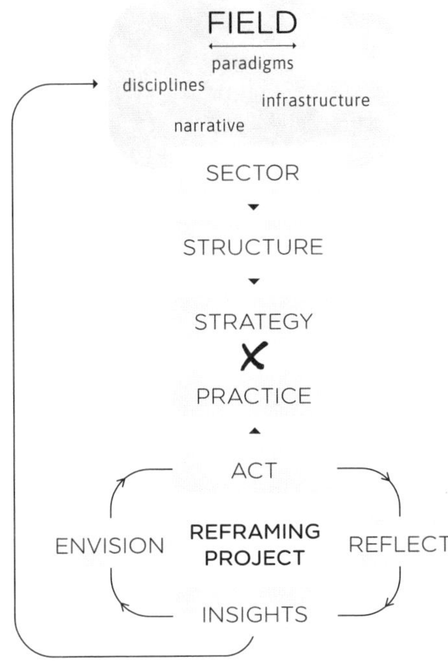

2.3d The Game Changers model.

2.5

CHANGING MINDS

If we want to create a 'new normal', we need to address the 'old normal'. Chances are the Game Changer is working in an established field, and that established field has practices that have developed over time. Emergent technology will have helped to make those practices more efficient, and chances are that education in the professional practice won't have changed much at all in the last decades. This is normal, the science historian Thomas Kuhn (1969) explained how 'normal science' refines existing knowledge within the paradigm, not by making new discoveries, but by creating more precise and reliable observations within the set of underlying assumptions that is held by the field.

Whole careers pass by, and 'excellence' is rewarded within the paradigm by recognizing those who achieve more precise and reliable methods, not those who challenge the very assumptions that underlie the paradigm. Normal science reinforces the assumptions and resists variance. This resistance can be implicit, where the paradigm is so specialized that there are no feedback loops to the outside world (silo-thinking). It can also be cultural, where the Innovator might transgress by challenging assumptions and be told to 'stay in their lane'. Remember our Innovator has now leveled-up to be a Game Changer, so will avoid such pitfalls.

What we can also see from science is that there are exceptions to normal science. Paradigms can shift. In this case the Game Changer feels uneasy, they may be able to see through the assumptions, seeing that something isn't right, and then be able to reframe the situation and change the game.

Here again we find our Game Changer in a very vulnerable situation. While they may be 'right', there are whole organizations and practices that are established in the old paradigm. It is complete folly to even try to convince the old paradigm of the benefits of the new paradigm. They are already invested in the old paradigm, they might have children to feed, bills to pay, holidays to save for, and are doing very nicely thank you very much, and by the way, where is the evidence that this new paradigm will 'work'? And frankly, trying to change someone's mind is just plain rude and disrespectful.

It is good to pause here, and before we start attempting to change somebody else's mind, ask ourselves this question first (as on the aircraft safety card: 'put your own mask on first before helping others').

"When in my life have I actually changed my mind?"

When we advocate a shift in paradigm, we are basically asking people to change their mind on a very fundamental level.

On the whole, people find it surprisingly hard to come up with more than a couple of instances. Changing your mind probably doesn't happen very often. Then we can start unpacking this moment, asking some follow-up questions.

"What was this about?"

"What was the situation/moment?"

"What preceded this moment?"

"What came after?"

"Was there a specific trigger?"etc.

These are important questions - if we want to create deep innovation, we will need to deeply understand this.

This IS the key process of innovation and change. Yet we tend to pass it over, hardly think about it, presuming that giving strong arguments in favor of our view will do the trick and sway the others to our position. We argue constantly, in the belief that argumentation actually works to convince the other on a deep level.

It is worthwhile spending some time reflecting on your own 'conversion experiences'. These conversion experiences may also be quite revealing in explaining how you intuitively try to influence others because they sit well with your own life experience and character. And make us pause and think about what the other might need to change position.

2.6

COLORS OF CHANGE

To understand the dynamics of change itself, the Game Changer will need have a literacy in the field of Change Management. Normally Change Management is engaged to manage a specific, predetermined, top-down change, often in the form of a restructure, or function change. The Game Changer does not operate in this way, they are inviting their organization to create a space for innovation, and in doing so will come up against the same resistances that the Change Manager experiences.

To capture the dynamics of organizational change, Vermaak and de Caluwe (2018) have created a meta-model of change paradigms that sheds light on the challenges/ forces at play when working with organizational cultures around change. To just skim the surface, Figure 2.6 contains quotes to explain what the Colors of Change stand for.

All of these colors are valid and useful and create a shared language for people reflect on their own modus operandi, and those around them. Just observing interactions with this framework in mind is an empowering thing to be doing, and a way of building open, mature, and productive discussion. The Game Changer understands that there is a kaleidoscope of colors at play, and can recognize when the balance is out. A field that relies too heavily on command and control will have a dominance of yellow and blue, with red helping to create resilience making white improbable, green will then perpetuate current practice. This is not a recipe for a healthy innovation portfolio.

The Game Changer can use this nuanced understanding to pinpoint the colors of change that need to be highlighted, or dimmed in order to create space for change.

YELLOW-PRINT CHANGE

"Yellow-print thinking assumes that something only changes when key players are backing it and that little will happen if key players oppose it. In this view, enabling change requires getting the powers that be behind it, whether their power is based on formal positions (e.g. board members) or informal influence (e.g. opinion leaders)."

BLUE-PRINT CHANGE

"In blue-print thinking, rationality--not power--matters most. The assumption that change happens only when you analyze first what the problem is, suggest the best possible solution, and implement it according to plan. Change is thus deemed a linear endeavor: you think before you act. The process is expert-driven: the activities are executed by those who have the necessary know-how experience."

RED-PRINT CHANGE

"In red-print thinking, the emphasis is not on power or rationality but on motivation. The key assumption is that change is not about policies and plans, but about behavior, and that people change their behavior only when they are stimulated to do so. In its simplest form this comes down to barter; the organization hands out rewards and offers support in exchange for personnel taking on tasks and responsibilities and trying their best. It can also go beyond that by taking an interest in people's wellbeing and creating an inspiring working environment."

GREEN-PRINT CHANGE

"In green-print thinking, everything is about learning. Changing and learning are deemed inextricably linked: they are thought to mean almost the same. From a green point of view, however, motivational (red) strategies only work when people are already sufficiently aware and capable to do something differently. The only way forward from a green point of view is then to dig deeper; to discover one's limits and expand and deepen the way we see and act in the world. The process is characterized by setting up learning situations, preferably collective ones as these allow people to give and receive feedback as well as to experiment with more effective ways of acting."

WHITE-PRINT CHANGE

"White-print thinking can be regarded as a reaction to the previous colors, in the sense that these still tend to view change as a planned affair, albeit to a different extent. In contrast, white-print change agents view change as constant and taking place of its own accord. The key assumption is that people can make the most difference when they understand and catalyze a change that is about to happen. In white-print thinking, change agents do not create evolution, but they do support transitions or stand in their way. They embrace complexity as an enriching view of the world that allows one to see what time is ripe for. They see self-organizing dialogical processes as an effective way to deal with the complexity and they take an active part in their emergence. The outcome of such change is unpredictable."

Figure 2.5 The Colors of Change (from Vermaak and de Caluwe, 2018).

2.7

THE STUDIO

Here our Game Changer will establish the infrastructure needed for authentic and sustained strategic innovation. The Game Changer will need to articulate what their innovation strategy will be, and how it will function. Chapters 3 and 4 shows how our Innovators and Game Changers have implemented this thinking in their own contexts. It can be nuanced, but it can also be a very literal translation of the Innovation Studio.

The Innovation Studio has four types of activity (experimenting, learning, communication and growing) and are organized into four 'spaces' each in dynamic relationship with one another: the Lab, the Academy, the Podium and the Temple, adapted from Dorst (2025):

The Lab is the infrastructure for re-framing and experimenting. The Game Changer strategically initiates framing experiments within the organization. These framing experiments have three functions:

1. The organization's current approach is de-framed, which can identify misalignment in the current frame
2. They allow the organization to authentically and meaningfully explore their raison d'etre - the value(s) they wish to create in the world
3. It is the engine-room for new bottom-up initiatives, and the vehicle for new practices to be brought into the disciplinary matrix of the organization

The insights gained through these experiments help to create the new Field - synchronizing the top-down processes with the bottom-up initiatives.

The Academy is the infrastructure for learning within and outside the organization, as well as across the wider innovation ecosystem. The Game Changer will help their organization to strategically shift practices, as well as engage with the professional fields that are holding the current paradigm and emerging practices.

The Podium is the infrastructure that makes sure we change in constant open dialogue with the relevant context. The Game Changer helps their organization avoid new unquestioned assumptions creeping into the new practices, making them less than realistic and in the end creating risk (untested assumptions are the major cause of risk and failure).

The Podium needs a strict rhythm of activities ('What are we going to show?'...'What are we going to do?'...'Who should be there?'...). This creates a continuous strategic discussion on what matters, and on the nature of the quality the Studio is developing.

The Temple is the infrastructure for (personal and organizational) growth, anchoring the deep change and the new paradigms into the core of the organization and its people. The Game Changer will establish a reflective, contemplative space for deep reckoning, inviting professionals to make the change real on a personal level.

These elements need to be present - all of them, and all the time. The Studio is not an 'innovation department' but a network of people that come together as needed. It should involve people from across the organization (and beyond).

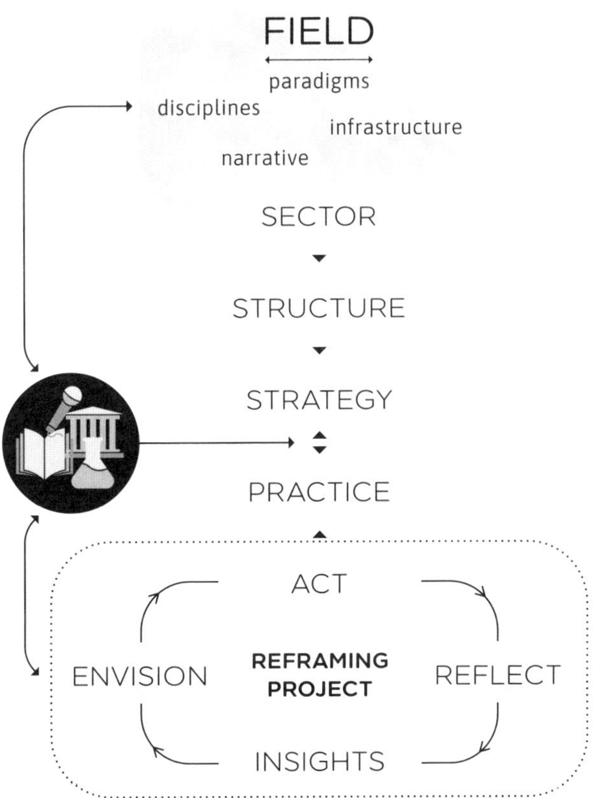

Figure 2.6 Placing the Studio in the Game Changer's model.

2.8

TOOLS AND METHODS FOR STRATEGIC INNOVATION

REINVENTING STRATEGIC INNOVATION - THE HOW

The journey to create a Strategic Innovation Studio can be cut up in three distinct stages: (1) digging for paradigms, (2) re-framing and experimentation and (3) creating the strategic proposition. These stages will be clearly recognizable throughout the case studies in the next chapter. We will briefly introduce them here, to give a sense of what activities they entail.

Stage 1. Digging for Paradigms

In 'Digging for Paradigms' we are seeking to understand the underlying assumptions and key practices that are at play within the situation at hand. This stage is inquisitive in nature, seeking to understand what is, and what has been. It ultimately results in a deframing of the situation. In deframing we show how the issue is currently framed and point to the stated values at play, the working principles in use, as well as the current methods and actions that make up current practice. The inquisitive nature of this stage means that we are seeking to understand, rather than trying to find absolute truths. Ideally this shouldn't be done as a solo activity, there are so many possible tools that can be used to build this understanding (interviews, literature reviews, etc) that can be done as a collective effort. Doing this as a collective, or with each participant bringing a piece of the overall puzzle makes it fun, engaging, and insures against one viewpoint becoming the accepted truth.

Sometimes this act of collaboratively formulating a deframe of the situation will unearth or point to a misalignment between the stated values of the organization and the lived experience of how this plays out - then it is abundantly clear that there is no possible way of expecting to achieve the stated values with the current actions. This stage can be cathartic and provides the launching off point for re-framing and Experimenting. It highlights the gaps between what currently is, and a desired future state.

Stage 2. Re-framing and Experimentation

In this stage we are moving into a propositional mindset. While still maintaining the curiosity of stage one, we are moving from trying to understand 'what is' to proposing 'what could be'. This stage builds on the momentum created by involving multiple people from the organization and their varied life/professional experiences. The tools in this stage support going deep into the understanding of the values at play.

Again by working collaboratively with mixed methods and bringing together different perspectives the group can start to explore new frames together (Appendix 1). In this stage it is key to start doing. Run small experiments to test the re-frames. A re-frame is a hypothesis that can be tested firstly by talking it through, and if it seems like a good idea it should be tested. Develop the concept further and sense check it. If it still seems fruitful then find a way of testing it in the real world.

Stage 3. Creating the Strategic Proposition

Stage 2 will have required significant boot-strapping. You will have asked people for their time and resources. You will also have a number of outcomes from your framing experiments. Bringing these two things together; outcomes and resources means that you now have the ingredients to put together a Strategic Proposition. Please note: this third stage is NOT about doing more experiments, on a project level, or about trying to implement the results of the re-framing experiments from stage 2. This stage is about stepping back, and thinking strategically about the infrastructure needed to bring these frames and this type of thinking forward. This is the Strategic Innovation Studio. Most likely, your organization already has elements in place that can built into this new infrastructure, but perhaps it is missing one or two. This is the time to do the strategic thinking needed to get the Innovation Studio right, but don't let perfect be the enemy of progress. Start where you can and build momentum, and gradually bring more people in as participants. Together, you will develop the elements of the next generation strategic innovation practice.

The three stages we have just outlined are little more than the backbone of a complex development process. The tools and methods we will outline in this section are the flesh on the bones - we hope you find them useful and inspiring. Then, in Chapter 3, we will finally get to see this in action, in the case studies of the pioneers.

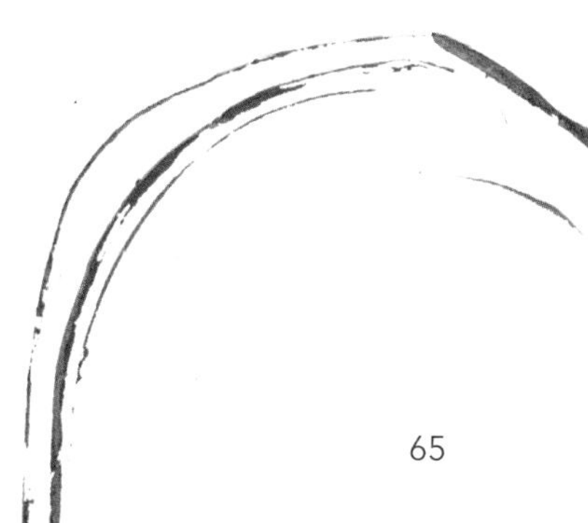

STAGE 1. DIGGING FOR PARADIGMS

DEFRAME

The ultimate aim in digging for paradigms is to understand the paradigm your organization is in, relative to the challenges it faces. This act of deframing is supported and informed by the other tools in this section. It is useful to just get started with deframing, and to build a deeper understanding of the organization and how it relates to its challenges over time.

To deframe, apply the practices framework to your own organization, or topic of interest. Is there a clear 'problem frame'? Is there an articulated 'action frame'? What are the actions? What are the methods in use? What are the working principles? What value is being created/is at stake? See Appendix 1 for an example.

It may be that you can identify opportunities for innovation just from this exercise. Perhaps the actions that your organization does made perfect sense when they were put in place, but now aren't achieving the value your organization strives for, or perhaps there is misalignment elsewhere. How would we know, unless we look?

HIDDEN RULES

For strategic innovation to succeed and lead to impact, it needs to be based on fact, on candid and clear knowledge of the real practices in an organization. We are not that interested in what people say they do (that is often aspirational, to put it nicely) but in what actually happens.

In a very enlightening paper, Jane Bower and co-authors (1997) describe their 'hidden rules' analysis of the offshore industry operating out of Aberdeen. They take on a wealth of primary and secondary information (interviews, mail, documents) to painstakingly describe both the 'open rules' (the official rules that say what should happen) and the 'hidden rules' (how the sector actually operates). For every 'open rule' they then take some situations where the difference between these was obvious and discuss them with various stakeholders. The result is both insightful and at times hilarious.

Some highlights:

- There often is great agreement on the hidden rules, everybody knows them
- People look a bit guilty, 'found out' when they are brought into the conversation
- The contradictions between open and hidden rules sometimes lead to misunderstandings, especially for outsiders (especially where the 'open rules' lead to false expectations or acts that are based on misguided anticipation)
- The 'outing' of the hidden rules is also seen as liberating, cathartic

On the other hand, the hidden rules can lead to common secrets in the sector, which then can lead to defensiveness across these organizations. And, as Chris Argyris (2000) has shown time and time again, defensiveness stifles innovation. The hidden rules need to be surfaced for radical innovation to happen. But how? We have seen above that this can be done by the serious probing research. It can also be done more creatively and playfully:

A communication consultancy from Rotterdam, Renewmedia, got to work with a client organization that was on the verge of going through a huge transformation (basically, a new technology was coming in that revolutionized a whole sector). They approached this by making short film clips of people within the organization, talking about what they do - based on the observation that you may have an image and think you know what your colleagues are doing, but this often wrong. They made sure the short film clips were always interesting and a bit funny too, with great out-takes. A new clip was put this out on the firm's intranet every Friday afternoon - and everybody would be watching it, straight away. This helped people familiarize themselves with the bigger picture of the organization, and provided a good, common basis for reflection. Gradually, more of the new and upcoming practices were mixed in, and discussion were started on what they would mean for the organization.

The key to understanding the hidden rules at play in a situation is a subtle shift in listening; we can understand what they are when we don't concentrate on what people say, but on HOW they talk about something....

More on this later.

RHETORICAL PERSUASION

How does your organization reason? What truth claims does it make? Start observing how communication happens, both in meetings, but also in written communication. Can you observe any of the below reasoning patterns?

Reasoning pattern	Observed	Notes
Cause to effect An observable action leads to an observable event.		
Effect to cause An observable event happens, an inference is made of the causal action(s).		
From symptoms A number of observable events are happening, a cause is proposed.		
Criteria to application A set of desirable criteria are highlighted, and a course of action to achieve them is proposed.		
From comparison or analogy Conclusions from one situation are inferred onto another situation.		

FALLACY

Sometimes we can slip into thought patterns that make no real sense. They may seem reasonable, but they are fallacies. Be on the look-out for these faulty reasoning patterns.

Adapted from Larson (2010).

Fallacy	Observed	Notes
Post hoc ergo propter hoc: An event happened after an action, it is argued that the action caused the event. The fallacy being that correlation between two (or more things) doesn't imply causation. After this, therefore because of this.		
Ad hominem: A person is attacked in an effort to discredit their argument. Playing the wo/man not the ball.		
Ad populum: Arguing that because something is popular it is valid. On the bandwagon.		
The undistributed middle: It is argued that because a concept shares attributes with another discredited concept, that it itself is discredited. Guilt by association.		
Straw man: Propose a weak version of opponent's argument, then knock it down.		
Partial facts: Painting things in a light that supports your own argument. Telling one side of the story. Quoting out of context.		
Appeal to sympathy: Using prejudice or stereotype to undermine the counter argument.		
False dilemma: Presenting two sides of the argument as if they are mutually exclusive. Zero sum game.		
Ad verecundiam: Arguing from authority or tradition. Because I say it is so, It is so. We have always done it like this.		
Begging the question: Evading, redirecting the question to another topic.		
Non sequitur: Using irrelevant arguments to distract.		

REPRESENTATIVE REDISCRIPTION

Adapted from Howard Gardner's Changing Minds (2004).

In our Strategic Innovation practice, changing minds is not about persuasion, it's about providing people with new ways to engage with a situation. Each of the following modes offers a different path into re-framing and re-understanding a challenge.

1. Story as Entry Point

Use narrative to frame the issue. Stories invite empathy, create coherence, and anchor abstract ideas in lived experience. A good story opens space for change by showing what's at stake.

2. Examples That Count

Introduce quantitative or specific examples that ground the issue in real-world evidence. These serve as boundary objects, making the abstract tangible and the complex comprehensible.

3. Make the Structure Visible

Draw out logical connections. Map how key elements relate. Expose contradictions or assumptions. People shift thinking more easily when the structure of an argument is made explicit.

4. Engage with Deeper Purpose

Ask what really matters. Explore the values and existential drivers behind the issue. This invites people to connect with the challenge at a more personal, meaningful level.

5. Design for Aesthetic Insight

Use form, image, or experience to express and explore ideas. Aesthetic approaches bypass intellectual resistance—letting people feel the issue before they think it through.

6. Work in the Situation

Create interventions that are hands-on and context-embedded. Mindsets shift most reliably through action; making, prototyping, applying ideas and seeing what happens.

7. Create Conditions for Collective Learning

Facilitate collaboration. Put people in situations where they must co-create. This generates new perspectives—not from outside—but from within the doing.

8. Mobilize Through Meaningful Incentives

Create challenges that reward new ways of thinking. Mind shift becomes more likely when resources, recognition, and real-world support follow. From large-scale funding programs to internal innovation days, incentives shape the seriousness of engagement.

GROUNDED THEORY

Grounded theory was developed by two sociologists (Glaser and Strauss) in the 1960s. It is said to contrast with the hypothetico-deductive method in that it asks the practitioner to suspend judgment and allow understanding to emerge through the application of the method.

We have found it a useful method to understand an issue at the values level. These values can then be used to re-frame a situation (see §2.2)

To begin with conduct several interviews and record them. In the interviews you will be asking someone with some expertise on the topic for their understanding. Remember to ask for permission to record, and if you are doing this as an academic study you will need to gain ethics clearance from your university.

Print out the transcripts of the interviews and read through them to identify the codes. The method can also be used on artifacts like board reports, or other documents.

There are three levels of codes; open, axial and selective codes.

Open code

These are the words/concepts that stand out from your transcripts/ artifacts. They may stand out because they occur multiple times, or because they 'seem' important. On the first pass of your transcript you may find it useful to highlight these concepts.

Often there will be 15-20 open codes in a 1 hour interview.

Put each transcript/artifact through this process. You then take the outcomes of this coding to the next stage of coding.

Axial code

Take your open codes and look for patterns across all of the open codes. It could be useful as an interim step to summarize each of your open codes into one or two words, and to write them on post it notes. Then group words that have a similar meaning.

Give each of the groupings a name that is descriptive of the grouping. You may find it useful to abstract away from the context that you are investigating for this step, and to focus on the meaning of the words.

For every 20 open codes you may find that there are 3-5 axial codes.

Selective code

In this step you are looking for relationships between the axial codes, and to find a central concept. Glaser and Strauss were fairly strict in directing you to find/nominate one selective code. We've always found it useful to be less strict about this. However, if you have more than 3-5 selective codes at this point, then you may like to spend a bit more time thinking about the patterns and relationships. From this thinking you may be able to get it down to 1-2 selective codes.

UNDERSTANDING MISUNDERSTANDINGS

The colors of change model is very much a living body of work. More colors have been added to the original five presented above (see §2.6), and many case studies have been published in which the colors have been applied, alone and in combination.

It is important to realize that these colors of change have deep roots; they touch the very logic that people use to reason with. In Figure 2.7a the thoughtful consultant and author André Schaminée compares different thinking styles that people use in change conversations. This is a telling comparison, showing the enormous potential for misunderstanding each other across these divides.

For instance; a 'design thinker' might table an inspiring example as evidence of the merit of a new direction, while the others wouldn't even recognize it as such - in their worlds, only rational explanation or evidence of support count.

	COGNITIVE knowledge and truth	NEGOTIATION power	DESIGN THINKING learning
SOURCE	logic	ideology	emergence
APPROACH	thinking (rationality)	wanting (morality)	feeling (empathy)
CORE VALUE	objectivity	inter-subjectivity	subjectivity
BASIS FOR JUDGMENT	evaluation	argumentation	aesthetics
STARTING POINT	definition of the problem	conflict	engagement
RELATIONSHIP TO SUBJECT	distance	influence	taking part
BASIS FOR AUTHORITY	explanation	connection	inspiration
RESULT	knowledge	agreement	new meaning and value

Figure 2.7a A comparison of styles of thinking (after: [Schaminée, 2018]).

STAGE 2. RE-FRAMING AND EXPERIMENTATION

THEME ANALYSIS

Here we draw on Hermeneutic Phenomenology (van Manen, 1990). To understand the nature and the structure of a Theme, personal experience is key. Consult your own experience or interview people about theirs. For example, to take up the Theme of 'Identity forming' as it surfaced in the Kings Cross project (see Appendix 1), you could explore questions like:

What are your own strong experiences with forming or changing your identity?

What triggered these?

How did it feel?

What were you thinking?

What did you do?

Did other people play a role?

To enrich this picture we can then turn to the arts: music, visual art, novels, theatre and film are a great source of both deep understanding and practical knowledge. Good art can provide universal insight, not as abstract knowledge but expressed in a very concrete and personal way.

On a slightly more abstract level, one can consider the psychology and sociology of the theme -

How does identity relate to our deeply felt beliefs and values?

What feelings are involved with identity?

What mental models, knowledge, learning processes, thinking, etc. is an identity actually based on? What are the elements of a person's identity?

What are the physical expressions of identity?

What external factors can have a positive or negative effect on the personal experience of identity? How can relationships affect identity?

The experience of a Theme like identity is also dynamic, it changes over time.

How is identity formed?

Are there discontinuities in the development of identity or is the change smooth and gradual?

When does the forming of identity go 'wrong'?

Themes like identity are layered, and to attain a deep enough understanding they need to be researched thoroughly in various ways. Scientific literature can be too aloof and abstract, but it is very helpful for some themes.

Philosophers literally devote most of their life to thinking about specific themes - for identity, the existentialists (e.g. Camus) and phenomenologists (e.g. van Manen) are great starting points.

What generally works well as a strategy is to start by focusing on personal experiences. We all have deep knowledge of these universal human themes, they are inside all of us. It is just that we normally don't think or talk about them that much. They tend to come up only in the deepest conversations with our best friends, or at perhaps in eulogies at funerals. Why don't we talk on this level more often?

INTRINSIC MOTIVATION

In his work on paradigmatic shift, Kuhn mentions a 'back door', as it were, where people can be swayed to adopt a new paradigm by appealing to a different, deeper motivation.

For our purposes, this back door is probably the front door; if reasoning only gets us so far, what else can we do to support people to make this 'leap of faith'? Both in academia and in the commercial world, there has been lots of research into the deep, intrinsic motivations that actually drive people's behavior.

A list we find useful is of '15 positive drivers'. These are just the top 15 (in alphabetical order) of a longer list that was based on extensive survey of people from around the world.

ACCOMPLISHMENT
A sense of satisfaction that can result from productivity, focus, talent, or status.

BEAUTY
The appreciation of qualities that give pleasure to the senses or spirit.

COMMUNITY
A sense of unity with others around us and general connection with other human beings.

CREATION
The sense of having produced something new and original, and in so doing, to have made a lasting contribution.

DUTY
The willing application of oneself to a responsibility.

ENLIGHTENMENT
Clear understanding through logic or inspiration.

FREEDOM
The sense of living without unwanted constraints.

HARMONY
The balanced and pleasing relationship of parts to a whole, whether in nature, society, or an individual.

JUSTICE
The assurance of equitable and unbiased treatment.

ONENESS
A sense of unity with everything around us.

REDEMPTION
Atonement or deliverance from past failure or decline.

SECURITY
The freedom from worry about loss.

TRUTH
A commitment to honesty and integrity.

VALIDATION
The recognition of oneself as a valued individual worthy of respect.

WONDER
Awe in the presence of a creation beyond one's understanding.

Figure 2.7b 15 Positive Drivers (Diller et al, 2005)

These deep inner motivations are important, as they sit in the lifeworld of people, crossing disciplines and modes of thinking. We can FEEL such intrinsic drivers, and as innovators we can appeal to them. They are profound, they are what makes us tick.

In our portfolio of innovation projects, it is the ones that had a real closeness to the positive drivers of the participants that were the most stable, went the furthest, and had the most impact. This makes sense: the fact that they were personally important to people in their own lifeworld gave these projects an inherent strength and stability that other projects didn't have ("nice ideas"). The more of these positive drivers that can be built into an initiative, the better.

NOMOLOGICAL NETWORKS

In a dictionary, a concept is defined by describing it in simpler words.

That is not really useful here: if we want to achieve a rich understanding of a deep human theme, it is better to look at an abstract concept (e.g. identity) as it is related to other concepts (a nice image would be to say that it is 'suspended' between other concepts).

In making a nomological network, we put the central concept of the theme (in this case: 'forming identity') in the middle and surround it with concepts that have a relationship with it. These relationships can be very varied; synonyms, antonyms, loose associations, metaphors, or even proverbs that the concept plays a role in. Deep human themes operate on different 'axes'; intrinsic vs extrinsic, individual vs social, etc.

As said, we have found that a dictionary is not that helpful for creating this richer picture of the concept - but a thesaurus is.

Then to progress to Frames we strategically choose some of these terms that are close to the theme, and map the patterns of action (Practices) that are associated with these terms. Please note that 'strategically' in this case means that we choose terms that are relevant, related, but in a non-obvious, slightly oblique manner - this is crucial in order to arrive at a new approach to the original problem situation. Choosing ones that are too obvious or too close to the theme probably means not shifting the thinking and eventually falling back into existing solutions.

STAGE 3. CREATING THE STRATEGIC PROPOSITION

LEARNING ON THE JOB

It is often hard to learn from projects, because they are all so very different. Knowledge you have picked up in one project can't often be applied in the next one, so how do you learn? This is true in an education setting, as well as for professional practice.

At Stanford University's Center for Design Research (which sits within the Faculty of Engineering) they have found a workaround for this problem by creating a new design curriculum layout. The students receive a really complicated design assignment, and have to come up with a design and a model of it in just a couple of days. When they have finished, they get the same assignment again, but now with two weeks to complete it. Finally they get it for a third time, with the six months that you realistically need to develop the product.

What happens? Well, in a few days you can always make something, but it isn't going to be very good - it will only be a sketchy embodiment of your first idea. In two weeks you are able to generate more ideas, and do some research. You cover some ground, but you'll mainly discover how much more needs to be done to really achieve a good design. So, it comes as a relief to get the six months you need to do the job properly. The students now benefit from all the things they had learned about the problem and solution in the first two run-throughs of the project.

This method of working out a project several times has also been adopted by design agencies. It is wonderful way to embark on the exploration and learning that is part of any design project. And forcing yourself to create a complete result (model) in every run gives very good feedback on the possibilities and difficulties of various lines of attack. Design firms also often try to get the client involved in these 'pressure cooker' sessions, so that the client learns what to expect in a design process, and the foundation of a good cooperation with the client's people can be laid before the real project begins.

It is always a pity that you only understand what you should have done at the very end of the project. This method is a way to generate that knowledge early on, so that you can begin your project with the benefit of hindsight.

LIFEWORLD

What do you navigate by in complex societal issues?

By the values that the system should achieve - and we have mentioned before that in the end, value only exists (gets experienced and realized) in the lifeworld of people. So in creating value, we need to intimately know what the lifeworld of people we are working for is like.

In the reality of our Lifeworlds, striving for an important value inevitably will go to the detriment of others. This shows exactly if something IS a real value - if we are not ready to sacrifice anything for it, it cannot be really important. Our lifeworlds are complex places, that are full of these tensions. Good art, such as novels and movies express these all-too-human tensions in deep ways. That touches the core of our humanity.

Extending this sacrifice to others goes to the core of what makes a society. While value is realized in the lifeworld of people, societal value is realized in their social space. Often this social space needs to be extended before a new approach will be accepted. We have learned in societal projects, say in a neighborhood, to go there and always ask two questions of the people we meet. The first question is, (1) 'What do you need/want?' - and in the answer, everybody sounds like an egotist, but then, we asked them what they themselves wanted. Therefore it is very important to ask a second question: (2) 'What would be good for the neighborhood/street?'

The difference between these two answers shows how much people are ready to sacrifice for the other, how much they hold back on their own interests for the common good.

This is the social space, and it shows their true compassion and humanity. At times, these answers can be noble, beautiful and heart-warming. Social space is about sacrifice, not about self-interest. The Burning Man festival has picked this up an amplified it to an extreme; at the core, the whole event is purely about the social space that people can create together (see the Burning Man rules Appendix 2).

In shaping the change itself, we need to create interventions that not only address the values in the lifeworlds of the people concerned, and their social spaces, the change should also be in tune with lifeworlds of the professionals involved. To give the word to Dick Rijken:

"PROFESSIONAL LIFEWORLDS

There is a tendency to contrast the notion of 'the lifeworld' to that of 'the system world', with an underlying suggestion of 'lifeworld good, system world bad'; customers, citizens, or patients are often seen as 'victims' of cold, technocratic systems that don't really care about them. The reality is not that simple. 'Systems' don't exist without people who order them, design them, and work within them. All systems express values - explicitly (because they were designed to express them), or implicitly (when they just happen to favor certain values over others). This is a daily reality for professionals who work in these systems. They are part of those systems, and have different kinds of agency within them. And they are also people with their own values and emotions. Their professional practices - what it is that they do on a daily basis - are important events in their lifeworlds. Understanding the lifeworlds of professionals is just as important as understanding those of patients, customers, or citizens. Many professionals genuinely care about their jobs, and find meaning in them. They want to make a difference in the lifeworlds of real people.

Many workers in health care or in education see their work as their 'calling', and expect their jobs to be a source of meaning or purpose in their lives. When the reality of their professional practice does not allow them to experience personal values like 'caring for others' or 'inspiring young people' on a daily basis, they feel alienated in their professional life.

Making systems more meaningful often requires a stronger connection between the values of people who work inside them and those of the outside world. We want a car mechanic to truly care about our car, teachers to truly care about our children, doctors to truly care about our health, and we want all of them to feel that they act on those passions on a daily basis. If an organization has a hard time finding employees, they are advised to rethink the alignment of the values expressed in the lifeworlds 'on the job' of their professionals with the personal values of those professionals. Don't expect a care worker or a teacher to find meaning in spending hours and hours to satisfy organizational values like accountability or efficiency. For many people, professional life is not a role playing game where they act out a role in a script that was written by others."

CREATING STUDIO PRINCIPLES

To make innovation and change happen, we will need to work in ways that are different from functionally defined relationships that organizations create to scaffold their structure and run their processes. Business as usual relationships are about the efficient running of the machine, and they are not the ones we need for creation and change. We need to find a way to organize ourselves away from normal, formal, transactional relationships in a way that we can't easily fall back into them (there seems to be a gravitational pull towards the practices we call 'business as usual').

We have learned that to achieve deep innovation and change, it is important to spend time to co-create "the new rules of the game". As an example to show what we mean by this, please have a look at the 'principles' below, that were formulated by professor Dick Rijken for a social research and design lab in the city of The Hague. Please, as you read this, imagine how different the practice of an organization is that abides by these rules...

Rules for The Hague University Lab, 'The Pavilion'

Dick Rijken

The Pavilion does research into a meaning-led approach to complex problems. This is fundamentally practice-based research: asking fundamental questions to (and about) practice.

We approach social problems in various domains like safety, education or governance from an artistic mentality. We are looking for methods and techniques that enable students and professionals from various domains to work in such a meaning-centered way.

0 - There are nine rules

No more, no less. Ten is too much and eight is not enough. This is rule number zero, so it doesn't count. All rules will be strictly enforced.

1 - Only nice people [Fight Club]

We are working with passionate people, that also have a sense of humor and do not make things unnecessarily difficult. We are dealing with very serious problems, that can only be dealt with from a playful mindset. Nice people have a broad scope of interest, and they are always curious about what others are doing. Where possible, we help each other. Asking questions about the definition of 'nice people' is not nice.

The use of terms like 'innovation', 'management', 'valorization', 'social cohesion', implementation' etc is kept to a minimum. We will only use difficult words for difficult things. What we can say, we will say accurately and about all other things we remain silent.

2 - It's about meaning [Yes Men]

Many complex problems are hard because they consist of people, organizations and their relationships. We are fascinated by technology, but will always search for the human and social meaning behind the questions, and use this approach to create new perspectives. Nobody is waiting for us to come up with solutions that have no meaning. Meaning first - this is non-negotiable.

3 - Nobody is the boss

Everything is allowed, in particular the things that cannot happen anywhere else. Everybody can do what they want and if this causes practical problems, then we solve those collectively. Everybody cleans up after themselves and makes coffee for others. There are no limits to the agreements we can reach. When in doubt, see rule 1.

4 - Quality

Nothing is done sloppily. No spelling mistakes or typos. Everything can always be better, but the perfect is the biggest enemy of the good. We are never content, except when something is finished - then we are happy with what we have done, and the learnings we can take to the future. See rule 1.

5 - Think big, do small… and doing is thinking

We never just solve a problem, but will always search for the bigger story around or behind the issue. We will publish all we can, once we are convinced we have learned something that would also be interesting for others. We are not very interested in abstract ideas about life in general, or other questions that cannot be resolved in a concrete manner. Everything we do is deeply thought through, and feasible in execution.

Thinking is doing. We learn through experimenting, trying out and learn from our mistakes.

6 - Taking responsibility

An idea is good when we can take it forward ourselves. If not, then not. Anybody who has a plan, takes care that it is implemented. If you have a great idea that should be implemented by others, you make sure they can do so. See rule 1.

7 - Feeling and thinking: beautiful is good

We are working intuitively, but we know what we are doing (although this may take a while). Intuition is important for judging and deciding, and very useful as a starting point for incisive thought. When we show results, we make clear that feeling and thinking are equally valuable. In content and form. No bureaucratic language, but also no PowerPoint with pictures that do not add feeling to a bunch of keywords.

In everything we do, we try to add beauty, even when that is not needed. Beauty is important. It doesn't arise on its own. That's why. See rule 1.

8 - Take risks wherever you can

If you don't make mistakes, you are not really trying. Experimenting is doing first, and then learning. As long as nobody dies in the worst case scenario, anything is possible. Lack of courage has caused us much trouble and prevented much good. Saying sorry is appreciated, doing better next time is preferred. See rule 1.

9 - From the outside in

Everything we do because of the potential meaning it has for the outside world. So we drag the outside world into the lab. Partners, users, stakeholders, all are equally welcome to participate in everything we do. If the outside world doesn't get it, or isn't ripe for it, we should explain better. We do not work on request (see rule 1 to 8).

These rules create a completely different world of practice, where new things MUST happen.

Just think about your own environment, what principles would be needed to get into a completely different groove? In Appendix 2 you will find some more lists of rules and principles, set up by remarkable individuals and organizations, that have inspired us in this. You will have to make your own.

How to create your principles

Normally, we hardly pay attention to the way we work together, and therefore assume a certain type of relationship to be productive. The very act of sitting down together and taking the time to create principles that are different fosters a positive culture in the Studio and beyond.

These principles should be challenging: different enough from business-as-usual so that nobody can fall back into their 'normal' patterns of practice. They should be strongly anchored in people's positive drivers, especially those drivers that are normally not part and parcel of their professional lifeworld. The principles should also be surprising, light, and humorous.

These workshop sessions can be hilarious (in putting up a mirror to how we are working now) and at the same time they can be liberating, as people start to realize and think through what could be done differently if we just agree to do it. And the creation of the new rules of the game naturally involves taking responsibility for your own side of the relationship, challenging yourself and the other to find a different dynamic. Taking care of this together creates a new bond between people. And in our experience, these rules are often referred to later on, and taken very seriously. They are very much needed; all of us have the tendency to slip into the normal (functional, transactional) mode, especially in times of stress. Then we do need to be reminded that the Studio is a different space.

CHAPTER 3

PIONEERS OF A NEW PRACTICE

INTRODUCTION

We are now coming to the main course on the menu of this book, the cases and projects that show what happens when these concepts and models are brought together by strategic innovation professionals, working in a concrete context. The proof of the pudding is in the eating.

In the following sections you will encounter these compelling stories from the cases, large and small, across many different sectors. They are worth reading one-by-one, and take some time to let them sink in. You will see that there are clear patterns that emerge across these cases, as organizations and disciplines struggle with the same issues. But the paths they take and the practices they apply are interestingly diverse and different. Reading through them, one cannot help but be inspired - they are all good stories, but they really hit home when you (as an active reader) take the time to connect them to your own situation and practice.

After all, this is not about these cases, but it is all about reinventing your own approach to strategic innovation!

3.1

CARE FUTURES LAB: CONVENING FOR CARE

Steve Sullivan, Lara Doltz, Matt Whale, Erin Bennett

COLLABORATION BEYOND PROJECTS

The Care Futures Lab emerged in early 2024 as a response to the deep-rooted challenges facing Australia's care and community services sectors. Recognizing the limitations of traditional, siloed approaches, a coalition of organizations came together around one central idea: systemic change is only possible through collaboration. From the outset, the Lab was not designed as a static project with fixed outcomes, but as a living, evolving ecosystem–a lab and, eventually, a movement–committed to imagining and enacting new paradigms of care.

Convened by three consultants from strategic design agency How to Impact and one from a leading care provider, the foundational workshop in February 2024 brought together practitioners from aged care, disability services, youth mental health, community development, and humanitarian work. This deliberately diverse gathering set the tone for an open-ended, experimental process. Rather than trying to "fix" the system, participants were invited to suspend assumptions, re-frame challenges, and reflect on what truly matters in care. A provocative insight quickly surfaced; Why do we continue to treat care as a solution to a problem?

This shift–from solving to sensing, from delivery to relationship–marked a foundational turning point. Participants expressed a shared desire to move beyond compliance-driven service models toward a system grounded in trust, relationships, and experimentation.

HOLDING THE TENSION: CREATING FLEXIBLE COHERENCE

As coalition builders, our role was to nurture both common and uncommon ground–to support the emergence of coherence without collapsing the diversity and complexity that made the Lab powerful. We recognized the clarity that reductionism can offer, while also remaining alert to its tendency to prematurely close off new ways of thinking.

Rather than begin with predefined outcomes or narrow goals, the Lab adopted a "Beautiful Question" approach, inspired by Warren Berger (2019). These questions served not to resolve ambiguity, but to hold space for it–inviting curiosity, imagination, and multiple perspectives. A Beautiful Question is not just rhetorical; it is a way of setting direction without determining a fixed destination. In many ways, the Care Futures Lab aimed to create the conditions for new questions to emerge– questions that awaken new ways of seeing–by their asking alone–and quietly unsettle the status quo.

DE-FRAME AND RE-FRAME: CARE PRACTICES

One of the Lab's core practices was the deliberate act of "de-framing" – challenging assumptions about what care is, who it's for, and how it should be delivered – followed by "re-framing" care as an interconnected, co-created social practice.

	De-frame The Current Practice of Care (What We're Leaving Behind	Re-frame Future-Facing Practice of Care (What We're Growing Toward)
Values	• Care as a cost, driven by efficiency and compliance. • Services built around problems, not people.	• Care as connection and human flourishing. • Support as liberating internal capacity for change. • Efficacy over efficiency. • Trust, relationships, and humanity as foundational values.
Principles	• Short-term, siloed thinking due to funding cycles. • Risk-averse and compliance-driven decision-making.	• Start with people, not services. • Long-term, place-based thinking. • Experimentation as practice. • Relationships as scope; learning as method.
Methods	• Service delivery silos. • Pilot-fatigue and transaction-heavy processes. • Processes that assess rather than understand. • Reliance on standardized pathways.	• Post-service care. • Bespoke-by-default relational work. • Community-led connection. • Long-term exploration spaces inside organizations–labs, residencies, "care commons." • Funding design: flexible, scaffolded, and regenerative, not extractive. • Front-line autonomy with learning loops. • Community-rooted care with iteration built in.
Actions	• Apply ➔ Deliver ➔ Report ➔ Restart. • Tick-box interventions. • Caseworkers overloaded with narrow remits. • Support given only after crisis hits.	• Enable ➔ Stabilize ➔ Step back. • Build trust, reduce barriers. • Support intrinsic change through everyday action. • Host cross-sector wisdom exchanges, not just strategic partnerships.

THE CHALLENGE: PARADOXES OF COLLABORATION FOR LONG-TERM IMPACT

The Lab encountered a landscape of paradoxes–tensions that illuminated the gap between current care systems and the futures participants longed to create. These were not puzzles to be solved, but deep systemic contradictions–calling not for quick fixes, but for reflection, imagination, and bold re-imagining.

The Paradox of Risk:

Organizations spoke of innovation, yet moved cautiously, hemmed in by the scaffolding of compliance and the fragile architecture of funding. There was a yearning to "design for uncertainty," to open the door to the unknown–but also a quiet fear that truly listening might unveil needs too vast, too human, too costly to meet. The risk wasn't just in action–it was in knowing too much.

The Paradox of Evidence:

In a world built on proof, the most transformative ideas arrived without credentials. They knocked softly, untested and unseen. Yet the demand for data cast long shadows, favoring the measurable over the meaningful. Certainty was a prerequisite where it should have been a reward. Innovation asked for faith; the system asked for guarantees.

The Paradox of Identity:

Many organizations wore their functions as identities—defining themselves by services offered, not by the deeper why that called them into being. In that narrowing, possibilities withered. Roles became cages, and purpose drifted. Though hearts longed for new paradigms, the courage to let go of old names, old maps, was harder to summon.

The Paradox of Clarity:

To manage the unmanageable, problems were boxed and labeled—homelessness, addiction, unemployment. Yet in naming, the whole was fractured. The living tangle of causes, conditions, and connections was stripped away. Clarity came at the cost of truth. Systemic change called from the margins, but definitions kept the center still.

The Paradox of Structure:

The sector itself, designed to care, was structured to compete. Siloed, fragmented, and often adversarial, it strained against the very interdependence care requires. While the Lab imagined networks of mutual learning and place-based wisdom, the dominant architecture reinforced division. The system's design betrayed its purpose.

These paradoxes didn't block the path—they were the path. The Lab became a rare space to dwell in these contradictions as opportunities to unlearn.

EXPERIMENT: INQUIRING INTO CARE STRUCTURES, RELATIONS, AND VALUES

The Lab encountered a landscape over several months, the Lab became a space of sustained inquiry—holding a wide range of collective conversations, design workshops, and reflective dialogues across organizations, sectors, and lived experiences. Rather than rushing toward consensus or action, we deliberately stayed in the discomfort of exploration, testing our assumptions and language through cycles of engagement. The guiding "Beautiful Question" created a container within which multiple sub-questions could emerge—each reflecting a different layer of the care system.

We explored questions of structure, asking:

- *How do we create the infrastructure to embrace risk as an essential ingredient for sector impact?*
- *What structures and funding models are needed to enable collaborative care ecosystems—within, across, and beyond traditional service domains?*

This revealed a recurring tension: the current system rewards predictability and short-term outcomes, yet what's needed is long-term thinking, space for experimentation, and trust-building across difference. We saw the necessity for new governance models, shared funding mechanisms, and physical and relational infrastructure that could hold collaborative innovation over time.

We also delved into questions of relationships, provoked by one simple yet profound inquiry:

- *What if all people had a support network before they needed it?*

This question shifted conversations from reactive service provision to proactive community building—surfacing the importance of early connection, reciprocity, and informal care networks. We explored social intimacy to re-language connection in a youth-led project and how social capital is created, who holds it, and what prevents its formation. It led to broader discussions about moving "upstream" in care, where resilience is built not through interventions, but through everyday relational ecosystems.

Then came the questions of values, which proved to be the most generative—and challenging—of all:

- *What values and cultural narratives shape our societal relationship to care?*
- *What language do we need to describe care not as burden or cost, but as a shared and vital part of life?*
- *What values and assumptions must we unlearn to imagine different care futures?*

These value-led explorations opened space for cultural critique and visioning. Participants interrogated dominant ideas about independence, productivity, and crisis-driven care. They began to experiment with new language—terms like "relational infrastructure," "radical reciprocity," and "interdependence" became part of the shared lexicon. Across these sessions, care was no longer seen as a transactional service, but as a cultural practice, a relational ethic, and a shared responsibility.

Throughout this extended period, we resisted the urge to collapse the inquiry into a single model or theory of change. Instead, we allowed the complexity to breathe—surfacing tensions, paradoxes, and patterns across different community contexts. This iterative exploration created the conditions for a new framing to emerge organically, rather than being imposed.

A UNIFYING FRAME: NEIGHBORHOOD WELL-BEING FOR BELONGING AND SOCIAL CAPITAL

When we talk about social "problems", the conversation often begins with familiar challenges; housing affordability, access to services, and social connection. These are real and pressing issues—but they also reflect dominant paradigms that limit how we understand and respond to community life. Too often, responses are shaped by service delivery models that address symptoms rather than root causes, reinforcing siloed thinking and reactive interventions.

In response, we arrived—through collective sense-making and iterative dialogue—at a different kind of framing: the question of neighborhood well-being for belonging and social capital. This offered a shared direction rooted in place, people, and possibility, while remaining open to diverse interpretations and locally grounded action. It enabled us to hold the tension between common and uncommon ground, creating space for a community of practice that extended beyond traditional cross-sector collaborations. By centering relational assets like trust, reciprocity, and care, the frame shifted the focus from transactional services to a deeper, systemic conversation about values. It invited us to see care not just as crisis response, but as a living social fabric—woven into the rhythms of everyday life—and opened new pathways for knowledge sharing, mutual learning, and collaborative experimentation.

AN EMERGING INFRASTRUCTURE: FROM A LAB TO MOVEMENT

After 15 months of collaboration and new organizations joining, the Care Futures Lab unfolded as a "movement". A new kind of infrastructure was beginning to emerge—not imposed but grown organically through practice. Across community gatherings, cross-sector workshops, and ongoing reflection, we began to see the contours of a shared ecosystem forming—one that offered the necessary structure without constraining creativity.

In parallel, our colleagues at the TD School at UTS had been developing a framework that resonated strongly with what we were experiencing. Designed to support innovation ecosystems working at the societal "midfield"—where community, government, public services, and the corporate sector intersect—this model offers both infrastructure and rhythm for long-term, values-led systems change.

Rather than functioning as a linear process, we saw our community taking the form of four interrelated modes of engagement–each supporting a different layer of transformation:

Temple - Reflecting (and Inner Growth)

This is the space for deep reflection, where values are surfaced, mindsets are examined, and inner transformation is prioritized. It's about asking the hard questions of ourselves and our systems. It's also about recognizing that others share our frustrations and aspirations. As the emotional and ethical grounding of the ecosystem, the Temple mode helps ensure that change is not just functional, but also personal.

Academy - Learning (and Capability Development)

Here, the focus is on building the muscles for systems change–developing shared design language, frameworks, and capabilities across sectors. This might take the form of design workshops, futures thinking tools, peer-learning, and action-inquiry. The Academy mode ensures that innovation is not only experimental, but teachable and transferable, enabling new leaders, organizations, and communities to take part.

Lab - Experimenting (on Shared Challenges)

The Lab is the engine of collective experimentation, where actors come together across traditional boundaries to design, test, and iterate on new ways of seeing. It holds the space for both rigor and risk, allowing for the kinds of bold prototypes that push systems thinking into tangible, situated action. Here, collaboration becomes concrete–and care becomes a collective practice.

Podium - Sharing Insights (and Inviting Critique)

In this mode, the ecosystem turns organizations outward–sharing stories, learnings, and failures with each other, and inviting constructive critique. It's about transparency and humility: surfacing what's emerging, what's messy, and what might be possible. By communicating through public dialogues, the Podium mode helps ensure the work remains accountable, visible, and generative beyond the ecosystem itself.

Holding the Center: A Rhythmic, Living System

What's powerful about this framework is not just its components, but its rhythm. These four modes–Temple, Academy, Lab, and Podium–don't follow a step-by-step progression. Instead, they form a living system that breathes in and out over time.

A cycle of learning, doing, reflecting, and sharing. Each mode strengthens the others, and together they build the conditions for resilient, relational infrastructure–not just for care, but for community transformation at large.

We did not set out to build this kind of infrastructure. But through our ongoing work it became increasingly clear that this is the infrastructure we are growing–together. It's already taking root in the ways we gather, how we hold space, and how we make meaning.

REFLECTIONS AND LESSONS LEARNED

Agency is distributed.

One of the most profound lessons of the Care Futures Lab has been the importance–and challenge–of facilitating for emergence. This meant resisting the gravitational pull of the current paradigm; the need for predefined outcomes, fixed deliverables, and neatly packaged solutions. Instead, we committed to holding the tension–between structure and openness, between clarity and ambiguity, between leading and letting go. Facilitating for distributed agency required creating enough scaffolding to support participation, while leaving space for dialogue, surprise, and self-organization to take root. It demanded humility: to trust that outcomes would emerge not from control, but from collective sense-making and co-evolution. In many ways, our biggest success was not what we produced, but what we protected–a space where new relationships, insights, and paradigms could unfold on their own terms.

Hold structure lightly.

In cross-sector collaborations, there's often a push to clarify roles, responsibilities, and governance early on–to create structure and reduce ambiguity. This can help teams work efficiently in the short term. But over time, too much rigidity can become a barrier to trust, adaptability, and shared ownership. What we've seen through the Lab is that coherence does not require tight control–it emerges through rhythm, relationships, and reciprocity. Sustained collaboration demands a willingness to let roles shift as needs evolve, to blur boundaries between "facilitator" and "participant". It requires cultivating an ecosystem mindset, where coherence is maintained not through fixed structures, but through shared purpose and accountability, and the ability to adjust course together. The real work is learning to navigate this fluidity without losing focus.

The most profound shifts often remain invisible.

In cross-organizational collaboration, the most meaningful shifts often happen beneath the surface. While reports tend to highlight shared outcomes or joint deliverables, the real transformation often lies in what's harder to capture: a shift in mindset, a new language of trust, the softening of boundaries between roles or institutions. Through the Lab, we saw how powerful it can be when organizations begin to relate differently–not just coordinating tasks, but co-creating meaning. These changes don't always come with metrics, but they are what make deeper collaboration possible. They show up in how decisions are made, how risk is shared, and how learning is exchanged. We're learning to recognize and honor these invisible shifts–not as side effects, but as the very signs that collaboration is working.

Framing is political.

One of our greatest challenges was creating coherence and a sense of shared space across a deeply diverse group of organizations. Participants came from vastly different contexts: a small digital-only youth mental health organization; multiple teams from large, faith-based aged care and community service providers; a mid-sized, place-based network; and a small disability-focused organization. Each participant carried their own strategic priorities and short-term mandates. In this complexity, our most powerful move was inviting people to step beyond their immediate contexts–to temporarily abstract from their specific audiences and agendas. This shift allowed us to avoid collapsing into incrementalism and instead focus on a space of shared potential.

Still, the frame had to feel relevant–it needed to resonate with each organization's reality to sustain their engagement. This is where neighborhood well-being offered something rare: a framing that was clear, locally meaningful, and generative across difference. It provided just enough specificity to anchor the work, while remaining open enough to invite imagination, alignment, and continued collaboration.

We need a new kind of evidence culture.

There's a growing call across care sectors to innovate–yet this invitation is often paired with requirements for pre-validation, proof, and risk-aversion. Funders and institutions want bold new models, but also assurances that they will work–before they've been tested. The conditions for experimentation are undermined by the very systems calling for change.

What's needed is not just more evidence, but a new kind of evidence culture–one that values emergence, story, and pattern recognition alongside traditional metrics. It also requires new forms of trust between innovators and institutions; a willingness to back learning as a legitimate outcome, and to see experimentation not as risk, but as responsibility in a changing world.

3.2

COMPLEXITY-FRIENDLY BY DESIGN: EMERGENT PRACTICES FOR MENTAL HEALTH

Steve Sullivan

INTRODUCTION: ON THE CHALLENGE OF BECOMING 'COMPLEXITY-FRIENDLY'

We live in a world of boundless complexity, rapid disruption, and uncertainty. The world that has emerged from global, industrial, and technological revolutions, is complete with paradoxes and ambiguity. Interconnectivity and interdependence have shifted the operating landscapes of many organizations. This new context feels oddly familiar, and yet it is frustratingly elusive to label. Our capacity to understand and effectively deal with it is outpacing the normal rate of change for many of the systems that we rely upon as a society - food, care, health, and energy. They are losing their fit for purpose. To make leaps in progress, we need to let go of things that do not serve us well. No longer do we have the comfort of falling back on management myths of best practices, prediction, and control. Tradition, hierarchies, and linear cause and effect mislead and distract us from progress. Time and time again, the world reveals our ignorance when we apply single interventions for 'problem solving' in complex situations. The notion that we can 'solve' climate change, an aging population, or poor (in this case study) mental wellbeing, ignores the ever flowing and changing world of relationships. Our systems have to continually fall apart and come together in new ways. A dogmatic adherence to process will not support the shift to new paradigms. Our practices need loosening if they are to have a catalytic effect on the wider system. We must start with a greater awareness of how and why we act if we are to shift the way that larger systems work. The values, assumptions, and beliefs that underlie our practices are the smallest units of change we can affect. They are the kernels of systems change. The practice of Strategic Design, which emerged from the intersection of design, living systems and cybernetics in the 1960s, helps seeing into the anatomy of practices. Through reflective and participatory methods, it acts on the borders of traditionally defined disciplines to nurture emergent practices. Holding many worldviews in the in-between space, it facilitates the mixing of knowledge by removing the distance between actors who, at the deepest level, have shared values (Dorst, 2018). By constructively blurring boundaries through Integrative thinking, new forms of possibilities can emerge for action.

YOUTH MENTAL HEALTH IN CRISIS

I recently experienced the boundless complexity of youth mental health. In April 2021, I received an email from a colleague asking to write a proposal for a leading on-line mental health service for young people in Australia. The organization had a vision to become a safe and immersive on-line space for conversation and community. They wanted help from our design and technology consultancy, How to Impact, to explore new services for young people who don't access help when they need it. From personal experience, I suspected mental health issues were on the rise. Over the years I've observed the surprisingly indiscriminate nature of poor mental health. Friends, family and peers from of all walks of life, dispositions and character have been affected, seemingly at an increasing rate. The numbers backed up my hunch, almost 40% of people aged 16–24 years have experienced a mental health problem. This especially challenging for young people who are often experiencing mental ill-health for the first time. There is an urgent need for innovative, youth-centered services for everyone.

Setting the scene: Design as a mode of intervention

As a consultant, it can be daunting stepping into a new organization. It's like a private chef hired to cook in someone else's home, only that you're stepping in mid-way through their preparation. You quickly get a sense for the space, what equipment we're working with, and the range of ingredients in the fridge. Then there are the concerns of who we're cooking for and how much time we have. What's going to get us to where we need within the constraints; what's practical here? You can forget about an easy-to-follow recipe. Even when there is one, half the challenge is understanding if we should stick to it or where to improvise.

This initial synthesis is a rite of passage; as an outsider, you must earn the right to step into the kitchen. The organization had already done much preparation work, even running a pilot for a new service. The oven was already warm. It was my great privilege to navigate what we should put in there, within a set time and budget, of course. This is the art of not only synthesis, but also sacrifice. In an organization of deep expertize, humility, and care, there are many perspectives and possible paths, but ultimately, less is more, for coherence and clarity. It's knowing when to lead and when to step back. This wasn't just about designing a new service, this was to be a punctuated equilibrium, a radical change in practice. Defining impactful digital experiences and new service models was the easy part, the real challenge was finding the pace for meaningful change. This would be a process of building relationships, redefining boundaries, and ultimately, helping an organization built on risk-aversion, embrace risk in the name of progress.

THE CHALLENGE: PARADOXES OF THE SITUATION

When dealing with complex adaptive situations,

how

do you create progress when you can't solve a problem?

How do you focus your efforts for innovation,

when

we can't predict what will create meaningful progress?

How do you deliver services that are personal

while

being relevant and inclusive to everyone?

How do you offer the necessary human connection for authentic care,

while

maintaining safe, professional service boundaries that aren't stifled by formality?

How do you take an evidenced-based approach,

when

the evidence shows much of what we do now does not create the progress we seek?

First experiments in designing an on-line peer support service

The organization had many potential service concepts for their vision of conversation and community. Finding the leverage point for impact required difficult, and at times, heartbreaking conversations with young people. I heard the hopes and helplessness of their struggles. Faced with humanity at its most vulnerable, my usual personal motivations of integrity and pride became obsolete against a sense of duty. Young people's support networks ranged from outstanding to crises in of themselves. Many people are ill equipped to understand their experiences. Concerns of being a burden, rejected or abandoned, were not only prevalent but also realized for some young people. Traditional support services could be cold too. Imagine sharing your most intimate secrets only to be cut off, because the time is up. Your follow up session? You'll need to reintroduce yourself. A general sense of frustration existed. Young people lacked agency, they didn't feel understood, and didn't want to be 'fixed'; they wanted relief. They wanted someone to walk alongside them.

We spent seven weeks co-designing on-line support environments that gave power back to young people. Using participatory methods, we invited a network of community and experts to shape a new service. We explored creative activities, gaming, potential community contributions, and strengths-based interactions. Our focus gravitated toward an anonymous peer chat service that had previously been explored by the organization: experienced workers shared the importance and rarity of having a conversation with a mutual peer.

Changing the game

I selfishly wanted to create something never seen before, but this was a lesson in listening. By valuing the lived experience of others, I came to understand how peer conversations could help a young person feel heard, reduce their isolation, and create hope.

This wasn't about creating something new; it was about removing the old barriers that get in the way.

Our experimental approach moved in a rhythm of reflection-action-reflection. We created peer support pretotypes, prototypes, and even an experiment that simulated an on-line guided chat for self-reflection. This helped identify where anxiety was elevated in on-line conversations and led to calming and reassuring interventions. Design decisions were a collaboration between a team of young people, peer workers, designers, researchers, marketers, managers, and clinical psychologists. By week seven we had co-produced a pilot for a peer chat service, live on the organization's website.

Following this period, we desperately needed a change of pace. Making decisions as a 'sprint' was not sustainable. We moved to a new process to continue co-production. This continued for several months until an official launch. The service continues to help young people feel heard, connecting them with trained Peer Workers. A new lived experience practice emerged, changing the boundaries of how care is delivered by the organization.

Much exploratory work is needed to become a system shifting organization. Catalyzing change through revolutionary ideas; the kind that shift all layers of the current system - the fundamental values and power, institutions and resources, local relationships, and micro interactions - needs wide and inclusive participation, imagination, and experimentation. Forming future visions that provoke action will require dedicated resources and effort. In the face of such an enormous task, optimism is not a fool's errand; small is big when a little idea tells a larger story. When it's unclear on how to move forward, that's exactly when we need many little seeds for change. We can be a visible attractor, pointing others to alternative possibilities.

Change needs to happen from within the organization, otherwise it will be rejected like a foreign object entering the body: it might make its way deep inside, but eventually the organization's defensive system will create enough resistance and attempt to degrade it.

TOWARDS AN INFRASTRUCTURE FOR ONGOING CHANGE

If we are to be an experimental lab, perhaps we should be a lab of conflict. Not in the sense of petty arguments, but in a deep diversity of direction. The change we need is too great to rely on convention or consensus. If what we're doing makes sense to everyone we may be in trouble. We'd aim for coherence, not commonality as we explore multiple adjacent possibilities. We'd find common ground while making room for disagreement. This type of exploratory work thrives in openness, patience, and bit of nonsense. The aim is not unnecessary risk, it's to highlight the risk of not trying new things. Our lab would support a portfolio of competing visions and ventures, through diverse minds, methods, and missions. Using an open-source philosophy for participation, we'd generate multiple project models with overlapping networks.

Our first step is to create an arena for unconventional collaborations. We would need to be accessible for many, while retaining the sensibilities of a fringe dwelling. A setting that clearly sits outside of the constraints and norms of organizational life. Makers and thinkers of different domains - science (empirical), philosophy (conceptual), arts (evocative), in situ (contextual), and introspection (personal) - coming together to incubate transdisciplinary knowledge. A place for learning and mixing worldviews, led by a compass, not a map. Our space would transverse physical and digital realms. By using Ethnographic Experiential Futures (Candy & Kornet, 2019), we can engage youth communities to document their images of the future. By increasing the accessibility, variety, and depth of available images of the future, we'd probe and provoke how things could be. Stories and future images could be shared in regular forums, hosted in physical spaces, and on a bespoke website. We will make our process and prototypes public, inviting critique as we frame, shape, and scale new possibilities. This is the promise of co-production at scale.

A set of guiding principles will co-evolve between the actors. As a starting point we may take inspiration from Nick Cave and his astute observations of the role of good faith conversations which "affords us, among other things, the great privilege of being wrong; we feel supported in our unknowing and, in the sincere spirit of inquiry, free to move around the sometimes treacherous waters of ideas. A good faith conversation strengthens our better ideas and challenges, and hopefully corrects, our low-quality or unsound ideas." (Cave, 2022).

REFLECTIONS AND LESSONS LEARNED

When you listen deeply, boundaries between people blur. Understanding the aspirations of young people seeking support for their Mental health revealed universal human values that we all felt. There was a symmetry between the needs of the people in the organization and that of the young people they served. Everyone wants to feel heard. Like a young person seeking support, practitioners in the organization want to be involved in making decisions, they want to feel listened to while retaining their agency in the things that matter to them. They have concerns about other people holding power who don't understand them, who don't appreciate the nature of their environment, their environment struggles, their hopes, their environment, just like a young person seeking support.

A sign of growth is having more tolerance for discomfort and less for the status quo.

OUTTAKES:

We can't always sprint to deep change. Systemic innovation shifts boundaries of identity and future possibilities. Strategic Design invites many contributions to make images of the future feel-able, discussable, and actionable. Through dialogue and visual thinking, designers reflexively explore deep values, goals, and pathways. They are concerned with revealing how patterns of a system help or hurt our intentions for change - how they emerge, flow, interact, reproduce, disintegrate, and decay. Strategic Design honors the many faces of truth, asking questions of questions, framing and re-framing our place in the world. This is the messy business of Strategic Design, bridging layers of new and old practices for progress in systemic innovation.

3.3

YOUTH ENGAGEMENT IN SURF LIFESAVING – A THEME ANALYSIS

Mark Elizondo

Surf Life Saving has been a cornerstone of Australian culture for over a century, fostering community connections and promoting safety along the country's coastlines.

Central to this legacy is the "Nippers" (Junior Surf Lifesaving) program, which introduces children aged 6 to 14 to surf life saving principles. Participants develop practical skills like swimming, first aid, and rescue, while also learning values such as teamwork, leadership, and environmental stewardship. By age 14, the Nippers earn their Surf Rescue Certificate and become Volunteer Surf Lifesavers, joining senior members in patrolling duties.

As a member of the local surf club, I have noticed the decline of membership of Cadets - ages 14-18. A notable challenge exists in retaining youth members after their first year of patrol. A survey conducted for the 2022/2023 season (not publicly released) revealed a significant decline in Cadet (ages 14-18) participation, with some Sydney Surf Clubs experiencing a drop of 22% to 50% between the 2022/2023 and 2023/2024 seasons, indicating a critical gap in retention. Employing grounded theory, abductive learning, and hermeneutic phenomenology, this study seeks to construct a structured and in-depth understanding of these experiences from the cadets' perspectives.

SYNERGIES

The combination of Grounded Theory and Abductive Reasoning facilitated the exploration of emergent ideas but also contribute to theory development. Thematic patterns, combined with inferences drawn from observations, challenged existing interpretations and refined theoretical understandings such as the value of intergenerational relationships through mentoring and community, or leadership opportunities and role clarity. Instead of rigidly sticking to one explanation, this combination presented the opportunity to explore multiple possibilities and intuitively reason when trying to make sense of complex, unexpected discoveries.

Abductive reasoning facilitates the iterative dance between theory and data. For example, it can be theorized that a small cohort of non-sport Cadets remain engaged not only for a service-oriented reason but as a strategic means to leverage. These Cadets are using opportunities in volunteering to develop their qualifications, future-proofing their prospects beyond surf lifesaving. This insight suggests that Cadets view their involvement as an investment in transferable skills, demonstrating a proactive and strategic approach to personal and professional development.

Hermeneutic Phenomenology (§2.8) helps to focus on the lived experiences of participants, enriching the understanding of the highs (such as their concept of belonging and social capital) and lows (such as the uncertainty of the transition) of youth volunteering. It offered evidence and examples that supported the narratives and themes emerging from grounded theory. This often involved active listening with a clear intention to understand the meaning behind the youth's experiences.

THE RESEARCH JOURNEY

Systemic coding in Grounded Theory (§2.8) can have limitations, particularly where themes or codes are adjusted or when new data emerges. It was crucial in this process to make deliberate decisions about when to halt the development of certain themes, especially when there was an over-saturation of interview data. Over-interpretation in Abductive Reasoning can result from creating loops of excessive interpretation, which may lead to shifting narratives. During the interviews, it became evident to many of the Cadets that the social aspect of getting food—before, during, or after their scheduled patrol—was an integral part of their social connection. The structured nature of Grounded Theory helped balance this by maintaining fidelity and control over iteration. The Hermeneutic Phenomenology interpretation of meaning of the various experiences of youth volunteering is multifaceted. As the youth evolve physical or socially, their motivations change and various observations can contradict as well as complement each other.

THE INSIGHTS

This qualitative research on youth volunteering within a local Surf Life Saving Club provided valuable insights into the lived experiences of cadet volunteers. The analysis revealed key themes, including leadership, connection (both interpersonal and systemic), community, belonging, pathways, and the influence of early formative experiences as Nippers on long-term commitment. Notably, the study underscored the significance of the transition period—a liminal space in which cadets navigate their evolving identities within and outside the club and ultimately decide whether to continue their involvement.

This liminal space that they occupy often involves uncertainty as they explore their identity within the club and search for a sense of belonging and purpose. The challenge lies in supporting Cadets through this pivotal stage to maintain engagement and ensure their continued contribution to the Surf Life Saving community.

3.4

A DIFFERENTIATED APPROACH TO DEVELOPING GREAT PLACES

Sarah Neilsen

INTRODUCTION: QUESTIONING THE PLANNING PROCESS

We are a developer.

When we plan buildings, shopping centers, precincts, or homes we impact generations of species and humans and what we chose to do in each moment can cast a long shadow. The hunch that started us off on this journey was that there was a bigger opportunity in developing land to ensure that we meet the needs of humans, and the broader ecosystem to deliver a much greater value than is currently being realized.

In addition, we knew that we cannot continue to look at land with limited visions and of immediate use and purpose if we wanted to create a true legacy for future generations. There is much available to us if we understand the true size of the prize, by approaching the process with our personal and organizational values front and center, and take a deliberate and conscious approach to the creation of community.

If we wanted to win more work, attract more third-party capital, partner with governments in the future then we needed to understand the needs of the whole community, and this was where the concept of the societal midfield (see §5.2) started to lead to some other ways to think about how we could influence the design of place. This is where we identify where governments, organizations and not for profits have gaps in the current system which puts humans and nature in a more vulnerable position and where us as the developer can look to make a bigger contribution.

This story related the beginning of a journey, creating a new field of practice that will influence change across the current system and has the needs of nature and humans sitting at the heart. One of the key challenges (as well as opportunities) is going to be to articulate the commercial value of creating better places that meet a much broader need - and then being able to articulate how this can be a catalyst and halo for delivering profits that are a multiplier of traditional development approaches. By working with Elders, students, communities, governments, not for profits, consultants and organizations striving to make a difference, we collectively have the most amazing opportunity in front of us.

A LAYERED APPROACH TOWARDS ACHIEVING BROADER VALUE

We know that by creating more exciting, connected, and inclusive places, we will deliver not just commercial returns but ways to positively contribute to a more regenerative approach to nature and social needs. In an environment rich in disruption across retail, office, and mixed-use precincts there is an overwhelming need for some new approaches and one of the biggest challenges that we encountered was a dormant fear amongst our peers and work colleagues partly due to these shifting landscapes. The business could see that we needed new roles and new ways of unpacking how we were undertaking developments and operational management, but it was how we continued to find ways to demonstrate some alternative approaches whilst being considerate of how this was making people feel about how their own value and purpose.

It is the historical structures that we have been traditionally operating within that is now not always addressing the complexity of the challenges and with silos of power spending more energy exerting control versus being curious, questioning and listening. It seems that the current paradigm structure is not working for the networked nuances of the issues that we are facing in the world today.

The realization in the first lab was looking at town centers and the key themes that we could ensure were important when developing or re-imagining retail assets. Through a process of hermeneutic phenomenology involving stakeholders from across the business in areas like transactions, technology, innovation, and project management four key themes came to life. During this process a key differentiation between customer and community emerged as we had traditionally been describing these groups interchangeably, yet we learned that they needed their own identity and focus. The data within our business is primarily on the customer which was all collated and designed around the transactional relationship and there was a broader opportunity about unpacking the needs of the more vulnerable members of our community that could help shape places that appeal to a much bigger audience. It was this subtle realization that led to the inspiration and catalyst for the second lab.

Through several experiments involving students and elders, we unpacked three layers that we saw were critical in the creation of great places and this resulted in (1) a visual layer, which unpacks what is seen, (2) the relational layer being about what is felt in the space and the (3) third being the metaphysical layer which is what is energetically at play within an area. The metaphysical layer is where we wanted to begin the process so that we truly understood the broader opportunity and true connection to all living organisms, the relationship of time and history in the creation of place.

INTRODUCING THE LAYERS OF VALUE

The next step was about how we then tested this information and found ways to integrate this into the organization. We needed to socialize these three layers and the detail that forms the structure for these areas of focus. We set about convening teams across marketing, design, research, and social sustainability as we started to debate the merits of the information collated to date. The process started to iterate and evolve into something that became the work of many. It was during this process that we started to see how the work had more layers and breadth than any individual team could produce. There were moments of frustration as our work was pulled apart, adapted and integrated with other frameworks. Having witnessed teams get very precious with their own work, this served as a continual reminder that we needed to trust the process and let the rich diversity of this team engage with the information to ensure greater organizational relevance and ultimately a wider adoption and ownership.

CHANGE PARADOXES: WHAT IS HOLDING US BACK?

The obvious contradiction that we kept seeing was that:

We needed to innovate
and test new ideas

but

we would need to demonstrate
the evidence for why this
should be supported.

(If it hadn't been done, how could we demonstrate empirical reasons for why the idea would work to address a certain challenge?)

We needed big bold visions

yet

the best way to test something was to start small and find a congregation of supporters all coming together for a united purpose

(Demonstrating evidence for small initiatives is then of course still challenging to demonstrate that a larger investment would be successful).

On a more personal level:

if we learn the most through failure

then why

are we all so intimidated to do something that might not work.

How do you build the muscle to want to keep putting new ideas on the table and take the embarrassing risk

if

it is to fail in environments where it is all about the successes.

We have all heard numerous success stories of the multiple failings prior to some great breakthrough but the message is only told once there is a positive outcome as we can't seem to stomach the reality of what lead to this more desirable point. The question that needs to be asked is if we can find more avenues for what might be considered as successful as the measures may need updating and could be around areas of social impact, driving better cohesion, circularity, or a myriad of new tools to garner whether a project or innovation was worth the effort, then maybe we will enlist more support for testing the untested.

FIRST INTERVENTION: WORKING WITH STUDENTS (TROJAN HORSE)

One of the interventions that we designed was working with three student groups from both Macquarie University and the University of Technology Sydney (UTS). Whilst the work they produced was of a high quality it was the exchange between our teams and the students that shone an interesting light into the conversation. Prior to the arranged meetings between our teams and students, people had complained about why they were being asked to meet these groups, yet after the interviews and discussions the energy and excitement was palpable. It was these sparks of vitality that we had spent considerable time trying to uncover in our respective organizations and so once it became apparent, we wanted to understand more deeply what was lighting our teams up.

Some observations:

- The students from the UTS Bachelor of Creative Intelligence and Innovation (BCII) noticed in many conversations that at some stage they were asked not to repeat what was said to the outside world... it wasn't that the information was in commercial confidence, it was these people's personal views and thoughts on how we could approach things for a better business outcome. The question of course was why were not able to uncover these thoughts amongst ourselves, within the organization. What we found interesting about this was that a more honest conversation was occurring with people sharing their ideas freely and there was no concern about hierarchy as both parties were genuinely interested in challenging the way that each was unpacking the situation.

- The students could be dismissed as naive and lacking experience, so they were never perceived as a threat, whilst their ideas being fresh and without political maneuvering allowed a more interesting conversation to transpire. It was the elegant simplicity of how they had approached the challenge that we set, that often shone a light on areas that were right in front of us professionals. In each scenario we set complex and networked issues that we were struggling to navigate through like the future of work or affordable housing and by seeing these perspectives from these different angles really helped us see where the little kinks in our system were hidden.
- Another more tangible benefit is the fact that the students will be the future benefactors within these precincts and places and they were talking about slightly different needs. The process of exchange was very different from traditional consultancy relationships as these were unpaid placements, so the relationship was based on time, energy, listening, unpacking, questioning and learning, all traits that a great organization possesses.

We have continued to engage with this process of working with different student groups into the business as the benefit for both the organization and the students provides a powerful igniting of conversations, ideas and new processes of thought in a relationship that is nonthreatening and more based on playful questioning.

SECOND STEP: LISTENING TO THE ELDERS (DESIGNING WITH COUNTRY)

We had begun the process of working with a group of elders from the Dharug nation and as the knowledge started to come to light, we could see many areas where we needed to change our approach to land or country in order to deliver a more healthy, inclusive and vibrant place in order to inspire a more connected community.

There are multiple layers to be considered when working with elders and designing with country.

The first lesson we learned was to think beyond the borders of the parcel of land that we owned or were responsible for. Initially as we presented a plan of the site showing the developable land mass this was where we learned our first valuable lesson. The second time we had a yarn with the elders we showed a plan with a 5km radius around the proposed development and yet again this was still falling well short of how we needed to look at connecting on this deeper level. Since then, we have started to understand root systems of trees and what they are connected too, ridge lines, historical river systems, materials beneath the soil and how the night sky is seen and interacts with the area. We have learned about how plants, animals and humans would pass through these places to ensure that as we are designing these places we take the role for being true custodians for the land in which we have the responsibility to care for.

"If you can see the relational forces connecting and moving the elements of a system, rather than focusing on the elements themselves, you are able to see a pattern outside of liner time. If you bring that pattern back into linear time, this can be called a prediction in today's world."

Lines in the sand - Yunkaporta (2019)

We know that by working in this way, we create more enduring projects, educate ourselves and teams on connecting more meaningfully with country and build a more prosperous future with first nations people. This is changing the landscape for how we consider our supply chain the businesses we chose to support and ongoing land management processes. Apart from all playing a role in working to heal country, create greater equity of wealth for first nations people, we also envisage that this will be more appealing to our partners, customers, investors and stakeholders. A renewed relationship with the land inspired by first nations knowledge and how we see it is critical in transforming into a more dynamic approach to creating a better legacy for future generations. By deeply understanding more of the biosphere and elements of nature we have an opportunity to create truly inclusive places considering everything from root systems to the galaxies above.

BUILDING A CAPACITY FOR DELIVERING BETTER PLACES

Convening a multi-disciplinary team within an internal lab environment proved to be very rewarding. The work was teased apart in an environment of constructive debate and then as we emerged with some new tools, we then tested this across various stakeholders around the business. The work had the original bones of what was created in the first intervention, but it was through the richness of the process with the lens of other professions within the organization that the framework became more dynamic. It has delivered a framework for an enterprise approach to delivering better places. As we continue to work through the areas, we allow teams to bring more depth and adaption in how we delve into the three-layer approach that was unpacked during the series of labs.

We envisage that this iterative process becomes a unique capability to convene teams on the unpacking of networked and dynamic complex matters.

The process has been widely supported and we have created a unique proposition in the unpacking of place which allows us to demonstrate how we can deliver a broad reaching appeal for the creation of better futures throughout the life cycle of the project.

REFLECTIONS

By working with relationships in both the formal and informal networks it is the accrual of trust that is critical to build a more dynamic organization and a culture built on creating a better way to live.

The ability to create an environment to experiment, learn and forge a better path forward together is only possible when you have an organization of supportive leaders who deeply believe in making a meaningful contribution and leaving a lasting legacy for future generations.

With this wisdom and insight and from this moment forward my hope is that the seeds that we have planted during these labs inspires the developments that we undertake to move us towards a future that is truly uplifting.

3.5

THE ESSENCE OF CHANGE

Monica Mayer

What is the anatomy of change?
In the start of my Reinventing Strategic Innovation journey I hit a conceptual wall: how to bring about change. In discussions and reflections I realized the essence of change is actually quite simple - when I broke "change" down into its smallest elements I saw the core factor is in connection, a connection that shifts an individual's perspective, state of mind, sense of self. If what we see as the macro change around us is a wave that eventually travels close enough to shore to break and become the ocean of "the way things are done", then the catalyst for that wave of change is the agitation of the molecules of water that then form momentum to shape and grow a wave.

At the heart of Reinventing Strategic Innovation is an effort to generate that connection; to reintroduce or re-balance the creative and interpersonal. If we look back at how most western institutions and corporations have been set up and designed, they contain at their very core a necessity to approach their operations and services in an impersonal, prescriptive, linear way, perhaps resonating with a feeling at the time that this was the more professional, impartial, and effective way to deliver services. In the interest of efficiency and impartiality, many of our institutions have swung too far in that logical direction and lost their effectiveness. As a consequence of the focus on the objective and detached, they have omitted processes and capabilities that can help with the very problems we need to address in today's society - those same capabilities that can allow for innovation, creative problem solving, and behavior change.

Strategic Innovation brings a dramatic re- focus back on the personal and relational - but we still have a way to go in bridging the gap between a more aseptic, established institutional approach and these strategic innovation practices, often referred to less appreciatively as "soft skills" or "creative and design techniques". The latter are still seen by many C-suite and institutional leaders as less credible or lasting than traditional, linear, prescriptive methods. There is a direct conflict with the current approach, rooted in risk aversion, regulation, project plans with defined timelines and linear progress. To progress in making change, we need to re-discover the essence of business - whether selling a product, delivering a service, or promoting behavioral change - it must center on the meaningful connection to the individual. If we can reintegrate this perspective and skillset into decision-making and operational processes across various sectors, and balance that with the risk management, funding, and timeline expectations of the current approach, we regain the ability to transform.

My background is in health - more specifically western health. Those who've had experience working in or being treated by the western healthcare system can attest to the fact that it is based on an industrial system approach to moving us as patients into, then out of the system when ill. We often have caring clinicians facing us in a clinical moment, but the broader system has trapped them as well into a transactional, illness-focused assembly line. This industrial processing of diagnoses and the detached vocabulary of pre-determined treatment protocols has perhaps served a purpose in allowing treatment to be scaled and may have been intended to protect the health care worker from emotional attachment to the patient.

However, the myriad symptoms of a burnt-out, ever-diminishing workforce, worsening outcomes, growing incidence of chronic disease and an inability to sufficiently fund healthcare are clear indications that a change in approach is needed. A hierarchical approach to acute illness that centers on diagnosis and treatment (usually with a medication or one-time intervention) is not proving effective in improving whole health, on an individual level or system-wide. Shifting the approach to one of empowering the patient as a partner in true care (guiding a whole human from a point of risk or illness to a lasting, improved state of being) is essential to the future sustainability of the health system. For acute illness and injury there will always be a need for surgical interventions and prescriptive medicine, but today's system is buckling under the weight of chronic disease, which is dependent on human behavior to prevent and/or manage.

So how do we then engage the patient in leading their own lasting behavioral change? Preventative health is the obvious way to go in the battle for health system sustainability - most would agree with this concept. And yet when the rubber hits the road it is not funded in holistic, meaningful ways to effect individual or systemic change. The preventative health initiatives often lack any mechanism for connection: they are just a flier to get a screening, or an ad about the dangers of smoking or gambling, or a "digital front door". Each of these assume patient engagement without addressing it. Why?

I've heard many policy makers say preventative health "doesn't work", discouraged by lack of proven results in pilot efforts - and in reality, often a long-term view isn't possible due to political and funding cycles. There is not a shortage of pilots to test new care models or approaches. However, to improve and scale initiatives to deliver the outcome of overall better health requires a discussion as to how to better design, integrate, and deliver these interventions to encourage behavioral change over time. Where is the moment of connection, inspiration, motivation of the individual? Where is the relationship that will sustain and grow the change? In the current campaigns, the linear, transactional approach often leaves a gap in engaging the patient in the change, inspiring the change required to prevent or manage a disease. Let's acknowledge that each change starts at the individual level with relationships and experiences, then grows into a series of changes as momentum grows, and sometimes into a movement or broader evolution: the wave referenced above.

This brings us to the core challenge in building a health care system that promotes health VS illness, that actually cares for humans. Many are already attempting to bring this about. The missing aspect is the integration of these efforts, but more importantly, an emphasis in each of the interactions on connection - the spark of inspiration and motivation in an individual, requiring an emotional connection, however slight. This is still seen by many policy makers and analytical thinkers as "soft", maybe unnecessary, and might even be deemed ineffective compared to more pragmatic approaches - and it requires a recalibration of risk and expectations.

One example can be demonstrated by feedback I received in explaining my most recent work on a project with Black Dog Institute (that researches the early detection, prevention and treatment of mental health disorders). It relates to a project aimed at building awareness and support for young women who self-harm through an arts-in-community-health installation. The visitor travels an experiential journey in which they are invited from a recreational, retail context into an interactive, reflective space, presented with lightly informative content, and engaging with provocative, alluring imagery that resonates with their own movement to shift perspective and mindset, if even for a moment, to spark an emotional shift. The visitor is then invited into a space for guided facilitation of crafts to embed their personal experience through making. The goal is to build public awareness, empathy and offer an alternative, human, even beautiful rendition of this condition as a human experience. When people hear this described, the most frequent response is "But what impact will this have on the problem of self-harm? How is this helping?".

The question indicates that an effort of this sort isn't worth the investment if it can't prove dramatic change in the moment - it seems the expectation is that there be more of a silver bullet in solving this "problem". When I explain that this public awareness change must begin with self-awareness change, and self-awareness change requires its "light bulb moment" of an epiphany, seeing the self, others, or things in a new light, so that new concepts and ideas can take root, many still aren't convinced. If I ask people to consider their own experience of growing awareness, building empathy, and changing behavior they can usually see their own changes through this lens, and in doing so no longer consider it "soft" or ineffective. Most realize that there is no other way to bring about change, other than to spark this individual change through connection with an idea, the self, or other individual - but this isn't the first instinctual reaction of most people. We have been taught in our western society that these are not serious methods, when in fact they are the only way to effect change - they are essential aspects of any policy, business case, or service design.

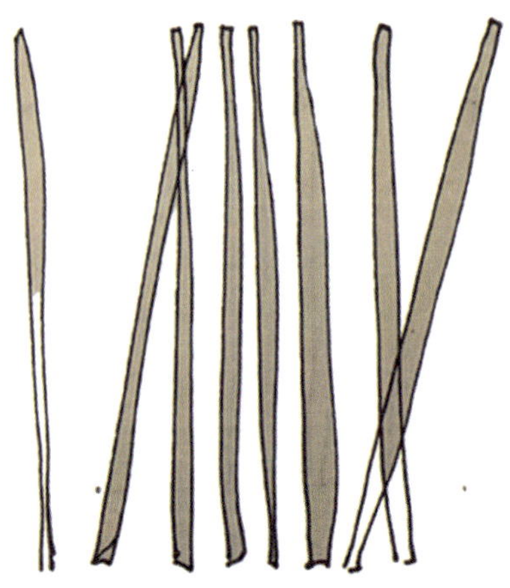

3.6

BEYOND PERFORMATIVE TRANSFORMATION

Abigail Schoenheimer

INTRODUCTION: THE LIFE AND TIMES OF A MANAGEMENT CONSULTANT

I am a Management Consultant, and I have been one for 13 years. I hate introducing myself in this way, because people either glaze over with no idea of what this means or narrow their eyes in cynicism because they know exactly what it means. I started life in the Big 4 consulting firms and have also worked for a few boutique firms. I've worked on very diverse clients from investment banks to hotel chains and Fast Moving Consumer Goods (FMCG) and across different kinds of engagements: Operating model transformations, Risk Culture Remediation Programs, Product Innovation, Platform Migration and Executive strategic alignment. My lack of deep expertize is simultaneously a frustration; I often feel unskilled, unqualified, an impostor; and a badge of honor - I am semi-convinced the 'experts' aren't expert anyway, and at least I can offer a fresh and impartial perspective.

I have been told I am temperamentally suited to the Consulting life (whatever this means) but have always been somewhat ambivalent from a values and principles perspective; not because any individual firm or person that I worked with or for has acted in a morally questionable way, but rather I am constantly left with a nagging and mild, dissatisfaction with the impact I am able to have. In all my roles and on all my projects, I felt that I was bumping up against 'something', though this thing shape-shifted depending on the situation.

On the flip side to my lived experience of the work is the surrounding rhetoric: worked on engagements that were 'ground-breaking' or 'cutting edge', using approaches and methodologies that were supposed to be challenging the status quo. And though we received great feedback from clients who were no doubt grateful for our interventions, I could not shake the idea that no matter what I did, however ambitious and whatever my intentions; no work I did was any match for the institutional forces at play in these large organizations. I could tweak around the edges, but ultimately, they would return to their status quo. My professional frustration therefore became my provocation;

"Despite significant investment in transformation, (both in direct monetary terms as well as in the focus of leaders, staff and other stakeholders) in most critical ways the organization of today looks and feels no different than it did 15 years ago".

In other words, I was aware that there were unacknowledged paradoxes at play and as the constant 'outsider', operating at the edges of the sectors, disciplines, areas of expertize - I was somehow closer to these barriers.

I tried dragging people over to my vantage point, gesticulating wildly at the absurdities of what I was seeing and experiencing. The more enlightened of my colleagues sympathized, occasionally railing against the same paradoxes as me, but eventually they would wave it off and return headfirst into the abyss with a wry smile and a shrug of helplessness.

In embracing the thinking in this book, the case for why and how the challenges of our contemporary world are substantively different to those of the past (as articulated in the Prologue and Chapter 1) hit me like a tonne of bricks. This explained a lot; the issues that I had been working on were examples of this new generation of challenge spaces; how to transform an organizational culture to be more risk aware; how to convince organizations to trade off short term profits for long term sustainability. Of course our old core consulting methods couldn't keep up. It was evolutionary mismatch theory at play; the environment had changed, and we had not. We were never taught to lean into the complexity, rather we were taught to strip it away. No wonder I was left with a lingering doubt about my impact, I probably wasn't having one.

DIGGING INTO THE PLAYING FIELD

The phenomenon that I have observed in my working life; this cultural and structural inertia of the corporate sector, appears equally applicable to large scale organizations across industries. So, why do large organizations, supposedly designed to make rational decisions to maximize productivity and value, continuing to invest such large amounts of money and resources into such ineffectual activity? In order to explain the paradox I delved into the implicit and explicit sides of both the language and lived experience of transformation. This draws on Bower's 'hidden rules', highlighting the difference between the real and stated principles that govern organizational transformation. Or to be more specific, the difference between 'What we talk about' (The stated rules) and 'What really matters' (the hidden rules). I identified three primary disconnects at this value level. Looking at the patterns across these three; a metaphor emerged; that of a 'performance.' This explains how the rhetoric around organizational transformation has evolved and morphed, without any underlying change in the organization itself. I have therefore come to see transformation as a kind of 'theatre', one in which all the actors know that they are engaged in a make-believe process, with no real impact. I have called this "performative transformation".

Disconnect 1: Clarity vs truth

In performative transformation; narrative is used to create 'clarity' that abstracts from 'truth'. Over time this contributes to the widening gulf between what people see and hear 'on the stage', and what they experience.

A recurring principle in the change management theory literature is around clarity; clarity of vision, clarity of purpose, clarity in leadership communication. It is spoken about as if it were a given and that not painting a clear enough picture of the future is a barrier to effective transformation. This clarity, should be helping to people to come to an internalized 'understanding' of what is important, but ultimately seems to be failing to do so. This is likely driven by two key factors;

The inherent difficulty of creating clear and concise messages out of complex and dynamic environments and objectives

The stated need for creating a clear vision assumes there is a clear vision of the future and that it is shared by everyone. This of course ignores the reality that the future is unknowable, affected by innumerate forces and ultimately not within the control of any one person, or even group of people.

The world of work is becoming increasingly complex; the factors that we expect people (and especially leaders) to take into consideration in their behavior and decision making, continue to grow. To add to the challenge;

these factors are, at a surface level, sometimes in tension. Take for example authenticity and professionalism.

Leaders are expected to always remain professional, yet are increasingly called upon to simultaneously be authentic. Yet, despite the complexity and tensions at play, corporate communications rely on simple messaging and 'key take aways' to give people clarity about what is important for them to remember.

In contrast to this focus on clarity in the literature deeper reflection on the lived experience seems to yearn for some kind of truth, expressed through adjacent ideas such as honesty, belief and cynicism. These principles are not generally explored or addressed in the context of large organizations, but they matter to transformation. Given that transformation is often experienced as somehow unsuccessful, it is note-worthy that concepts of belief and honesty are not addressed, breeding an unspoken cynicism. Perhaps because these concepts require nuance and active engagement and cannot be expressed through pithy one-way communications.

Disconnect 2: Progress / achievement vs purpose/meaning

In performative transformation, it is understood that the narrow objectives of the financial system e.g. growth and financial value creation can no longer be relied upon to act as incentives for individuals. There is talk about people needing to find meaning and purpose, but at its heart the organization still exists for the same reason it always did. Thus the immediate requirements of value and growth to continue to trump meaningful consideration of individual or organizational meaning and purpose. Conventional wisdom on successful transformation has typically focused on the need to show people 'What's in it for me?' A deceptively straight forward hypothetical relationship between benefits and behavior. However, we know this relationship is not as predictable as claimed; with many examples of people behaving in ways that are ultimately not in their best interest at all. This has led organizations to reconsider how they talk about transformation, and indeed the organization in general.

Contemporary transformation efforts will often center principles of 'meaning' and 'purpose.' This can be seen in the increasing popularity of activities that work to articulate these concepts. In theory, the idea is that if people are in some way connected to the underlying purpose of the organization that they are more likely to invest the time and commit to the activities and behaviors that are necessary to drive transformation.

However, this rhetoric is not matched by evolution in the underlying purpose of the organizations themselves. At their heart, organizations continue to exist within the same system, for the same reasons; shareholder value, growth, and success in the market.

Today, the true focus on these (supposedly outdated) principles is abstracted with statements that speak to customer and community value; as the expectations of these groups demand it. However, the underlying rules, the ones that truly guide behavior and decision making, have not changed. Ultimately, organizations still decide which programs of work to invest in, based on business cases and quantitative (often directly or indirectly commercial) measures, rather than any questions about what 'should' be done. The system holds people and programs 'accountable' only in a very narrow sense. Another consideration goes back to the very reason for this recent focus on purpose and meaning; which is the assumption that it will help people to feel connected to the organization. The theory behind this is sound, behavioral economics holds that affecting people's behavior is easier if you can affect their true emotions. This is the basis for much of change management theory which focuses on creating commitment to change by influencing emotions. The use of language such as 'burning platforms' is an attempt to engage people at this more visceral level. However, once again; whilst the theory and practice of change management is guided by the need for emotional engagement; in the context of the organization this rings hollow; largely because emotions are not typically encouraged in the workplace. On the contrary, displaying too much emotion is generally associated with a lack of professionalism. This is a fundamental paradox between the theory of organizational change and its application. Viewed through this lens, the lack of meaningful behavioral change at the individual level is not surprising; in the bluntest of terms, they don't 'care' enough, and this is because they're not truly encouraged to.

Disconnect 3: Power vs Security

In performative transformation, notions of hierarchy are played down in favor of the appearance of the consideration of individual needs and diversity. This transformation narrative focuses on the security and comfort of the individual as critical. In reality however, inherent power structures continue to dominate. One of the most confounding paradoxes in the case of transformation is that though the system demands 'growth' and 'value', there is a generalized acceptance of the status quo; i.e. that transformation spend will be wasted on unsuccessful programs. One way to understand this is through the notion of personal risk taking.

In this way, people's comfort (emotional) and security (rational) are served by maintaining the fundamentals of the existing approach to change, despite personal experience of challenges or outright failure in pursuing these approaches. In this kind of an environment, some kind of 'bravery' is seen as needed to take a stand, not just to suggest a new approach, but to challenge the existing processes, structures and individuals involved.

As with the other disconnects explored, there has been increased awareness on the importance of bravery, courage and vulnerability. This can be seen in the rising prominence of the concept of psychological safety which is increasingly seen as a key ingredient for successful teams and organizations. Leadership development courses have begun to focus on this, with the aim that leaders will demonstrate the right kind of behaviors and create the right kind of environment that people within their teams feel 'safe' and 'secure' enough to question and to challenge. The diversity, inclusion and equity agenda is important to this set of stated principles as well.

However, despite the acknowledgment of the theoretical benefits of providing diverse peoples with the sense of security needed to try things differently, underlying questions of power and ego remain pervasive in large organizations. In fact, there is a sense that leaders have begun to weaponize this language to maintain their positions of power. For example those leaders in large organizations that are now more 'fluent' in the language of vulnerability, care and purpose; but who continue to be driven by the same drive towards status and power that remain so important in hierarchical organizations. Contemporary organizations do not refer overtly to the importance of these hierarchies, in fact the common rhetorical insistence on 'flat' structures and cultures is an implicit acknowledgment that overly hierarchical organizations are perceived to be in some way outdated. However, the system in which these organizations operate continue to demand strict hierarchies, primarily as a means of assigning accountability for outcomes. Take for example the mismatch between management rhetoric which lauds creative, learning organizations and the reality of the demands of shareholder expectations in which all decisions must be accounted for rationally. In this system the paradox remains; failure through conventional approaches is tolerated whilst failure through experimentation is not.

In summary then it appears, there is a veritable 'gulf' between the narrative and rhetoric around organizational transformation, and people's lived experience of it. To cope with the disconnects dominating this experience a sort of cognitive dissonance is required. This cognitive dissonance causes what appears to be irrational behavior; an obvious example of this is the decision to continue to invest (commercially and personally) in transformation efforts, despite dismal track records and less than enjoyable professional experiences. What is obvious is that the proposed solutions, variations on the same themes enshrined in traditional change management and leadership theory, are unlikely to yield different outcomes in the future.

PARADOXES OF THE CONSULTANT

"The rhetoric surrounding organizational transformation is maturing in line with broader social progress,

whilst

the values ultimately driving behavior and decision-making remain the same"

"It is commonly accepted that most transformation efforts fail,

but

the processes and practices surrounding change efforts remain constant"

"Practitioners embark on new transformation programs with outward enthusiasm and stated optimism,

hiding

a cynicism in their ultimate ability to bring about meaningful change"

"Those most disillusioned by the Consulting Sector opt out of the system,

leaving

those who are unaware or willfully blind to the current shortcomings to somehow drive transformation"

"Change is ultimately driven by learning,

but

consultants feel that they are paid for their 'expertize', making it difficult for them to be seen to be actively engaged in a learning process."

DE-FRAMING AND RE-FRAMING CONSULTANCY PRACTICE: FOUR EXPERIMENTS

Experiment 1: Innovation Salons

In order to more holistically understand Performative Transformation and the potential role of the Consulting Sector in addressing it, I was clear on the need to involve a diverse group within my personal and professional network. I held a series of 'Innovation Salons'; lightly facilitated informal, talk-/work-shops to further explore and evolve my thinking. These salons allowed me to begin to understand how some of the abstract concepts that I was exploring might translate into tangible actions and therefore impact. Each of the salons had a different focus, but common to each was a twin-purpose;

To test, challenge and progress my thinking on performative transformation, learning and innovation ecosystems

To create the time and space for participants (and myself) to reflect more deeply on their practice

These are the focus areas of each of the Salons, expressed through the critical questions:

Salon 1: Values in Action

How does performative transformation show up in your organization?

What values do you perceive as driving true behaviors and decision making?

What values might drive genuine transformation?

What re-frames might be fruitful given transformative values?

Salon 2: Value and Impact

How aligned has your real-world impact been to your personal values and imagined future?

What are the forces at play that have amplified / moderated your impact?

How might the Consulting Sector re-imagine its role, impact and future?

Salon 3: Addressing the Learning Gap

What are the fundamental but forbidden questions that you / your organization might be avoiding? Why?

What are the implications of this avoidance?

What will you commit to surface these questions?

Given the complex nature of the challenge of performative transformation it was unsurprisingly invaluable to have input from a range of academic and professional disciplines (Participants included consultants, designers, change managers, risk specialists, organizational psychologists, behavioral economists communications experts and HR professionals.) Despite differing professional backgrounds and work histories, there was a profound shared sense of frustration at the existential challenge of making meaningful change in large-scale organizations.

I found this to be simultaneously heartening and slightly dispiriting, however I was struck by the palpable energy that seemed to be created when people were given the opportunity to frankly discuss what was generally undiscussable. These salons reinforced the need for these transdisciplinary forums in transforming professional frustration into productive networks of action. Though not a silver bullet, such a network might serve as a blueprint for one way of inspiring bottom-up change. With little infrastructure required, the critical success factor appears to lie more in the questions asked, than solutions proffered, a theme that continued to emerge in other experiments (see below).

Figure 3.6

Experiment 2: Examination of corporate values

In this experiment I sourced the stated corporate values of the organizations making up the ASX100, which represents a cross industry sample of Australia's large-scale corporations. After capturing each organization's value set in a database I clustered and categorized the values to explore the key concepts and arrived at some primary observations;.

The stated values of Australian organizations are not most readily observed / experienced in cultures, behavior and decision making.

One of the questions that emerges through this exploration is the underlying purpose of these value statements. Do we think they should be descriptive i.e., what do we value; or prescriptive, i.e., what do we think we should value. At present they seem to be a strange hybrid of the two i.e., what we think, you think, we should value (where 'you' represents some notion of the broader external group of stakeholders; including the community, customers, regulators and shareholders. This (unspoken) framing means they are limited in usefulness as either descriptive or prescriptive. This seems further support for the 'performative' nature of the institutional narrative, and in particular, the corporate ritual of identifying, articulating and communicating corporate values. That is, whilst claiming to represent some sort of 'truth' (be it descriptive or normative), it is actually an extension of brand and how the organization wishes to be seen. The gap between what an organization explicitly values, versus the experience of the majority of stakeholders within and outside of that organization is palpable, resulting in a degree of cynicism in how these values are discussed outside of formal channels.

A different set of values might be more appropriate for driving true organizational transformation. Setting aside the descriptive versus normative debate and returning to the underlying question of how organizations might move from performative to genuine transformation, there is also a question of which values might better serve these companies. Exploration and discussion with a transdisciplinary group identified a set of values that might drive more genuine transformation. These were Curiosity, Humility and Bravery.

These values do not necessarily align to the most commonly recurring concepts in the top-line categorization of the ASX100, which focus more 'basic virtuous human descriptors' than specific and differentiated principles of behavior. Cross-checking these more 'transformational' values to the ASX100 database revealed that though some of these organizations had articulated one of these concepts within their broader value set, none had combined these in order to articulate (either descriptively or normatively) a set of value drivers that might drive more successful and genuine transformation.

Experiment 3: Honesty (Fundamental but Forbidden Questions)

In this experiment I explored the concept of honesty, as a potential valued-level lens to address performative transformation. I sought to understand how a variety of different practices view honesty, particularly philosophy, psychology, behavioral science and communications, to understood its role in transformation. From a philosophical standpoint honesty stands out amongst the ancient "virtues' as being less binary, i.e. being honest is not always better than being dishonest (for example to protect someone / their feelings.) This challenged honesty's usefulness as a construct in the context of organizational transformation. Examining the opposing phenomenon of 'dishonesty' also challenged my notions about how behaviors like lying and cheating might be contributing to the performative experience of transformation in practice. Emerging research seems to question the conventional 'rational motivation' theory which posited that people will lie / cheat to the maximize benefit offset by the likelihood and consequences of being caught. Rather, a more nuanced picture of dishonesty is merging whereby people will cheat up to the point that they can still reasonably convince themselves that they are honest.

Examining the slippery notion of 'truth' through the prism of communications professionals demonstrate how the concept of honesty could so easily be manipulated. In particular I was struck by a quote that illustrated the subjective nature of 'honesty' that highlighted the dynamic rather than static notion of truth. Rob Ford, a notorious politician, when challenged as to the truthfulness of a previous statement replied, "I wasn't lying, you weren't asking the right questions." This provided a powerful re-frame away from honesty and truth as an somehow 'pure' ends in and of themselves, by focusing on a willingness and ability to ask questions as a key means.

This led me to develop a new construct of 'fundamental but forbidden questions' at the center of my exploration and discussion. I see two primary question types;

The questions we do not ask because we are afraid that we (and/or others) won't like the answers

The questions we do not ask because we are afraid that we (and/or others) won't know the answers, or be unable to find them

Conversations with the innovation network reinforced the importance of these questions as I worked with individuals and groups to articulate the 'fundamental forbidden questions' that were not being articulated or discussed within their organizational context. Some examples included: "How should a 'Profit for Purpose' in the care sector balance its drive for shareholder value with outcomes for patients?" and "How does an organization care for employee wellbeing without adding to the pressure (and therefore further endangering the wellbeing) of managers and leaders?". What is common across these and other fundamental but forbidden questions is a (sometimes unstated) difficulty in making trade-offs between competing priorities, stakeholders and time horizons. These questions also tend to be closely aligned to broader societal conversations and challenges and therefore complex, political, and sensitive. Performative transformation can be seen as a natural result of this failure to ask the tough questions in not even asking the questions, organizations are free to pretend that they do not exist, instead carving out adjacent questions that do not pose the same existential threat and channeling energy and resources into addressing these; which often miss the systemic causes, and therefore don't drive meaningful change.

Experiment 4: Futures worth wanting; re-imagining Consulting

Despite my exasperation with the Consulting Sector; I believe there is a role for Consultant's (should we choose to accept the role) in attempting to address Performative Transformation to help our clients along the journey to genuine transformation. However the current paradigm of the sector will need to shift.

There is strong resonance between Science and Consulting; perhaps because the sector is so much a product and reflection of the Scientific mode of thinking (see Chapter 2). Just as post-modernism reflected a rejection of the scientific assumptions about the world, and humans as objective observers seeking only to understand and communicate existing truths and meaning, so too does the Consulting Sector need a new frame at the existential level. Whilst the Consulting sector has traditionally seen itself as a custodian / facilitator of client outcomes, using objective knowledge and truth to enable their clients to realize value and impact, I propose a more post-modernist function of the sector as one that does not shy away from actively creating meaning.

But in order to do this there is a fundamental question about how the practice of consulting tends to imagine the future. The centering of Science as the basis for the Consulting sector is instructive. The focus on positivism / empiricism in this scientific paradigm encourages a view of the future that aims at prediction, based on current trends and forecasting; rather than other approaches which center more imagination and hope, based on post-positivist paradigms. Using Gidley's Future model, I formulated a matrix to explore the Consulting Sector balances positive (hope) and negative (risk/fear) imaginings of the Future with the impact they might have at an organizational, and broader societal level.

Within the Consulting Sector there is a lack of emphasis on the 'Imaginative Focus' quadrant. This is partly due to the 'indirect' impact that Consultants expect to have, through client outcomes. In traditional models, Consultants rely on the client 'brief' to determine their impact, in other words they have traditionally been relatively agnostic in terms of ideology. To create futures worth wanting, I envision Consultants moving away from passive 'facilitative' roles where the clients provide the 'why', towards consultants themselves playing a role in defining their vision for the future. Consultants should therefore be using their own tools (such as futuring itself) to challenge their future value and impact. This relies on a more post-modern philosophy in which Consultants give themselves permission (or confer upon them an expectation) that they are not simply empty vessels that uncover existing meaning and reveal current trends (e.g., empirical/positivist) but value and meaning creators through whose work value is created through a normative process (e.g., critical/postmodern).

THE ARCHITECTURE AND INFRASTRUCTURE OF TRANSFORMATION

Transformation can be framed as coordinated learning process, experienced at scale. This means that to create a new field of practice for the Consulting Sector and address performative transformation, creating authenticity around learning loops must be critical. Learning loops, in theory, are not new to the sector; processes exist at each level of the organization (and beyond) that point to existing (if not necessarily effective) infrastructure.

For example:

At the individual level, performance management processes through goal setting, feedback and coaching are meant to encourage personal development.

At the team level, project debriefs, post implementation reviews and lessons learned sessions are designed to facilitate collective learning.

At the organization level, 'knowledge sharing' is conducted across teams, spreading the reach of team level learning, external experts are brought in to share 'best practice.'

At the sector level, there are events such as conferences and publications such as white papers that lay out the emergent practice from across organizations, disciplines and industries.

What appears to be missing from these learning loops are the values of humility, curiosity and bravery, and the asking of forbidden questions, reducing all the so-called learning to its most performative state. Interestingly, it appears that as one moves through the levels above, the systemic disincentive to genuine learning become stronger, reducing the true curiosity, humility and bravery needed to ask and attempt to answer fundamental but forbidden questions.

In considering how to establish more effective learning loops within and across these different functional levels, the primary consideration is perhaps then less about new infrastructure and rhythms to house the learning loops and more about the practice of individuals and groups within those existing processes. The job to be done is therefore to re-frame these existing organizational processes, using the Practice model (see §1.2), to place learning as the ultimate value, alongside curiosity, humility and bravery as enabling principles. For example, in the corporate sector at the individual level there is an existing, deeply embedded rhythm and process which can be leveraged in the form of performance management. However at present, the methods and actions associated with these processes are driven by a set of values and principles that may differ between reality and rhetoric.

See below for an example:

Value	Explicit: Personal Professional development, Learning Implicit: Progression, Recognition and Success
Principles	Explicit: Organizational Principles / Values Implicit: Justification of self, positivism (data and evidence)
Methods	Coaching, reflection, goal setting, metrics, feedback
Actions	Developing achievable goals in line with team/ organization priorities Demonstrating progress in line with capability frameworks

Table 1: 'As is' Personal Development Practice.

Therefore, what could or should be acting as a kind of Temple (see §3.5) in which individuals take time to reflect on themselves, their impact and their growth, remains another forum in which they need to validate, justify and promote themselves; a rather unholy trinity. In order for this infrastructure to represent a more authentic learning loop, I would propose a re-imagining of the practice (from top to bottom).

Values	Authentic learning to drive progress / desired impact (as defined by individual)
Principles	Curiosity, Humility, Bravery
Methods	Coaching, reflection, goal setting, feedback
Actions	Asking the fundamental but forbidden questions of oneself and others; for example; What did I think I knew, that I know now I did not What do I still not know? What do I not have control of that I would nevertheless like to influence? What is the value and impact I want to create in the lived world? How might I unintentionally create adverse impacts? What can I do to avoid / mitigate these? What do I need to change about my mindset to drive positive change?

Table 2: Re-imagined 'Temple' Practice.

In doing so, it is interesting to note that the methods themselves do not need to be radically transformed, having values and principles that reposition the purpose from self-justification to genuine learning in turn changes how those methods manifest at the action level. For example, feedback as a method might change drastically FROM asking colleagues to provide feedback on progress against stated objectives / aligned to a capability framework

To engaging a wide range of stakeholders in a feedback conversation around fundamental but forbidden questions e.g. "How did I negatively impact your world?"

REFLECTIONS AND NEXT QUESTIONS

For now, I remain convinced that proposing additional infrastructure within the existing organizational paradigm will not be sufficient to drive the change in practice I think is needed to drive genuine learning and transformation. This is due in part to an inherent and fundamental paradox in trying to address performative transformation; efforts to change the system (including new infrastructure) risk being co-opted into the performative structures; adding activity and rhetoric without fundamentally addressing systemic challenges. The question remains; what kind of informal infrastructure might we experiment with to drive the change in practice within the formal structures within organizations?

In contrast to the systemic and deeply held paradoxes on the sector and organizational levels, I felt that my first steps at building a new practice should center around the Temple element of the Studio, allowing for individuals (outside of the confines of their organization) to formulate the fundamental but forbidden questions that feel most important to them in order to more deliberately create value and impact through their practice. The Innovation Salon represented an experiment with this; a diverse group of Consulting practitioners from different industries and specialisms to explore how using principles of Curiosity, Humility and Bravery, might inspire a mindset shift that could act as a call to arms for more deliberate practice. Using the value and principles contained in the Temple Practice above, I designed a session meant to drive more awareness and self-reflection from participants on their desired impact on the world, and how this might shift their decisions and behaviors as consultants. The interactive, facilitated discussion-based format proved effective. Participants agreed that being given physical space and dedicated time to genuinely reflect on their own values, decisions and behaviors was a valuable exercise and were keen to repeat the experience on a regular basis as a way of more consistently including deliberate reflection into their practice.

This loose, informal and highly decentralized experiment is not the concrete kind of infrastructure that lends itself to the action plans and implementation timelines that I (and many others) would find comforting. A clear path forward might offer solace, however this is the fundamental temptation of performative learning and I must resist. Rather, in the spirit of curiosity, humility and bravery, I conclude with a sample of the fundamental but forbidden questions that I am left asking. It's relatively easy to identify the questions that are not being asked by others; all teams and organizations have their taboo subjects.

But what are the questions that I struggle to contemplate myself... At the moment, they include:

- Can system be changed from without? Though the concepts of performative transformation and fundamental but forbidden questions resonated strongly within my self-selected network am I 'preaching to the converted?' Surely, the real challenge lies in changing the minds of those still working within the status quo system.
- Will there be any lived world impact to my work? Or am I adding to the interesting but ultimately pointless criticism of accepted theory and practice?
- How can we affect change at scale? Bottom up change might be personally rewarding but will not address the fundamental questions of what drives behavior at the institutional and sector level. For example; the basic business model of Consulting Firms remains an inhibitor to truly disruptive change.

This level of self-reflection is not for the faint of heart; these questions follow me, haunt me and exhaust me. But maybe that's the only way I'll actually learn.

3.7

THE IMPROVISING ORGANIZATION: STRATEGIC EDUCATION IN PRACTICE

Dr Steve Barry FHEA

Amidst his characters' manifold struggles with the realities of ecological destruction, one groundbreaking idea reverberates throughout Richard Powers' (2018) stunning novel The Overstory - that trees are social creatures. As Powers' dendrologist Patricia Westerford devotes her life to showing, those strong, silent, perhaps even institutional figures of our natural world are in constant dialogue - sharing information about environmental changes, warning neighbors of threats, and even transferring nutrients on a needs basis to support the holistic well-being of their ecosystem.

As a musician and lecturer, this feels oddly familiar. For us improvisers, the relationship between the individual tree and the collective forest is always in play. Even as each musician pursues their own independent creative goals and ambitions for musical self-actualization, they do so most often through vital and often ensemble-based collaboration, shaped and amplified by the contributions of others.

Yet it's remarkable how quickly a change of environment - say from the bandstand to the educational institution - can uproot these enriching practices of emergent co-learning. The more I've reflected on this in recent years, the more I've seen just how powerfully context frames behavior, how easily those values or *qualities without a name* can be lost in translation from the ecological world of practice into the construction of knowledge in the institution.

For example, the history of jazz highlights time and again that innovation stems from musicians' direct responses to the shifting ecology around them. Yet jazz curricula have often focused more on canonical artifacts than on the situated creative processes that produced them. In our degree program, I noticed this product-orientation could hinder students' ability to develop transferable techniques across varied performance contexts - put simply, they couldn't see the forest for the trees. By recently reorienting our curriculum to zoom in and out more rhythmically between conceptual methods applied actions, students now report that their learning feels both deeper and more interconnected across the program. This zooming approach has also opened to door to deeper collective interrogation of the "why" - the values that lay behind certain curriculum content.

I've noticed a similar translation gap with my teaching colleagues. Onstage, those mycorrhizal networks of collaboration are clear in the real-time adaptation and collective intuition of spontaneous performance. As we migrate into our siloed teaching studios and lecture rooms, though, the very frames of and buildings around teaching and learning can hinder or outright prevent these kind of interactions, even within disciplines let alone between them. In jazz the "jam session" - where musicians gather to spontaneously find and solve performance problems together, in configurations decided on the spot - plays a vital role in sharing and advancing creative ideas.

Yet it's so easy to miss the opportunities of this model in the institution, where the values of rigor and efficiency subtly dissuade activities without pre-determined outcomes - even as research continues to highlight the value of enacted and exploratory practices in generating new knowledge. In this light, we recently completed a year-long co-design project, rooted in staff and student dialogue and borrowing methods from the jam session model - and it has been remarkable to witness the camaraderie and shared ownership that has emerged through those dialogues.

These small experiments - and others like them - have made me optimistic that our institutions can reflect the creativity they seek to cultivate in the way they design, run and review their operations.

As the world becomes ever more open, complex, dynamic and networked, Universities are hearing the call to be not just vital trunks of knowledge, but also diverse, adaptive forests - full of individuals and micro-climates resilient and responsive to change.

Just as fields from architecture to computing increasingly turn to nature for inspiration, if not even outright solutions, perhaps the "best practices" we seek in our organizations are already all around us. The challenge, as always, may simply be knowing ourselves well enough to see them.

3.8

THE INFLUENCE OF THE COLLECTIVE/ THE INFLUENTIAL COLLECTIVE

Matilda Coy

Photo by olia danilevich.

INTRODUCTION: MEET THE GEORGIE COLLECTIVE

I am an inherently curious person, working across both creative and strategic spaces. I have been shaped by powerful connections, travel and art. Art that you idolize, art that you immerse yourself in, art that I create and the art that you wear as clothing. I had always worked in a transdisciplinary way, however I never had the vernacular or understanding to recognize the strength of this experience. After studying a Bachelor's degree at University of Sydney majoring in English Literature and Art History I moved to London, a cultural epicenter and worked in fashion as a marketing consultant and personal shopper. Recognizing the cultural magnetism of my favorite city I then moved to New York, to work in digital communications. After a declined visa I moved back to Australia to start a new career in advertising at a creative agency. During the Covid19 pandemic I transitioned into a remote role at a tech start up to work as a Brand Strategist. And finally transitioning into a Place Strategist role at a design and strategy agency. This range of experiences across various industries and sectors not only improved my professional practice but also set me up to become a business founder of The Georgie Collective.

The Georgie Collective is a women-only community that is a safe space for curious women to connect and grow with one another. Named as a tribute to my best friend Georgie who passed away in 2017 after battling with depression, an illness that eventually overcame her. My motivation is to make other women feel the same way she made me feel - safe, supported, and connected. The Georgie Collective is built from an honest desire to continue Georgie's legacy, based on vulnerability and love. We are a women-only networking organization without the hustle culture, that's focused on women's holistic health and building connection, where the only prerequisite is that you identify as a woman. The establishment of The Georgie Collective was deeply personal for me, inspired by my own journey and the broader societal complexities surrounding womanhood. The loss of my friend Georgie, who struggled with depression, served as a powerful catalyst for creating a safe and supportive community where women could connect and thrive. Motivated by my own experiences and a desire to address systemic challenges, I sought out a different way of thinking and doing, leading to the inception of The Georgie Collective.

The starting point: being a woman - in data

My ambition for this research was to validate and better understand how The Georgie Collective could support women. I wanted to comprehend how you could understand the immeasurable experience of womanhood. The learned behaviors that are present on a micro and macro scale - the internalized misogyny, the carrying your keys in your hand, covering your drink when you're out, the "text me when you're home" practice. Through inviting a range of diverse women's voices into the conversations I started to recognize the patterns that exist within the experiences of womanhood. I realized that it's in the moments of suppressed thoughts, the things left unsaid in meetings because you didn't think your idea was good enough, or the quiet mistakes made because you were too nervous to ask. I embarked on exploring several key themes, including engagement with mental health, relationship with connection, societal pressures, impostor syndrome, sources of creativity, fear, vulnerability, and the individuals' experiences with womanhood. Beyond these themes, my curiosity led me to delve into the paradigms and paradoxes that women navigate in today's society – encompassing systemic issues, daily stigmas and stereotypes, mental health challenges, and patriarchal pressures.

To paint the picture from a data perspective:

"Clinical studies in emergency departments and antenatal clinics indicate that between 19.3% and 25.0% of women will be subjected to domestic violence over their lifetime. Surveys of women attending general practice in Australia reveal varying partner abuse rates of 8.0% and 28% in a 12-month period." Therefore this indicates that there is a real need for female-only spaces for safety.

"More than two thirds, (68%) of women experience a mental health condition before the age of 25."

In Australia in 2023 the gender pay gap is still sitting at 13%. Which means "For every dollar on average men earned, women earned 87 cents. That's $252.30 less than men each week. Over the course of one year, that adds up to $13,119.60." - Note that these stats don't factor in the individual stories and experience with other aspects of discrimination; racism, homophobia, ageism, disabilities etc.

The anti female bias in medicine is still prevalent as there are still shadows and fall out of years of research on only male bodies which impact how women are treated. Noting that, "Doctors and nurses prescribe less pain medication to women than men after surgery, even though women report more frequent and severe pain levels."

As I delved into my research I realized that there are open and hidden rules at play in any complex situation, and

I had set out to understand the ever-complex experience of womanhood. I started exploring my problem space through in-depth interviews with women, and quickly realized the key hidden rule was that I was trying to bring the undiscussable nature of the issues, paradoxes, taboos and nuances into discussions.

THE PARADOXES OF WOMANHOOD

"Balancing independence and self-sufficiency with societal expectations of dependence

creates

a paradox in the experience of womanhood."

"Despite efforts to promote body positivity, women

face a paradox

with societal beauty standards that foster body dissatisfaction and pressure to conform."

"The tension of balancing motherhood and career ambitions

presents women with

challenging decisions and feelings of guilt or inadequacy."

"Women grapple with the paradox of being held to high standards of perfection,

contributing

to feelings of self-doubt in various aspects of their lives."

Institutional paradoxes that accompany these lived experiences:

"Creating temporary spaces for women outside patriarchal structures seems futile,

as

these spaces are transient and once we exit, safety becomes uncertain."

"Mental health is different for everyone making it challenging to offer effective services

but

the uniqueness of each person's experience makes it difficult for anyone to truly understand the struggles of another."

DE-FRAMING AND RE-FRAMING OUR APPROACHES TO WOMANHOOD: EXPERIMENTS

The underlying drive behind all my experiments is consistently centered on gaining a deeper understanding of women's experiences. To ignite curiosity, I consistently frame my experiments with questions aimed at stimulating thought and guiding structure.

Experiment 1: How do women engage with creativity?

Objective: Mary Lou Cook once said, "The greatest barrier to creativity is the lack of courage to take the first step." The connection with courage, confidence, and creativity are all interconnected. When we look at the rates of impostor syndrome in women, how can we expect women to have the courage to explore something as vulnerable as creativity... unless given permission. The intention behind this experiment is to carve out the space for women to be creative and reflect on the experience.

Method: Host a creative workshop in collaboration with a florist and invite women in to explore their creativity in a safe, judgment free space.

De-frame: In order to challenge the framing of this experiment within the confines of the question, it could be argued that this is an oversimplification of an experience. Whilst the event will not appeal to all women and is targeted at the women who are interested it could critiqued that it perpetuates a narrative around female creativity that does not apply to all women.

Re-frame: One could emphasize a more inclusive approach that recognizes the diversity of women's experiences with creativity. This involves acknowledging that courage, confidence, and creativity are not inherently lacking in women but may be influenced by various contextual and individual factors. The experiment's intention could be re-framed to underscore the importance of providing a supportive and inclusive environment for individuals, regardless of gender, to explore and enhance their creative potential. This re-framing shifts the focus from a perceived deficiency in women to the creation of an empowering space for all participants to nurture their creative instincts.

I think the biggest challenge for this experiment was getting women who don't think they're creative to attend the workshop. Most attendees loved the idea and felt comfortable walking around the space. There were a few attendees who had clearly boxed themselves into the 'uncreative' head space. These people required more time, attention and intervention. It was beautiful that everyone got to take something home - the impact of The Georgie Collective will sit as a reminder in everyone's home until the flowers died. I loved to think that there was a little bit of Georgie's spirit in every woman's arrangement. As the event looked beautiful people naturally took lots of photos which was great for branding and digital impact. Creatively flowers are the perfect medium for people to explore because you can't really do any wrong! It would be more intimidating to arrive to a blank canvas.

Experiment 2: How do women reflect and connect with themselves?

Objective: Explore the strength of women's individual voice alone and as part of the Collective.

Method: I asked women to write themselves a love letter exploring their experience with womanhood. The letter-writing task is one that takes personal courage and reflection, and as the curator of this task, I need to hold a level of responsibility. It was important that I consider the impacts of the circumstances of the experience for the engaged women.

De-frame: The individual's psychological safety of the women completing the task is an impossible measure as it is incredibly complex and nuanced. This experiment could be critiqued within the limitations for overlooking the broader systemic factors that come into play.

Re-frame: Could broaden the impact and understanding of physiological safety. This re-framing should consider the interplay between individual circumstances and broader socio-cultural factors that shape the experience of womanhood. The objective could be adjusted to emphasize not only the impact of individual circumstances but also the collective aspects that contribute to psychological safety.

Some key reflections: firstly, since submissions were digital, individuals had agency in selecting when and where to complete the task. Secondly, the structure of a letter introduced a level of formality to the reflection process. Additionally, there's a certain beauty in addressing a letter to oneself and witnessing one's own name as the catalyst for the task, which encourages a reflective, free-flowing stream of consciousness mentality.

MOVING FORWARD: BUILDING A MOVEMENT

What infrastructure will you need/ should be built to support the above going forward? What are key elements in the Studio? (Is there a Lab, Academy, Podium, Temple?). Which element would you build first? Based on the unique context and strategic goals for The Georgie Collective, establishing effective learning loops requires a thoughtful and tailored infrastructure. Below are the key elements:

Formalized space for collaboration - as the sole Founder of The Georgie Collective it's easy to feel isolated without the network for collaboration. Throughout my experience with the innovation ecology having a consistent collaboration space to challenge Ideas and future planning has been incredibly valuable and is a key learning loop that will need to be continued moving forward.

Formalized digital data infrastructure - understand the digital systems that support growth, collect data after each event, assist with scheduling, monitoring warm data, new leads, live feedback and be able to plug in the feedback forms.

Event activation evaluation - review event frequency and consistency. Develop the processes and ways of working to support this new rhythm around developing The Georgie Collective calendar for members.

Reflection and personal appraisal - this is something that has come up throughout my business journey, ensure that I develop a rigid reflection template which allows me the space to reflect on the event successes and areas for improvement. Also includes integrating more structured reflection sessions into the learning loop, both during and after the events.

Reflection in action - develop the process that turns feedback into actionable insights and improvement for future events. Add in the possibility for the feedback forms to not be anonymous but to co-design the events with members.

Collective Community - create a space for the members within The Georgie Collective to connect with one another. The need for the community to have a formalized infrastructure to connect with one another will empower them to connect and pay credit to The Georgie Collective without us having to organize the event itself. A growing ecology.

Communications Strategy - continue to build the brand through existing communications strategy. Main touch points social media and mailing list.

Operations, Documentation & Evolution - keep a comprehensive record of each learning loop, including feedback, changes made, revised strategies and outcomes to ensure that the business is always growing and evolving.

In my practice I have re-framed the structure of a Studio into An Ecological Community. Based on the naturally occurring plants & animals that interact in a unique habitat. To develop this new way of working I overlaid elements of Ikigai - a Japanese concept that refers to a passion that gives value and joy to life, with networked thinking.

REFLECTIONS, LESSONS AND FAVORITE THINGS

The key evolution for The Georgie Collective is shift from growth metrics to impact metrics. Meaning that for the Collective to grow it's essential that I focus on the impact that the events and the communications are having on individual women opposed to the number of attendees. This will also ensure creative output and powerful, organic growth. As a practitioner I understand that I transcend multiple spaces that will be impacted by the development of my innovation ecosystem. Throughout my journey I have developed two new ways of working that can plug into multiple spaces and develop innovative outcomes.

Creative Workshops – Based on the depth of creative study I've been able to curate and run creative workshops. They invite people to be creative by carving out the space and the permission to do so.

I have also developed my own Masterclass to be implemented in organizations as a consultant. This brings my own perspective and approach to the work. For each task I have developed a new framework: (1) The Teaser - provides inspiration to spark interest in the form of a teaser, (2) The Task - whether that's a method card or other action, and (3) The Thaumaturgy - the working of wonders or miracles, the magical insight that is found.

Lessons learned:

- All innovation starts with curiosity and pursuit for change.
- Rather than closing the loop on the day to day, we're opening future(s) opportunities through creativity and connection.
- Through my research I have constantly gravitated towards the impact of impostor syndrome on women and how it affects them across multiple spaces (not just work). I am exploring the idea of developing a suite of creative practices and methods that would work towards recognizing and in turn overcoming impostor syndrome on a micro level.
- My academic journey is innately human as I am an extension of my organization and visa versa. My journey has been emotional at times and has been peppered with some emotionally challenging conversations.
- To have creativity you need to create a space that is safe and inviting.
- While a community requires growth to achieve impact, excessive rapid growth can diminish that impact.

Thought Starters:

- What are our learned behaviors doing to us?
- Is innovation a way of thinking more than it is an output?
- What is your truth? Is this reflective within your organization?
- What makes you feel alive? How can I create something that makes others feel alive?
- Where do I seek inspiration?
- Reflect on today. What were your assumptions?

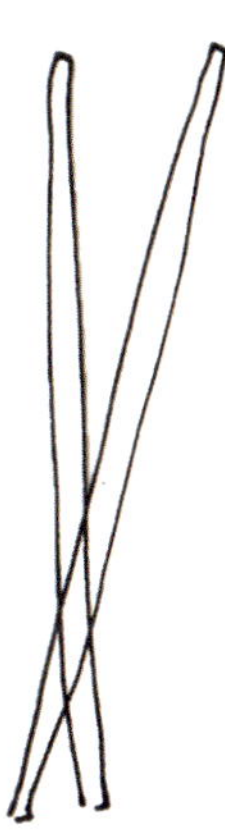

3.9

EDU CERE, TO LEAD SOMEONE OUT TO A PLACE

Christina Luzi

INTRODUCTION: WHY DOESN'T EDUCATION LEARN?

Education is one of the fundamental enablers of success as an adult. Schools are where individuals learn to communicate with others, they learn how to think critically and problem-solve. Across the world, education is fundamental to a country's long-term success and sustainability. It is these high stakes that continue to see education systems live under scrutiny all over the world. As countries evolve and professional landscapes change our society becomes far more dynamic, open, networked and complex. These changes are both an opportunity for evolution and innovation as they are a place for societal decay. Governments look to education to understand and solve these societal shifts. What is discovered is an out-of-date system that does not meet the needs of our changing world.

To add to this complexity is how the success of an Education system is measured. In Australia, standardized tests are the tool used by governments and the media to assess the current state of education. Australia on a global metric scale has continued to face declining results. These falling results challenge public perceptions of educators and cause a societal distrust of the education system. This distrust is evident in the falling number of graduates with education degrees and the number of graduates leaving the profession in the first five years. Whilst politicians believe that standardized test results are an accurate measure of the system, in reality, the system is far too complex and dynamic to be judged against these measures. The reality is, that if school systems continue to be led by strong educators who are highly skilled classroom practitioners, the Australian education system will continue on its steady decline. Until we can define new measures of success, attract a greater variety of graduates, and break down the old educational paradigm, we will continue to see the same issues emerge.

Like most Australian educators, I transitioned from my own high school experience into an education degree and then returned to the classroom as an educator. Like most educational leaders, my expertize in classroom pedagogy and natural leadership skills were the prerequisites for my progression into educational leadership. Unlike other industries, educational leaders are not required to have management degrees or leadership credentials. Perhaps it is this process that has led to the stagnation of the Australian education system.

This challenging space is one of the driving forces behind my engagement with creative intelligence. Through seeking interaction with other professionals from transdisciplinary backgrounds I have been able to develop my understanding of the complexities of leading an adaptive and developmental organization. Understanding the values of an organization and how these drive the methods, practices, and actions of an organization has been fundamental to allowing our organization to challenge the current educational paradigm and write the new measures of success.

THE CLASH OF PARADIGMS

Behind these organizational tensions is an age-old discussion between different paradigms at the basis of education.

On one side of the discussion, the 'teaching' side, education is framed as the transfer of knowledge, as 'what you should know'. This way of seeing leads us to a particular way of thinking about education, and an impressive well established action repertoire of useful practices. Education is talked about in terms of teaching of pre-determined subject matter, held in a structured curriculum to ensure completeness of the knowledge transfer. Quality of the knowledge transfer is tested by examinations in which students are compared on their ability to reproduce knowledge. Students are encouraged to do well by being in competition with one another in this well-defined playing field. They are trained for a set exam and will enter a profession that is predefined.

On the other side of the discussion, the 'learning' side, education is framed as learning, as conveying 'how you can get to knowledge'. This way of seeing leads to thinking about education in terms of exploration and growth, often using the metaphor of a journey to structure the actions that scaffold experiential learning. Active curiosity is stimulated. Hierarchical distance between teacher and learner is minimized, as it gets in the way of open discussion and reflection. The learning journey is different for different learners, the fact that they are hard to compare means that quality is largely measured in terms of levels of reflection. Learning is seen as both an individual and a group process.

THE PARADOXES OF TEACHING VERSUS LEARNING

Schools are places for students to learn,

yet

their voices are often neglected in their design and implementation.

Schools are no longer fit for purpose

yet

we keep reinventing the same rigid curriculum and expect something to change.

Students thrive when they feel connected to their school and peers

yet

this time is not mandated in the curriculum.

As communities grow and change the needs follow

however

we continue to implement traditional leadership structures that reinforce old molds.

We want our education system to change and evolve

but

all our time is spent on short-term fixes to our current problems.

We know future change starts with the students who are in schools now

yet

we don't trust or empower their voices.

We want education to change

yet

we train teachers the same and make it too hard for professionals to transition into education.

We want student agency and voice

yet

we continue to reinforce hierarchy of Principal, Leadership and student.

EXPERIMENTING WITH WAYS TO MOVE FORWARD

Re-framing student agency

As educators we saw students as the flowers and plants in a garden, we chose which plants and where they went, we tended to them and our gardening was the key to their flourishing. Re-framing this to imagine the students and the educators as both a plant and a gardener shifted our perspectives on the possibilities. Why was it that students could not nourish and tend to our needs to allow us to flourish?

This question led us to a series of experiments.

- Our first experiment was the collaborative design of our learning center. We had struggled for years to have our senior students use this library space effectively. Using a variety of creative tools including imagining the library as a character and exploring the tension points through narrative sensory reactions to sounds, smells, and textures in the space we were able to have the students diagnose what made the environment challenging for them to learn and collaborate. Students held private ideation sessions with architects and they created mood boards with visions of the color palette, layout, and furniture. What emerged was a harmonious space that met the needs of all the stakeholders in our community.
- From this experiment, we were able to highlight to the students the power and value of their voice and began to re-imagine other elements of College life. This was evident in how we elected our Student Leadership team. In the past this had been a role limited to most academic students, they were required to write a letter addressed to the principal and deliver a speech to the student body. Upon examining the process it highlighted the many hidden rules at play holding the old system in place. Student leaders represented the student body yet they had to have their worth assessed by the adults. The speech and the letter also limited the students who were able to apply and hence they really did not represent the entire student body.
- Our next experiment had Senior Student leaders pitch ways to build connectedness and community in our college. The students then had to collaborate with the other applicants to host an event for their peers. The students were able to see the individual's leadership in action and were able to participate in an event conceived by the students for the students. We then had these senior students hold an advertising campaign for the rest of the student leadership body. We saw a 500% increase in applications for student leadership.

By allowing our students to take on the role of the gardeners we were able to give them the autonomy to choose the garden bed, the location and the plants. They experimented with how the garden was nourished. The students still utilized our skills and expertize but we were the guest appearing in their program. The result of the success of these experiments is a genuine belief that our students can impact our community in positive ways and that they have something to offer the adults at the school. The frequency of student-led initiatives continues to increase and highlight the health of our innovation ecosystem.

RE-FRAMING: FROM SCHOOL TO ORGANIZATION

Schools have maintained the same leadership structures since they first emerged. There is a principal and their executive, pastoral care roles, and learning roles. In a world where we want schools to evolve, do these frameworks and roles fit? What if schools were seen as learning organizations. Would our roles and structures look different? How could we learn from innovative organizations and re-imagine the ways of working, thinking, and being to ensure our community is at the frontier of change?

Again, these questions led to a series of experiments:

- Our first experiment was to open up to our community the opportunity to have time and money allocation to probe into a "challenge space" in the school. Often the executives and leaders in an educational organization are charged with the responsibility of ensuring the compliance elements of schools are in check to keep their doors open. The result of this is time and energy is spent in the wrong places- reinforcing the constraints of legislation instead of negotiating ways around them. We had nearly 10% of staff come forward with a pitch for an area of the school they would like to explore and improve to ensure our community was at the "frontier" of education. The pitches came from a range of areas such as well-being, connectedness learning interventions, micro-credentialing and diversifying learner pathways. The result of this experiment was eleven smaller experiments taking place across our learning community. Using creative methods the individuals engaged various stakeholder groups, defined problems and co-evolved interventions to improve our learning community. Seeing the person behind the educator and invigorating their passion spaces allowed for organic evolution and change. It also led to sub-projects and new ways of thinking and being to emerge in our learning community.
- We took a similar approach to exploring existing wellbeing leadership roles within the community and if they were still fit for purpose. We asked the current leaders in the roles to consider who did their roles serve? In the industrial sector what similar roles were out there? How could their role evolve to meet the growing needs of our diverse community? What emerged were some inspired and fresh approaches to the relationships between learners and educators and different methodologies and perspectives from other industries. The roles continue to be designed with the values and lived experiences at the core of the position as opposed to the actions required to be undertaken.

Across both experiments it was evident that there is a willingness in our community to do things differently. The collaborative and team within team culture in our community breeds confidence to experiment. Engaging the people behind the roles allowed for fresh perspectives and a sense of duty to execute the proposed solutions.

WHAT DOES IT TAKE TO CHANGE EDUCATION?

It can be challenging to identify the differences between emergence and intentionality. The core success behind all of the experiments was removing the barriers of pre-conceived notions, enabling the "why" question and ensuring that we put the people and their lived experiences first.

If I reflect on the key enablers that saw the rapid evolution of innovation in our school, one could not pass the re-imagining of our College vision statement. In the past our organization had evolved as a result of key mantras such as "get on the bus", "fill the bucket" and being the best person you can be. These mantras or ways of being took a community which was fractured and stagnant to a community which was activated. Success meant being on board with the new direction of the school, showing one was on board through participation and the commitment to personal growth. We could see that these mantras had become our boundary objects.

Success was to be on board and to participate. We knew that a clear vision and mantra had been successful in creating change in the past, we just had to consider what we wanted to change in the next iteration of our College. We involved all the staff and students and asked them to articulate what they believed our College stood for and where it was going. From their answers we co evolved the vision statement below;

St John XXIII Catholic College is at the frontier of learning. Connecting and encouraging every student and staff member so that they can flourish and be the very best person they can be.

St John XXIII Catholic College will proactively co-adapt, co-create and transform in ever-changing local and global ecosystems.

The vision statement has become a key piece of infrastructure to change the collective thinking when enacting change and evolution. However, this alone is not the only infrastructure required. In a learning community with over 2,000 staff and students our organization is too large to rely on one individual to drive the ideas and implement the change. McCrystal's (2015) vision of a collective consciousness where shared vision and trust are the key enablers to organizational innovation is another fundamental element of infrastructure required. Within our organization we intentionally developed teams within the organization that had both independent and interdependent ways of working. This collective mentality saw the development of a shared consciousness and through intentionally developing these teams in their execution of ideas we saw their confidence and autonomy build. To continue to allow our organization to evolve we must reinforce and support the development and cohesion of the teams we have. Supporting them with both experience and youth to ensure that both mastery and naivety exist together. We want to reinforce that all levels of knowing are welcome and useful when being at the frontier, as it is through this connection that the organization will flourish.

LESSONS LEARNED AND NOT-YET LEARNED

In every organization there are hidden rules and legacies which govern how the organization operates, what is rewarded and what is not. The first step for anyone interested in shifting their organization to an innovation ecosystem is to stop and get on the balcony. From the balcony you will start to see all the hidden rules and legacies that act as inhibitors to the change you want. It was by doing this that I was able to see the residue of the past and how it was very much living in our present. It also gave me a great starting place to shift thinking.

Another key enabler was The Colors of Change framework (see § 3.4) and exploring how I navigate change and how those in my organization navigate change. This revelation was another enabling factor for the shift in organizational thinking. It allowed us to utilize different individual strengths and deploy them at the right time, a shared sense of success was experienced.

Happiness and satisfaction are the hidden fuel of change. When the individuals in the organization can see and feel the positive energy and spirit surrounding the changes in thinking the evolution is almost contagious. They evolve so rapidly, you have to keep up...

For those who respond adversely to these collective shifts, one must take time to stop and diagnose the loss. The loss must be acknowledged and the individual given the time needed to grieve this loss. Choosing to ignore this may lead you to create a new legacy that lives in the organization.

Lastly, one must simply begin. There need not be a blue print for success, all the rules do not have to be written one must simply Shoot, Aim, Fire. If one does not take the first step, there is no need for the ones that follow. Consider who will you take with you physically, intellectually, spiritually.

The qualities of the process in a way became the solution space.

3.10

THE HEAVY SUITCASE

Cecilia Warren

This tale is not a case study. It is just a case. A suitcase.

The landscape of its travel is not unfamiliar: a pebble in the shoe, a stone to rest on and a rocky cliff to set the edge of sight. I picked up the suitcase on route to a board meeting to lead a strategy session with fellow directors. In advance, I had borrowed a 'cliff' metaphor from this landscape. The company faced a strategic challenge that was akin to standing at the precipice of a cliff. This provocation injected conceptual metaphor theory (Lakoff & Johnson, 1980) into strategy and revealed hidden frames of perception.

The 'cliff precipice' invoked what cognitive linguists call an image schema (a preverbal cognitive structure based on concrete experience) related to the verticality of up and down. The physical experience of being lifted up and down is felt by our bodies in early development, before we can verbalize it into language. Once the concrete experience is embodied as an image schema, abstract concepts can then be mapped. A conceptual metaphor is formed when this preverbal, embodied knowledge becomes the 'source domain' to understand a more abstract concept, known as the 'target domain' (Ibid).

The other image schema that was evoked by this metaphor is that of the 'path' which is ubiquitous in organizational strategies. The path (or journey) is found in annual reports where 'headwinds' are used as the source domain for emerging financial conditions that threaten shareholder value. When a CEO outlines the company's 'north star', they are indicating the orientation of the company's journey. The linguistic structure of metaphor does not need to be explained for it to be used: it comes naturally.

The quiet metaphor signals in the foundational board conversation revealed an early 'gestalt' form of the strategy - a new path and new modes of travel (such as flying up into the air). This early, subconscious engagement in conceptual metaphors happened quickly and largely unobserved. It had the effect of cohering the group to a common orientation and language architecture for several years to follow. I was learning how conceptual metaphors could open the door to new insight, and protect against blind spot formation. However, it would be some time before I would realize the rich significance of embodied cognition, beyond its ability to frame and re-frame perspective.

I had over packed for the occasion. Inside the suitcase, I had numerous tools and methods for the strategy workshops that I had based and designed on the Dorst frame innovation structure (2015). I overcomplicated the use of these tools. Subconsciously, I relied more on my own framing than on the inherent wisdom in the group. When I should have built on the early conceptual metaphor work, I jumped into more complicated exercises that were hard to understand and complete. What many in the group wanted was a map. What we needed was a navigation capability. The early cohesion was still present, but ideas on how to get to the goal were splintering. The metaphor of a map provided certainty, while a compass invoked constant adaptation to the environment. While I observed this preference, I did not open the possibility of exploration for the group to explore why a map, or a compass may be better suited to the context. I had crammed too much into the suitcase.

One reason to over pack is uncertainty. A fear of unpreparedness? Perhaps a subconscious sense of weightlessness or insufficiency? Tools, frameworks, job titles, career ladders had become proxies for practice. I had a career arc that traversed corporate, government and research sectors, between two opposing poles of governance and innovation, and through five industries. I had adaptability, but no sense of my own practice. I had walked the edge of the cliff without knowing when my feet were on solid ground, and in some sense, had fallen off my own metaphor into a ravine of unclarity.

I had been musing for some time on a career decision which had no obvious or correct answer. I could stay and receive more resource to do my job, or embark on an unknown quest. I sought the counsel of an academic whose practice I respected. The response was Bob Dylan's invitation to sit at the edge of the "Grand Canyon at sundown" (Dylan, 1963). Unexpected, this was ambiguous enough to inspire me to strap my suitcase onto my back and begin the rocky quest. I hoped to make my way to the clifftop in time for the setting sun. As I tried to get my bearings, it became clear that I was looking for an imagined horizon. My sight was obscured by boulders and blocks of stone jutting haphazardly out of the cliff's otherwise sheer surface. I had to climb each ledge get a better view.

At the first plateau, I saw an array of trees that had burrowed into the valley. Some roots were as thick as the years of time they been in place, and some were weary, thin trails across a long, rocky surface. These trees had a sense of place. A relationship with the ground beneath that reached into the sky above and across the landscape of their living. Pragmatist John Dewey connected the disparate domains of governance, education and the arts as sites for meaning-making, found in the interactions between organisms and their environment (1925). Mark Johnson (2015) further examined how values, meaning and reasoning all start with the interactions of our body with our environment. Unaware that I had climbed a somewhat slippery, stony affordance, not a smooth corporate ladder, I lucked upon an earnest footing. I spotted a stone that had cleaved off the rocky ledge, as if to mark the occasion. I placed it in my case, knowing that the weight of it would remind me of this place. A transitory boundary stone from a site of meaning-making.

After more climbing than I thought was possible, I was able to pause on a second ledge. This one had enough room to lie down and feel my tired muscles cool against the hard surface. I could feel my body's vulnerability in this expansive landscape. There was a shift that occurred when I moved from being the victorious, vertical conqueror to the grounded, horizontal traveler situated in a broader context.

I became more aware of participation in my environment, and wanted to sense and to seek quiet interactions. "Human understanding is profoundly embodied. That is, it is rooted in how our bodies and brains interact with, process, and understand our environments in a way that recruits bodily meaning, neural simulation, and feeling to carry out both concrete and abstract conceptualization and reasoning" (Johnson, 2015, p. 7). I had sensed this when we explored conceptual metaphor theory in the earlier strategy session, but I had not yet felt its real weight. Without realizing there would be a convergence between avocation and profession,

I was also being mentored by a sculptor whose own deeply embodied practice had moved through formalism and minimalism into the body movement. Her sculptures have both real presence and formal structure, rather than optical re-presentation. I was able to see how metaphor materializes. Pathways to metaphor were reactivated through my hands. The physicality of 'wrestling with matter' through an ancient discipline was providing an unexpected ground for my embodied cognition to grow.

There was a third ledge that I nearly missed. When I was first introduced to the work of psychiatrist and philosopher Dr Iain McGilchrist, I did not immediately see the depth and breadth of his central proposition about attention. Dr Barbara Doran's arts-based research translation had revitalized my respect for creative intelligence as a critical element of practice (Doran & Watson, 2021). In a discussion about how we use tools such as artificial intelligence, I encountered the profound proposition that the way we attend to the world determines what we find. Our mode of attention is a product of brain lateralization between the left and right hemispheres. It results in two different types of attention: a left-dominant mode, and a right-left-right-patterning mode. The former sees narrowly, in parts, and grasps for its goal; while the latter sees a gestalt form and can place the left's view into broader contextual dynamics and relationships (McGilchrist, 2019). It is this right-left-right pattern that girds embodied cognition. It mapped the company directors' bodily experience of metaphor and re-framed a strategy discussion. Weary but revitalized, I started to sense deep layers of connection between my encounters with these rocky ledges: meaning-making, embodied cognition and attention. I chose a rock from this ledge, and heaved the stony suitcase onto my shoulder.

By the time I found myself at the fourth ledge, I was very hungry and my arms were sore. I thought I would stay for a while, so I lifted the stones out of the case and arranged them so I could sit with my back resting on them. There was a fourth stone already placed to serve as a temporary armrest. I found a sandwich in my pocket to fill my empty stomach and allowed my legs to dangle over the edge. I was thinking about whether Sisyphus ever stopped along his rock-heaving mission up the mountain? The narrative bookends his cyclical steps at the top or the bottom of the mountain. More visually, artists represent him in motion, carrying the stone up the mountain, along the journey. My load-bearing quest was revealing a mystery, as the metaphor became embodied. This was an invitation into practice, rather than profession. A practice is "an encounter with the world and with people and things in it" (Kemmis, 2019, p. 20).

I noticed a change in the light and finally allowed my eyes to sweep the visual field in search of an anchoring horizon. Across a vast chasm, I saw the sun setting at eye level, between two poles. The gargantuan trees from the valley below, now seemed like heads of broccoli in a bowl. Behind me, I heard a raspy voice reading a poem about someone called Woody... I turned around and saw a wide open plain of possibility. Inside, I felt walls that previously did not have structure. The inner horizon was being carved and I could sense the outer horizon). I was carrying the stones of my practice.

These four stones I had gathered were small pebbles of invitation from megaliths larger than any one human, at any point in time. They were ground to a size that I could hold, and I was grounded by them. I have turned these stones into the cornerstones of my practice. A cornerstone orients not only the building, but the way a building is made. I have founded a collaboration studio, create sense (createsense.com.au) to establish a site of interaction with these four megaliths of meaning-making, embodied cognition, attention and practice. I did not discover these, rather, I encountered them at the boundaries of my transdisciplinary practice where "stone is thick in its compaction of possibility, explosive in its release." (Cohen, 2015).

3.11

RE-HUMANIZING BY DESIGN

Ashkan Deravi

INTRODUCTION: THE DESIGN OF HUMAN EXPERIENCE DESIGN

Human Experience Design (HXD), or Experience Design (XD), represents a transdisciplinary domain that synthesizes insights and methodologies from various fields, including psychology, sociology, anthropology, design, technology, and business. At its core, HXD is dedicated to enhancing and optimizing interactions between humans and various aspects of their surroundings, such as environments and systems, prioritizing the experience as an evolving value over commodities, goods and services. (Pine & Gilmore, 1998). This design approach transcends traditional design methodologies, aligning itself with Human-centered design principles by understanding what the problem is really about. It is anchored in a deep understanding of the inherent problem, exploring unmet human values and meanings in the context of the issue (van der Bijl-Brouwer & Dorst, 2017).

The fundamental goal of HXD is to eliminate dehumanization, "any process or practice that is thought to reduce human beings to the level of mechanisms or nonhuman" (VandenBos, 2015, p. 291). Its focus is to foster a sense of belonging, thereby shaping experiences that profoundly influence individuals and groups. These experiences are about fulfilling human needs, providing a sense of purpose, enhancing well-being, and fostering lasting emotional connections.
The impact of these experiences is enduring, often resonating with people long after the initial interaction or event. This approach aligns with the theories of Chilean economist Manfred Max-Neef, who emphasized the importance of addressing multiple human needs holistically and integrated. HXD leverages this principle by creating synergistic satisfiers, solutions that simultaneously satisfy various needs, promoting well-being, sustainability, and equity (Max-Neef, 1991).

A critical aspect of HXD is its focus on integrating technology to amplify the human experience. The challenge lies in ensuring that technological advancements complement rather than detract from human interactions. In the modern digital era, where technology is rapidly evolving, HXD practitioners must be experts at navigating this delicate balance. Integrating technology in HXD is not just about leveraging the latest tools but understanding how these tools can enrich human life, making experiences more accessible, enjoyable, and meaningful. In addition to technological integration, HXD necessitates a profound understanding of human psychology and behavior. By drawing insights from psychology and sociology, designers can better comprehend how individuals interact with their environments and what drives their decisions and actions. This knowledge is crucial in creating solutions that are not only functional and efficient but also emotionally resonant and psychologically satisfying. Furthermore, HXD is inherently collaborative, requiring the convergence of multiple disciplines and perspectives. This collaborative nature is a defining feature of the field, allowing for a more comprehensive understanding of complex issues. Through collaboration, designers, technologists, sociologists, psychologists, and other professionals can share knowledge and expertize, leading to more innovative and effective solutions.

Human Experience Design is a dynamic and evolving field with immense potential for humanizing the future of human interactions. By integrating various disciplines and the thoughtful application of technology, HXD aims to create experiences that are not just functional but deeply meaningful and impactful. As society evolves and technology advances, the principles, and practices of HXD will become increasingly relevant, offering new opportunities for enhancing the quality of life and fostering a more sustainable, equitable world.

HUMAN EXPERIENCE DESIGN IN PRACTICE

In many large organizations, a prevalent issue is the existence of a "silo mentality." This term describes a scenario where various departments or sectors fail to share information or knowledge with others within the same organization. Such a mindset leads to a compartmentalized approach to operations, where departments focus exclusively on their quantifiable metrics, operating independently. This fragmentation often undermines the organization's overall objectives, as each department becomes preoccupied with its own goals and Key Performance Indicators (KPIs) rather than the collective aims of the organization. For instance, consider an organization whose objective is customer satisfaction. They might invest in design practices to develop innovative solutions that meet customer needs. However, designers in a siloed organization may face barriers to understanding and connecting with the target people due to restrictions imposed by other departments. Compliance departments might limit direct customer engagement, citing policy concerns, while software developers might be preoccupied with separate projects, hindering collaborative feasibility discussions. Additionally, development teams might prioritize meeting deadlines and budget constraints over maintaining design integrity, leading to a final product that fails to meet customer satisfaction criteria.

This scenario highlights the critical challenges posed by a silo mentality, especially in the context of Human-Experience Design (HXD). The silo approach is antithetical to the principles of HXD, which emphasize a holistic, integrated, and human-centric approach. Key issues include:

- Limited integration of diverse perspectives and transdisciplinary knowledge that is essential for innovative problem-solving.

- An over-reliance on conventional knowledge, neglecting the benefits of a broader, more inclusive approach.
- A lack of co-creation and participatory design, which are pivotal in understanding and meeting human needs.
- Assumptions about human interactions with products or services instead of empirical, human-driven insights.
- A preference for quantitative data, often at the expense of valuable qualitative insights that are not easily measurable.

To effectively incorporate Human-Experience Design, organizations need to adopt several strategies:

- Transdisciplinary Approach: Embrace the integration of knowledge and methods from various disciplines, creating a more synergistic work environment.
- Organizational-wide KPIs: Develop Key Performance Indicators that reflect the organization's collective goals rather than isolated departmental objectives.
- Focus on Lived Experiences: Prioritize real-world, human-driven data over internal assumptions and metrics.
- Embrace Human Qualities: Recognize and incorporate human elements such as emotions, behaviors, and needs into the design process.
- Humanizing Processes: Foster awareness and understanding of human experiences, focusing on why, when, where, how, and what aspects humans interact within solutions.

By breaking down silos and adopting a more integrated, human-centric approach, organizations can foster innovation, enhance problem-solving capabilities, and ultimately create products and services that genuinely resonate with humans. This shift requires a cultural transformation, moving away from isolated departmental success towards a unified vision that prioritizes human experience at its core.

PARADOXES IN THE SITUATION

"Organizations aim to enhance customer satisfaction through innovative design,

yet

often isolate the very designers who need direct customer insights to achieve this goal

while

the objective of a company is to operate as a cohesive unit towards common goals, departmental silos inadvertently promote a culture of isolated achievements over collective success."

"The advancement of technology in organizations seeks to bridge gaps and enhance efficiency,

but

when used in siloed environments, it often contributes to further fragmentation."

"Human-Experience Design advocates for an empathetic, human-centric approach,

yet

organizational silos hinder the empathy-driven collaboration necessary to truly understand and meet human needs."

"Organizations strive for innovation and problem-solving capabilities,

but

the silo mentality restricts the cross-pollination of ideas and perspectives vital for such innovation."

"The pursuit of quantitative metrics for performance evaluation is intended to drive success

yet

it often overlooks the qualitative aspects that are crucial in human-centric design and customer satisfaction."

"Transdisciplinary collaboration is recognized as key to addressing complex challenges in HXD,

yet

organizational silos create barriers that prevent this interdisciplinary integration."

"Organizations seek to create products and services that resonate with human experiences,

but

the compartmentalization within these organizations often leads to a disconnect from the very human insights required for resonance."

"The goal of organizational unity in pursuit of a common vision

is often contradicted

by the segmented operational approach fostered by a silo mentality."

RE-FRAMING TECHNOLOGY-CENTERED ENGINEERING THROUGH HUMAN EXPERIENCE DESIGN

The challenge we faced stemmed from a Technology-Centered Engineering (TCE) mindset, a common practice in many large organizations. This approach typically involves developing technology first and then finding a problem that it can solve (Antle & Silver, 2005). In such scenarios, the focus is primarily on the 'what' - the artifact itself - while neglecting the 'why', 'where', 'when', and 'how' of its use. Although technically proficient, this method often results in solutions that may not align with real-world needs and the human aspect of technology use. In contrast to TCE, Human Experience Design (HXD) encourages a paradigm shift - from viewing oneself solely as a designer to adopting an end-user perspective with a human-centric mindset (Antle & Silver, 2005). Metaphorically, this means embracing the mindset of a driver first. This perspective involves deeply understanding the driver's experience, including their emotions, fears, aspirations, thoughts, and feelings. Engaging with users, observing them, and immersing in their experiences are essential. This shift in approach highlights the critical role of empathy and focusing on the user in design processes. It's not just about product creation; it's about comprehending the human's context and developing solutions that truly resonate with their everyday life experiences for a human.

To present the value of the HXD perspective to the leadership team and internal stakeholders, we engaged an external agency to conduct a practical experiment. The agency's design team was tasked with immersing themselves in the lives, experiences, and environments of our end-users, with their activities live-streamed for our internal teams to observe. For example, in designing a new investment solution, the designers actively participated in investment scenarios, gaining firsthand experience of the investor's journey. This approach provided our internal stakeholders and designers with valuable insights into actual user needs and preferences.

The experiment uncovered a substantial disparity between our designers' and stakeholders' initial assumptions and the actual experiences of end-users. Features that were previously prioritized by the design team were not as significant to the users. Moreover, several user needs were entirely overlooked in the preliminary designs.

Based on these findings, we initiated several interventions. These included an overhaul of our workflow to integrate immersive experiences and end-user feedback at every development stage and establishing regular field visits for designers to better understand user emotions, fears, aspirations, thoughts, and feelings within actual context. We also created user personas to guide the design process and introduced empathy-building exercises to help all stakeholders empathize with the user and internalize their perspectives. Following these interventions, we noted a notable shift in our internal team's ability to empathize with users.

There was an increased emphasis on the importance of understanding end-users first, as reflected in internal feedback. Our design processes became more proactive in empathizing with users before initiating the design phase, ensuring alignment with actual user requirements. There was a noticeable increase in user satisfaction, as evidenced by feedback and usability testing results.

This intervention highlights the significant impact of empathy and elements of the innovation ecosystem in transitioning from a technology-focused to a human-focused approach. By prioritizing empathy and a deep understanding of users, we developed solutions that not only met technical criteria but also deeply connected with users, significantly enhancing their overall experience. This shift towards a human-centric design philosophy is crucial for creating meaningful and effective experiences.

THE ARCHITECTURE OF INFRASTRUCTURE

Building upon the intervention detailed earlier, a structured infrastructure is essential to support and foster the ongoing Human Experience Design (HXD) initiatives. This infrastructure, inspired the Studio Model (see §2.7) Lab, Academy, Podium, and Temple concepts, forms the backbone of an Innovation Ecosystem. Each element plays a vital role, emphasizing the 'Temple' as the foundational component.

Temple - Immersive Experiences and Respecting the Problem

The 'Temple' represents the foundational element of our approach, where a deep respect for the problem and understanding of the human aspect is cultivated. This space is dedicated to immersive experiences, allowing teams to empathize profoundly with the users. It's a place for contemplation and insight, where the complexity of the user experience is revered and understood in its entirety. Developing this element first is crucial as it sets the tone for empathy and user-centricity in all subsequent stages and creates awareness.

Academy - Understanding the End-User

The 'Academy' functions as an educational hub, comprehensively understanding the end-user. Teams learn about user psychology, behaviors, needs, and aspirations here. The Academy encourages continuous learning and development, ensuring all team members have the latest insights and techniques in user research and empathy-building. Regular workshops, training sessions, and knowledge-sharing events will keep the team well-informed of new developments in HXD.

Podium - Engaging with Larger Stakeholders

The 'Podium' is a platform for interaction with a broader audience, including stakeholders and the wider community. This space is used for presenting findings, sharing insights, and soliciting feedback. It bridges the internal design processes and the external world, allowing for transparency and collaboration. The Podium helps align the company's vision with user needs and ensures stakeholders are engaged and informed throughout the design process.

Lab - Design and Feedback Collection

Finally, the 'Lab' is where the actual design and feedback collection occurs. It's a space for experimentation, prototyping, and iterative development. The Lab is where ideas conceptualized in the Temple, educated in the Academy, and discussed on the Podium are put to the test. This space is vital for turning insights into actionable designs, allowing for rapid prototyping, user testing, and refinement based on feedback.

In conclusion, every component plays an essential role in assuring the success of HXD initiatives. However, the Temple, focusing on respecting and understanding the problem at a human level, is the cornerstone. It ensures that the entire process remains grounded in empathy and human-centricity. As this foundation is strengthened, the other elements - Academy, Podium, and Lab - can effectively contribute to creating experiences that are not only innovative but also profoundly resonant with humans.

REFLECTIONS ON THE STUDIO AND BEYOND

The central role of the 'Temple' in the Innovation Ecosystem underscores the importance of deeply respecting and understanding the problem from a human perspective. This approach is a powerful reminder that successful design starts with profound empathy and insight into human experiences and needs. It's a lesson in the significance of a human-centric mindset, not just as a design principle but as a foundational ethos.

Interdisciplinary Integration - The case study and the architecture of the Innovation Ecosystem highlight the necessity of integrating various disciplines. The 'Academy' serves as a testament to the importance of continuous learning across fields like psychology, sociology, and technology. This cross-disciplinary knowledge enriches the design process, ensuring solutions are well-rounded and deeply informed.

Collaboration and Communication - The 'Podium' and 'Lab' elements reinforce the value of collaborative efforts and open communication. Engaging with a broader audience and stakeholders is crucial for aligning the design vision with user needs and the company's objectives. This ensures the design process is transparent, inclusive, and grounded in real-world feedback.

Iterative Process - The 'Lab' represents the iterative nature of HXD, where prototyping, testing, and refining are continuous processes. This iterative approach is vital for translating insights into practical, human-centric designs, allowing for agility and responsiveness to feedback.

Strategic Structure for Innovation - The structured approach of the Studio, with its distinct yet interconnected components, provides a strategic framework for fostering and sustaining innovation in HXD. It illustrates how structuring the design process around specific functions - immersion, education, engagement, and execution - can create a more efficient and effective pathway to innovation and building a better human experience.

Respect for Complexity - The entire ecosystem, especially the 'Temple', teaches us to respect the complexity of human experiences. This respect is crucial in creating solutions that are functionally superior and emotionally resonant.

These reflections highlight that humanizing design processes and outcomes is about more than just following steps; it's about cultivating empathy, interdisciplinary collaboration, and respect for the complexity of human experiences. This ethos, embedded in every stage of the Innovation Ecosystem, is what truly drives meaningful and impactful designed experiences.

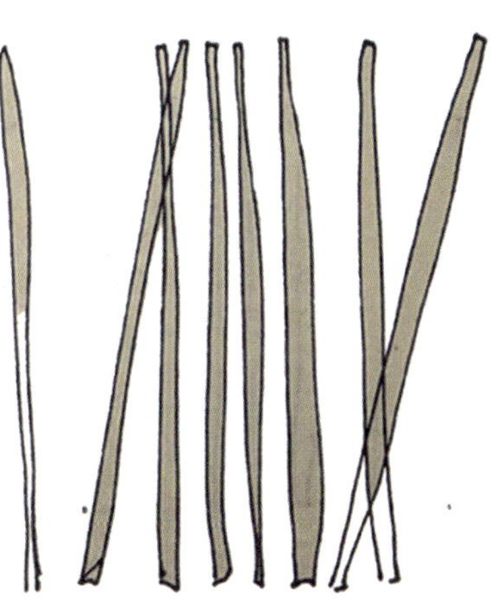

3.12

BEYOND CREATIVITY-AS-USUAL

Annalise Brown

INTRODUCTION: MY PROFESSIONAL CONTEXT

I have spent the last 25 years in the communications Industry, the last 15 working in large-scale organizations with multi-discipline functions, working closely with advertising (or creative) agencies. Having become a Managing Director at a very early age (34), I have spent the bulk of my career in a senior management position. The agency model appealed to me as I was always drawn to solving clients' business problems through creative output that directly helped business success. I enjoyed the opportunity to work across a wide range of industries and with a variety of people - both within different organizations and my agency ecosystem.

I also have a strong sense of justice - it's one of my core values. I was, therefore, always aware of the inequalities and constraints in the working environments I was surrounded by. I always thought I could use my experience and position within senior management to make changes to help those who experienced inequalities. However, over the years, I became increasingly frustrated with the definition of creativity within these organizations, together with their reliance on hierarchy. There seemed to be so many barriers to solving the overarching problem or challenge at hand–many which were created by highly mandated profit goals. I also observed that the remuneration model did not encourage innovation or creativity. We weren't remunerated on outcomes; we were remunerated on outputs. Our projects were costed based on the number of head hours each person involved in every project component would need to produce an output. When speaking to clients, there also seemed to be an acute disconnect. We were tasked with solving business problems but were remunerated on a set of hours to complete tasks. However, clients couldn't find another way of assessing if 'the job had been done'. We all knew what we were there to do; however, the remuneration model did not reflect this. Concurrently, I was acutely aware of the lack of diversity within these organizations. Most of the strategy and creative departments were Caucasian (mad)men from similar backgrounds and education. Senior management was similar, again white men, but wily enough to appoint women in senior positions with no power to try and demonstrate they had gender diversity at the top.
I felt that our systems, structures and processes had not evolved since industry stalwart David Ogilvy set up shop in 1948. To me, this meant a lack of diversity of thought within the agencies I had been exposed to. There was also little incentive for those with the power to make change as to do so as it would potentially destabilize their positions. Toeing company line was the modus operandi. There had to be a more compelling reason for these organizations to create real change.

THE MODUS OPERANDI

So how can we change the systems, structures and processes within communications agencies where we can foster innovation and creativity at the core?

The immediate hidden rules I found were around siloing of creativity and hierarchy, as well as the supposed corporate values not being adhered to. Creativity at the core was largely spouted as the driving mantra for most agencies but as mentioned investigating further it was growth and profit targets that had to be adhered to. I wanted to work with those from the industry across different businesses and capabilities to investigate the communications Industry. This included those within different departments and at different capability levels from different agencies. What I wanted to understand was where "real value and wealth creation goes to those who innovate and redesign themselves and their industry", why was this not happening in those presenting themselves as the leaders in both? What I found was there were many similar themes not just in the communications industry but many organizations. This was through the deliberate questioning of friends and colleagues in different industries. These conversations underpinned my further exploration.

Concurrently, were my thoughts around human centricity. Too many times in my career I had seen that humans were treated in the same way as another commodity input into businesses, a cost of doing business and a balance sheet item that needs to be reduced as a high cost of business in economic downturn. People were also treated differently as per their position. Information flowed from the top down and collaboration with more junior members of the team was not sought. Often company changes were made with assumed knowledge, rather than enrolling the input from those it could affect the most. My thoughts were: what if we treated our humans as an asset rather than a cost, one that we invest in as we would an expensive piece of machinery to upkeep, one that we continue to maintain and upgrade?

How do we create workplaces that are ethical, sustainable, and profitable. How do we create a workplace that instills creativity and innovation and also recognizes their people as assets?

PARADOXES

We are an industry with creativity as our stock and trade

however

we are assessed by growth and profit.

Creativity thrives on freedom and unstructured thinking

but

it's contained in structured, siloed structures.

Creative outputs often involve taking risks and pushing boundaries,

but

financial success and stability often constrain our thinking.

Creativity involves pushing the boundaries of tradition,

but

too much innovation can alienate clients who seek familiarity.

Creative works often aim for simplicity to be accessible,

yet

some of the most celebrated works are complex and require deeper engagement and collaboration.

We care about people before profit

but

we need to answer to shareholders. Shareholders who don't often understand the individual business problems or even the creative process itself.

GETTING OUT OF THE STARTING BLOCKS

Experiment 1

I firstly wanted to explore my own biases, where were they in the question and how I could understand different points of view. This is why I decided to interview key people from the different fields within the agency structures at senior levels to understand what they identified with and where their pain points were in relation to innovation and creativity. These were people I trusted and respected so therefore didn't feel I led in conversation.

Using the Future Ripple Method (FRM) each of the participants were asked prior to meeting to conduct their own situational analysis, asking where they saw the systems, structures and processes are broken down (or not) and what then might that lead to. The FRM is a process of assessing the most compelling factors within a situation and then playing them out with a series of 'if then, what' questions. Each of the participants were then asked to email through their assessment of the problem at hand. They were instructed according to the Future Ripples Method (Epp et al. 2022). The themes that were acutely apparent were ones of hierarchy, systems challenges, fear, and an inability to be able to look at long-term thinking. Post that exploration, I then wanted to engage with those in other industries; where did they see these issues sitting where there were blocks to innovation and creativity?

A further collaborative exploration workshop, using the same tool, was done with people from a Child Protection Association, a Creative Consultancy, a Production Agency, a Communications Consultant, an Innovation Consultant, and a freelance Creative... Each identified different issues, but each also seemed to connect to the same themes. These included hierarchy at the core, and that there was a need to change the ways of working. I now understood that this problem was not unique to the communications/creative industry but was apparent in many industries. Creativity and Innovation, in my opinion, creates change, open dialogue and thought provocation. Where they are not present these things were not happening in organizations.

Experiment 2

This stemmed from the development of an idea with another colleague where we wanted to develop a creative approach for senior leaders to take them out of their comfort zone, identify their challenges differently and focus on different approaches to problem solving. We wanted to use a different location to one they were used to, to stimulate different ideas and thinking, but also one which allowed us to easily demonstrate creative thinking tools. We also wanted to develop something that could be transferable. With another colleague we developed a program centered around the new Art Gallery of New South Wales, using its different levels and exhibitions as our inspiration. We overlaid the specific notions of creativity, future thinking, complexity, wicked problems and 'quality without a name' which focuses on a central quality which is the root criterion of life and spirit in a man, a town, a building, or a place. This quality is objective and precise, but it cannot be named (§5.4).

Each of the experiences also provided an opportunity for reflection, conversation, and further interactivity with the group.

This was the perfect storm of what stepping out of the comfort zone and inspiring creativity and innovative thinking is about. Developing our own way of transdisciplinary thinking, enrolling others to provide feedback loops and refine proof of concept that could then be used with real world application. Collaborating, iterating and combining our experiences to see this come to fruition was a truly enriching experience.

DOING WHAT IS NEEDED

After interrogating the systems and structures of multiple organizations I believe there is a need for organizations to change. This was confirmed by a colleague at another university: what they were seeing was that the top students were no longer being seduced by traditional top jobs, largely due to their differences in values together with a generational shift in expectations. Long gone were the days of working until midnight for a company that had a good name on the door. These new recruits wanted life balance, equity for work done and for them to believe in the companies they represented.

I sought to create a community of people who were dedicated to the stories we all tell, which allow us to relate to and learn from each other and have empathy. The ensuing approach is to put humans at the center of our organizations to create more fruitful, diverse and ultimately creative and innovative ecosystems. As a part of this thought process, I was lucky enough to have access to different colleagues from a diverse set of industries and experiences, and tapped into their professional opinions and where there were gaps in what we were currently experiencing. From wanting to use the tools I'd explored to assist the industry I had been a part of for my whole career, I now had the opportunity to widen the scope and the first step was the creation of a bespoke business. One that was born out of transdisciplinary thinking, creativity, and using different tools to unearth the real problems and possible solutions for organizations. More importantly, my changing perspective shapes the different approach that needs to be taken to each of these things. HUMANFiND is a human consultancy specializing in organizational change and communications.

We know the importance of authenticity in a world of fake news and AI. We've spent decades working with clients navigating reputation management, strategic communications, together with internal and external business solutions. What we've also learned along the way is how organizations change, the importance of culture and how we all have a different working cadence. Any shift in these can impact business exponentially.

This is a new consultancy aimed at addressing both communications and change, where the intersection is storytelling, but the understanding that both fail without authenticity, transparency and a commitment to values.

Core is the listening to clients, collaborating and iterating with them to come up with solutions. Each problem needs a different way to approach, but at the core is ensuring humans are thought of within each and every part of the decision making process.

REFLECTIONS

The only way that HUMANFiND would have been born was with the adoption of transdisciplinary thinking. My problem state when I started the analysis changed over time. The iterative process which changed my thinking of the problem state as I saw it and how I could have impact was inspiring. Being able to access minds from diverse backgrounds and experiences allowed me to step out of my bubble and explore themes more thoroughly. Working with the communications Industry and beyond allowed me to expand that thinking. Internal and external communication are key to the acceptance of organizational change. Over the years I have come to the belief that putting the human lens over the top of these things will be key to success. Sometimes we need to reacquaint ourselves with humans to succeed. Ultimately the key things to success are collaboration, leaning in and out and being able to check yourself at the door.

I started out on this journey wanting to change the Communications Industry, I am now setting out to change all organizations.

3.13

BREAK DOWN THE WALLS! RE-IMAGINING FINE ART EDUCATION THROUGH SKATEBOARDING CULTURE

Samu Carvajal

Artwork by Samu Carvajal.

Imagine walking into an art school and finding no walls. No fixed schedules, no separate departments, hierarchies, or any distinction between teachers and students. Instead, you discover an open space where disciplinary boundaries dissolve, learning happens through exploration and sharing with others, and artistic expression emerges organically. A place where the only requisite for acceptance is wanting to be part of that community.

As one of Australia's oldest ongoing art schools, The National Art School in Sydney has been facing a complex tension between tradition and innovation. Housed in a heritage sandstone building that was once known as the Darlinghurst Gaol, NAS' institutional structure sometimes seems to resemble its iconic architecture.

In the role of Creative Projects, Samu worked across disciplines, researching, documenting, and interviewing artists to understand the essence of what NAS is today. What started as a brand research soon evolved into a communicational re-framing project that looked into the fundamental values of art education: What is the role of an art school today? What is the importance of the artist in society? What does the art school of the future look like?

Traditional art schools are built on divisions, separations between disciplines, studios, and skill levels, with hierarchies and clear differences between those who teach and those who learn. Within these structures, an "excellent" artist is often defined as someone who has achieved technical mastery, is represented by a famous gallery, and has won art prizes.

This approach generates a paradox: art requires breaking with traditions, yet it depends on those traditions to move and rebel against. These traditions are built over time, yet we need new, challenging ideas to stay relevant. The institution simultaneously celebrates creativity while containing and measuring it against those established traditional frameworks.

To illustrate this paradox, we can understand it as a tree growing inside the brick walls of NAS. This new branch puts the solid structure of the wall in danger, cracking it and dissolving the sandstone. At the same time, this new tree brings life and renewal to the school. We might cut it over and over again, but it will keep growing and finding its way.

Skateboarding is about being fully present, an awareness of the here and now: feeling the board beneath your feet, the textures of the ground, the body in motion, and seeing the city anew, as one creative challenge. In a world obsessed with outcomes and measurable results, skateboarding reminds us that the true value of art might lie simply in the doing.

What if we took ideas from the skateboarding culture? What emerged through Samu's exploration was a radically different frame. In skate parks, boundaries dissolve. There is no separate section for beginners, no walls between disciplines (styles), and no locked doors. Knowledge is transferred horizontally, with the community itself being the curriculum. Every member is simultaneously the student and the teacher. As skateboarding legend Jeff Grosso once said: "if you are a fucking skate coach, you can go fuck yourself, cause that shit is for free, that's what you do with friends, you teach each other how to do a back D".

Through this new frame, values such as creativity, excellence, community, and tradition mutate. They become understood from a self-realization perspective in contrast to an external validation framework. This model challenges assumptions that recognition or commercial success are the primary measures of artistic achievement. It moves motivations from extrinsic (art world validation) to intrinsic (personal growth, love for the activity). It creates a fertile ground for ideas to cross-pollinate without institutional resistance.

In this re-imagined art school, painters mingle with sculptors, who collaborate with printmakers, who are in constant conversations with photographers and art historians. This space is always open, allowing artists to work whenever inspiration strikes. The absence of walls is not only architectural, it's philosophical. Newcomers learn by watching more experienced artists. Questions are asked freely and answered with generosity. Achievements are celebrated often and collectively without standardized requirements.

Just as skate parks simply provide a space for personal expression to happen, our re-imagined art school refuses to define what constitutes "good art". Instead, it offers the conditions for artistic expression to arise organically. Students follow their curiosity, at their own pace, to finally discover their unique artistic voice through immersion in the practice.

This vision for art education might feel too idealistic, impractical, or even impossible. However, skateboarders throughout the decades have specialized in making the impossible look easy. Maybe it's time for art education to attempt to land an impossible trick: creating learning environments where the joy of making overcomes the pressure to produce.

Skate parks are living proof that such spaces can exist, that learning can happen without formal distinctions between teachers and students, that communities can self-regulate without authorities, and that passion motivates more than grades or money.

The question is not whether such an art school is possible, but rather why haven't we built it yet?

We have forgotten to dance while the music is playing. We have forgotten that art is about the process, not the outcome. After all, both skateboarding and art emerge from the same fundamental "what if?" It's all about seeing the world not as it is, but as what it could be.

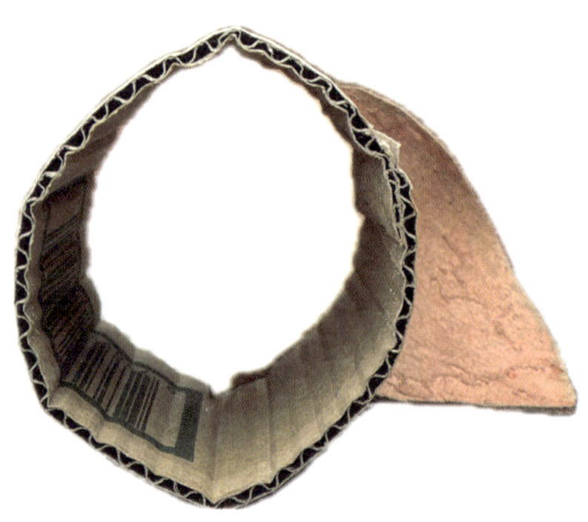

3.14

GROWING A GARDEN IN A PRISON. GROWING MYSELF AND OTHERS.

Phil Hugill

INTRODUCTION: THE EVOLVING ROLE OF PRISON IN SOCIETY

As a worker in human services in both Non-Government and Government I was excited and proud to Join New South Wales Corrections, an agency with a long history going back to the white settlement of Australia. The first settlement, at Sydney, consisted of about 850 convicts and their Marine guards and officers, led by Governor Arthur Phillip. They arrived at Botany Bay in the 'First Fleet' of 9 transport ships accompanied by 2 small warships, in January 1788.

The penal colony established in Sydney governed by military officers, originally Royal Navy Captains has left a legacy. An example of that legacy foundation today is at the annual Corrections Governors dinner, with the 'Passing of the Port' tradition derived from the Royal Navy. Carried out at the end of the evening with formal toasts to dignitaries present. You drink with your left hand to keep your right hand free to draw your weapon if attacked(!).

The agency has built an identity to protect the public, separating the criminal from society and therefore providing public safety. From 2 Jails in 1840 to 36 in 2022. From 4000 prisoners in 1978 to 12,500 in 2022. Of which there are 940 'serious offenders', so about 9% of the total prison population. In modern times public scrutiny of both the justice system including sentencing and the prison service has increased. Media coverage, social media posts and talk back radio often heighten

Artwork by Phil Hugill

a perceived fear of crime and this leads to calls for tighter laws, longer sentences and harsher punishments. My goal in joining NSW Corrections was to be part of a culture of rehabilitation, supporting prisoners to take pathways that would lead to their release as members of society able to contribute and do no more harm.

NSW Corrections has a proud history, as a traditional and safe public service that nevertheless has been caught between the paradox, to punish or to rehabilitate. The 'push and pull' of crime and its consequence plays out in the organization, every day: do we prioritize maintaining law and order, protecting property and possessions, safeguarding human life, and excluding from society the mad and the bad - or are we striving to rehabilitate, support people and return them to society as productive and law-abiding citizens? What does it mean to be a prisoner and what is justice today? And; how do I go about opening doors to change?

THE HIDDEN RULES

I became aware very early on that the prison system relied on rules both those written and articulated and more importantly the unwritten rules. There is a hierarchy within the system, the uniformed staff are identified by the stars on their uniform or lack thereof. Officers in the service tend to stay throughout there working career, and interpersonal relationships, family connections and team loyalty are all strong elements. For prisoners, connection to or affiliation with groups be that cultural, organized crime gangs, motorbike gangs, religious groups provide safety, belonging and connection. Hierarchy in both staff and prisoner can be both positive and negative, in that in a command and control environment clarity of hierarchy and decision making can and does ensure safety. On the downside those in power will always do all they can to maintain power and the weak, or isolated will always be vulnerable to exploitation. That said talking to prisoners I was often struck by the care and humanity they demonstrated to each other and their adherence to the rules both formal and informal, as it was with the majority of staff. In an artificial congregate housing environment, it's the rules that are the difference between order and anarchy.

My awakening came in the form of a health episode, having to undergo surgery and losing autonomy within a health system, made me reconsider how prisoners must feel. My cancer diagnosis and hospital treatment gave me a user experience of being dis-empowered and trapped in a room. Which resonated with me as I reflected on my work in NSW Corrections. My office in the middle of a jail, my window view being razor wire and 20 feet high fences and guard towers I felt I was a prisoner too, looking at those on the other side of the fence who were looking back. The environment I looked upon was restrictive and harsh, it seemed a dead sterile space.

PARADOXES: THE PUSH AND THE PULL IN JUSTICE AND PRISONS

Punishment versus Rehabilitation?

The say it takes a village to raise a child,

but

what if the village is a prison,
what children are we raising.

We convict people of crime and sentence them to prison, removing them from family, friends, culture and their normal geographical location,

but

expect a change in behavior?

How does locking people up with other criminals

lead to

better law abiding citizens?

If crime (90% is committed by those not defined as serious offenders), is driven by social disadvantage, addiction, poverty, unemployment etc

then why

are we not focused on those causes of crime.

We have closed institutions of congregate care for the disabled and mentally ill as they are recognized as negative ways to house people,

but

we build bigger prisons to hold more people.

If community is about inclusion, then prison is built for exclusion,

how

do we then reintegrate people into community on release having conditioned them to be excluded.

INTERVENTIONS: WHAT HAPPENED, WHAT LED TO WHAT.

For me I have not one case study but multiple variations on a theme, the theme being 'hope'. I started exploring how sound could affect behavior in a jail, the harsh metallic sounds that are common in a jail, be they doors clanging, air conditioning, loudspeaker announcements, alarms and keys jangling on guard's uniforms, or the sound of officer's shoes on the concrete floors. What if we replaced those sounds with soft noise, the sound of nature, rain falling on trees, birds singing or the sound of water on the seashore. The hope being that a softer sound would reduce noise, anxiety and therefore lead to improved behavior in jail.

That led to an idea, if nature sounds can make a difference, then is it the environment more broadly, trees, plants, growing things that could work. Then what could an actual green project achieve, growing a garden to grow people became an idea. That developed into the garden project, with prisoners and staff building and restoring an overgrown neglected garden within the Silverwater Correctional Complex in Sydney, the garden area surrounded by 3 jails with large fences and razor wire surrounding it, a harsh and sterile environment. The garden project was about giving hope, a wellbeing space, inmates and staff sharing a common interest, creating a living space, and growing people. As I socialized the garden project through internal communication, staff briefings other gardens started in other Centers, often with different purposes, a vegetable garden, or herb garden as examples.

I believe how we build environments shapes how people interact with each other. The garden project demonstrated this as I observed staff stopping and taking to prisoners working on the project. Leading to another evolution changing how we label people, i.e. no longer using the term inmate but prisoner "Think like a gardener, not an architect: design beginnings, not endings" (Eno in Hill, 2022).

This led to not one intervention but multiple variations on a theme. That theme is best summed up through this study and my work as being like a 'butterfly effect'. Using the work of Edward Lorenz who observed that a tiny change in a data formula around weather patterns had a dramatic impact, hence the metaphor that the "flap of a butterfly's wings might ultimately cause a tornado" (Lorenz, 1963).

For me the most powerful tool and method I used was the Practices model. It was at its core the simplest, just ask the service user, client, prisoner, patient etc what is it that matters to them. The Practices model details how; using four levels that in a human centered approach are used to develop a in depth understanding of the problem and therefore propose more human centered solutions, in my case by asking the prisoners what motivates them, what do they value and what will make a difference to them.

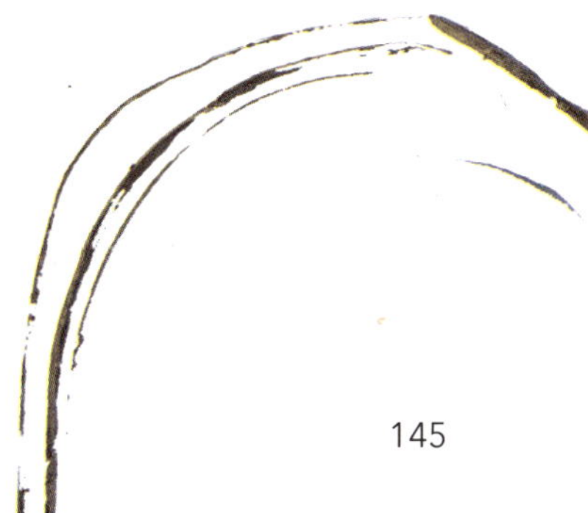

REFLECTIONS

The garden project was a success, as measured by its replication at other centers. It opened the doors to thinking differently. Change, systemic change in a large bureaucracy with a long and strong tradition does not happen overnight nor without resistance, therefore small incremental changes are more easily adopted and embedded.

The infrastructure required in the context of my work in corrections was a framework. I was attempting to introduce changes, small changes that could lead to a deep shift how we view, engage, and manage people in prison. My vision was introduction of a simplified classification system, and by introducing sounds of nature, more garden projects, changing the labels we use. Words matter: we have as a society spent many years defining these people as subjects, dehumanizing and therefore dis-empowering them, to ensure control.

A hope I had with the classification reform was to establish a positive pathway for people (prisoners) that by the use of different identifiers supports a different approach within the system, that is rather than seeing prisoners as subjects to be treated, to a view that is focused on them as humans that have potential and opportunity and hope.

Why try and make a change, why try and change a culture, why oppose a system, why invest in this, why try and make a difference, why? Because people matter, and hope is what sustains us. Though the reality is although crime rates in the Western world have overall fallen over the last decades, funding has gone to the criminal justice system rather than social supports in community, (Chambliss 2001). In this way the power is retained by the system. So, we maintain a system, developing and implementing a new initiative to address an issue but really, we are just perpetuating a system and repeating past mistakes, we "fall into recurrent patterns" (Lacey in Stacey & Griffin, 2002 p. 142).

3.15

EXAMINING THE GENESIS OF THE SUSTAINABLE BRAIN PROJECT

Isabelle Phillips, PhD

In the summer of 2023, I took a Creative Catalyzer course with Dr Barbara Doran from the UTS Transdisciplinary Innovation School where I also happened to be teaching. The Creative Catalyzer did not just interrogate critical theory on 'creativity'. The course also supported students' own creativity via drawing. Lots of it. Drawing with pens, pencils markers, ink, crayon, drawing upside down items, drawing without lifting the pen from the page, and drawing inside circles, drawing anything that emerged from the nib of the pen. Moving my hand across paper and watching the color emerge for weeks on end did something to my brain that I was not expecting. It connected disparate areas that had previously remained separated by contemporary notions of work-self and home-self. Some kind of neural lightning storm ensued. I became obsessed with a new idea for Australia and Australians. I experienced this as something happening to me, not something I was controlling. The Sustainable Brain Project exploded in my head. For a time, it became all I thought about and talked about. Shortly thereafter, it came to life in big cities all over Australia, in regional NSW and in Norfolk Island. Here, I will outline the unexpected connections that were gifted to me via diligently doing my drawing homework. I will also share the big questions and paradoxes underpinning the project, the flowering of the Sustainable Brain Project all over Australia and the fruit this is bearing.

UNEXPECTED CONNECTIONS

When I commenced the creative catalyzer course, I brought my work-self who had spent the past 20 years working at the nexus of performance and wellbeing, in various countries and many sectors. I brought knowledge generated from my PhD studies focusing on positivist, medicalized random controlled clinical trials and on socially constructed relational understandings of leadership. My work-self brought the experience of grappling with legislative drivers of change such as the recently emergent workplace wellbeing and psychosocial safety changes in Australia. Meanwhile, my home-self was grappling with my beautiful mum's dementia diagnosis, the complexities of her care and what to expect as dementia progressed. To resource myself, I dived into a massive on-line open course on preventing dementia through Tasmania University and discovered the depth, breadth and projected growth of this problem of dementia. My work-self and my home-self saw no cogent connections until my daily drawing brought these problems together. But there is a problem with problems.

THE PROBLEM WITH PROBLEMS

The Sustainable Brain Project acknowledges the problems highlighted by the World Health Organization (WHO). WHO claims that OECD countries are on track for health system overwhelm by 2030 as a dementia diagnosis is made every three seconds. We will need US $2 trillion to address dementia care, and 40 million new health care and social workers. A big problem, yes. But if we take a problem-based approach we might seek simply to nullify the problem. We might ask: how do we prevent health system overwhelm? We already know the answer to this question: prevention of health system overwhelm. With a problem-based approach our narratives remain stable, we serve institutional longevity over humans and health and, I for one, am already bored. What if we ask a different kind of question?

ASKING SALUTOGENIC QUESTIONS

Salutogenic questions have answers that are not immediately knowable, answers that are divergent and co-created, answers that bring about new narratives that can better serve our emerging realities. As such The Sustainable Brain Project is a knowledge-making vehicle, a creative social experiment designed to bring about novel and valuable social narratives to drive positive change. What if we co-create workplace environments that promote cognitive fitness and wellbeing? What if these were the very things that prevent dementia? What if communities of workers co-create it themselves? If you are still asking: But what is it? At its most concrete and mundane the Sustainable Brain Project can be simply described as a series of place-based training programs. Each program comprises eight two-hour sessions, conducted once every two weeks and enacted within existing communities (such as multiple levels of work within an organizational community). Already the Sustainable Brain Project has influenced communities all over Australia, and Norfolk Island, has influenced state and local government, not for profit and health sectors, and community and place-based groups. Beyond the concrete and known, the Sustainable Brain Project invites creativity and innovation via salutogenic questioning of communities around workplace wellbeing in the context of very real tensions and paradoxes.

TENSIONS AND PARADOXES

In response to a number of tensions the Sustainable Brain Project takes a both/and approach. We don't seek to resolve or solve any tensions, instead we work with both polarities acknowledging the complexities of co-creation. For example, we acknowledge problems. And we invite solution amplification. We engage in short, iterative sprints with a focus on rapidly boosting cognitive fitness. And we finesse long-term practices toward preventing dementia. We engage with neurobiological drivers of wellbeing and performance. And we engage with social constructionist ideas supporting individuals as the both main characters in their story and as the authors of their story. We bring individuals together. And we invite them to think and dialogue on positive change through a collectivist lens.

TILLING SOIL, NURTURING FLOWERS AND SAVORING FRUIT

For some decades I have been an avid journaler, a mindfulness and yoga practitioner. I have regularly accessed calm states, to examine and process my life via introspection. However, the experience of producing 'creative work' via drawing (§1.5) was a new experience for me. It has delivered something quite delightful. I am grateful for the diligence that my other practices have gifted me. Despite my 'sandwich generation' lifestyle I diligently made the drawings happen. Despite having no discernible skills as a visual artist, I did as I was asked, and put pen to page every day. I drew while my son played basketball. I arrived early to client gigs and drew in nearby cafés at 7am, I drew my dinner party conversations, my photo album, my movements around the city and whatever was in front of me. I drew from the sunny window seat in mum's nursing home apartment. Drawing did the work of 'tilling the soil'. The 'flowering' has been the Sustainable Brain Project artifacts the website, team, clients, organizational and community cohorts, the hundreds of participants and the joy of connection with all these wonderful people in this meaningful way. The growing 'fruit' is The Sustainable Brain Project as a knowledge-making vehicle for healthier ways-of-working for Australians. Place-based communities are changing up some entrenched ways of working in novel and effective ways. Stay tuned.

3.16

CREATIVITY BRIDGES TO BETTER FUTURES

Julie Batch

INTRODUCTION: ON PERMANENCY

"When we try to make impermanent things permanent, we cause ourselves to suffer when they eventually change."

- Brian Thomson

Humans have endured through our ability to protect ourselves, to make ourselves resilient. Castles surrounded by moats, shelters to keep us dry, battle armor for a fighting chance, vaccines to stave off viruses. These designs though have not been for defense, rather tools for advancement. Without shelter we are just another species, without armor no new lands, without medicine no longevity. When we put a protection in place, we increase our chances of success and our willingness to experiment. To move forward, go faster, deliver quicker comfort and find new opportunities. These protections are enablers, allowing us to take greater chances, to advance our kind more rapidly. With each new advance comes new risk. Buildings are exposed to the elements, fire unchecked can cause harm, and technology has the capacity to move more quickly than humans can comprehend. Marching forward, in a world with ever increasing complexity and accelerating change, it is easy to forget these were risk enablers and to see them just as defenses. Controls to maintain the status quo, to limit rather than provide a platform on which to advance. If yesterday's castles are todays institutions - we must not forget there was always a drawbridge to cross over a moat.

Search 'institutions', and you will find the expected description, accompanied by pictures of buildings. Solid structures placed with intent to stand the test of time, symbols of permanence and stability. This visual representation of permanence is a cornerstone of most institutions; hospitals, churches, municipal buildings, skyscrapers, Wall Street, Fleet Street. Symbols of intent, power, stability, longevity, progress. It's not just the exterior, of these institutions that has been built in pursuit of permanence. Inside people are housed, creating systems designed to last. Over time these people form habits, write rules and then reward and promote behaviors, creating more structure within the structure, commands and controls. When the rules don't make sense, people work around them, making short cuts to find the easiest way, etching their systems into the carpets like desire lines.

Over time, it's hard to differentiate the rules and intent at origin with the way we do things around here - the culture. In these institutions, built to last, where people and culture have etched lines into its very fabric, how do you change? When the world around you is shifting and the mechanisms that created these great long-lasting organizations are crumbling, and the risk enablers are inhibiting rather than enabling progress, what impact can one individual play in the system, to help an organization adapt and change.

We must search for mechanisms that might help unlock new potential, in organizations that have stood the test of time, and position them for the future.

THE HIDDEN RULES OF THE GAME

"You cannot solve a problem for the same consciousness that created it. You must learn to the see the world anew."

- Albert Einstein

Many leading organizations in Australia are long standing. In a country with a western civilization less than 250 years old, some organizations have been operating for more than 150 years. My organization is one of those, it serves more than half the population, has grown exponentially through acquisition, absorbed multiple cultures, has an abundance of technology, and holds a market position in terms of size and scale that makes it systemically important. It has excelled in the age of manufacturing. As society has transformed enabled by a seismic of technology, surrounded by rules, its capacity for change has been limited to ever shifting organizational redesign. It is very clear on the long-term risks to the business, very clear on the potential shifts that need to occur and yet challenged by empowering the system to change. In the last decade, attempts have been made. Our organization has set up structures to innovate. Like many others, these innovation forays have been independent of the core business. We built innovation on the side, recruited great people, had access to all the capabilities required. It didn't work. As we developed new technologies and new experiences, they got stuck when we attempted to deploy into them into the enterprise. Business champions were few and far between. Often the innovations challenged the roles and responsibilities of those we needed the most to deploy them. There were limited pathways to scale. Ultimately the rules that have kept the institution stable and strong over time succeeded to repel the change. Not intentionally, it just didn't know any other way and moreover, I did not teach it one. Looking across other industries that have disrupted themselves, even the successful ones are no longer quite as shiny. Governance failures, unsustainable growth trajectories, lack of diversification abounds. Even those organizations built in this new age are finding values, principles and behaviors are pre-requisites to success. Once or twice a century we have a revolution an uprising of the people, so disenfranchised by the system the only option is bloody egregious change. In the quiet times in between, we are always changing. We are capable of it. This is not revolutionary change but evolutionary, subtle shifts - of shape, of ideology, of influences. Changing from within.

Rather than fight the very system we are trying to adapt, we should celebrate what already exists within it, and consider what else we might inject into it, so it changes from within. There is a role of creativity of both the intellectuals and artistic kind to support this shift.

INSURANCE AND HOPE

Insurance was built on the principal of mutuality - the premium of many cover the risks of a few. If not for insurance, much of what we know today as trade and enterprise would never have existed. Insurance began through the support of trading of goods and materials between countries using ships. Before insurance, the risk of placing goods on these ships was too great because the chances of the ship sinking on journey too high. Producers of goods were reluctant to place their produce on a ship to gain access to a market that was otherwise beyond their reach. By spreading this risk cross entities and over larger spans of time - insurance created a bridge to better futures. Insurance companies make it possible for the world to make leaps into futures that would otherwise be deemed impossible.

Insurance is an intangible technology, it is one of, if not the single, most important technology we have invented. Our trust in this intangible technology has played a critical role in society's advances.

BUT

Sadly, today, insurance is not always seen in the same light, as an enabling of a technology that supports hope, rather as a conservative product that is purchased begrudgingly, as a necessity.

Looking at change (as a thing in itself)

"Be not the slave of your own past - plunge into the sublime seas, dive deep, and swim far, so you shall come back with new self-respect, with new power, and with an advanced experience that shall explain and overlook the old."

- Ralph Waldo Emerson

LOOKING AT CHANGE IN ORGANIZATIONS

Within organizations, Change is happening all the time, people, systems, policies, customers, competitors. Both the macro environment and the daily operating environment are subject to a continuous set of forces that leave it with no choice but to adapt. The change is both incremental and continuous. In these organizations, change occurs at the intersection of politics, position, and power. To move decisions through this system, multiple methods and levers are used to achieve an outcome. At times, these methods might be deployed for immediate effect or consecutively over a longer term, to shape a decision using influence.

Within our organization we have various, well established management systems. These include, annual budgeting cycles, annual business plans, multi-year road-maps, external consultant support, internal strategy resources, design capabilities, and innovation centers. Many of these are well oiled machinery aligned to share market and regulatory rhythms. Changing from within requires us to adapt these systems and inject new practices to drive different outcomes.

LOOKING AT COLORS OF CHANGE

I can't look at a colleague now without seeing their change aura. As well as the designated color, I am also associating those colors with creatures, yellow bellied black snakes, blue bird accountants etc. When engaging I am thinking about how they move, how they are motivated, what they need to make them happy. The pot of gold at the end of the rainbow might be that instead of focusing on the behavioral attributes as negatives and blockers, the colors enabled a celebration of their value and what might be possible if we could find points of agreement and enablement. It also highlighted how important each of these types is to the system and fighting them won't work - working with them might just move us forward. Within our company, colors of change provided a gateway to better decisions. Introducing a deliberate practice to defining decisions and the role individuals (based on their organization position play) could help us cut through more rapidly.

We observed time and again that proponents of different approaches could not easily switch their thinking,

Blue-print thinking is based on the rational design and implementation of change. Empirical investigation is seen as the basis for defining outcomes, and planned change (e.g. project management) is responsible for delivering them.

Yellow-print thinking is based on socio-political ideas about organizations. This type of thinking assumes that people change their standpoints only if their own interests are taken into account. Change is seen as a negotiation, and is achieved by forming coalitions.

Red-print thinking focuses on motivation: stimulating people in the right way is believed to induce behavioral change. Interventions range from reward systems or strengthening team spirit to an inspiring vision of the future.

Green-print thinking has its roots in action learning and organizational development: changing and learning are deemed to be inextricably linked. Change agents focus on helping others discover their limits and learn more effective ways of acting.

White-print thinking views change as continuous and pervasive. In this view, while change agents cannot control change, they can catalyze it. Change agents try to understand undercurrents, support those who grasp opportunities, and help remove obstacles in their path.

LOOKING AT LEVERS OF CHANGE

When focusing on this Gardner's Levers within our organization, I observed all of them at play. Interestingly, many of the Levers are entrenched and perhaps over-relied upon within specific areas or departments of the business. For example:

Reason is deployed frequently in Business Casing, particularly where funding or investment is required.

Research is utilized heavily in Strategy, lots of data to support hypothesis, often put together by external consultants.

Resonance is used frequent by our CEO, together with active use of the word "I", validating and directing the discussion.

Representational Re-descriptions or storytelling in our customer space with customer stories supporting change agendas.

Resources and Rewards is present in cross divisional programs including Game Changers where teams are incentivized to solve problems with non-salary-based prizes or recognition

Real World Events forms the basis of Scenario Planning including regulatory capital stress testing, including where external events are simulated within our portfolios.

Resistances shows up in our Risk Assessments - what could go wrong and how do we mitigate that.

LEARNING LOOPS AND CREATING THE SPACE FOR CHANGE

The existing rhythms of the organization are arranged around annual budgeting cycles. These are financially driven cycles aimed at looking backwards at actual performance and predicting future outcomes. These cycles use our internal views and project them outside in the forms of guidance, business plans and targets. It is a continuous loop, the first part of the calendar year defining the plan for the next financially measured period and the second half re-forecast and measuring before starting again as the prior year plans run through. Any new mechanism needs to recognize that this is entrenched and isn't going to change. Maybe it doesn't need to. Supplementing with additional learning loops create a more fulsome system that enables a more continuous process of learning and robust change.

CREATING LAYERED LEARNING LOOPS

Organizations are honed on cause and effect. Take and action, measure the outcome. Many of the systems in place are pinned there by budgets, frameworks, performance systems and extraneous forces. What propels us forward is an ever-increasing set of targets and metrics, however under frameworks designed in the 1950's, hardly anything ever changes, very rarely is anything new measured. It would be wrong to say these methods don't drive results, however they are highly attuned to economic returns. This could perhaps be described as single loop learning. Adding further loops to this process which recognizes the delivery and growth mechanisms of a traditional organization but supplements them with more qualitative, creative, customer centric practices could enhance outcomes and help shift our existing system from a delivery system to a learning system that adapts and changes in line with changing consumer expectations.

I propose three loops: (1) The Budget Loop (inside out): the existing budget process which set annually and measured monthly. This draws quantitative data together with external financial market analysis to define a set of measures and outcomes. (2)The Exploratory Loop (discover): Create space to ideate and explore leveraging elements of Coding, Methods, Boundary Objects explore the talent and capability within our organization to find new methods, analysis, and insights from sources of information that might not otherwise have been contemplated. The capability of our people, feedback from our customers and unifying practices that give permission to new ways of doing things. (3) The Re-frame Loop (outside in): drawing on the elements of re-framing, studios and colors of change utilize stakeholder groups both internally and externally to problem solve, define new hypothesis and solutions and product design that feeds Loop 1, creating a richer set of outcomes. Move these insights to actions by defining and endorsing activity through the thinking laid out in colors of change.

SETTING THE RHYTHM

In this model, the first and third loops work together. The annual budget cycle supplemented with an equally defined structure that allows outside in exploration and problem solving around relevant topical issues and longer dated outcomes - projecting forward in multi-year horizons, the outcomes of which are subsequently embedded in the Budget Loop. Connecting them are a series of Explorations- Loop 2, this loop uses the key disciplines to build a culture of innovation, using methods and actions that creatively solve problems. Bringing together capabilities from within the organization and celebrating them, ensuring there is appropriate time to implement.

The infrastructure to support the proposed three loop learning model is largely present in the organization but currently pointed at line manager derived initiatives versus finding opportunities throughout the system. The critical additional requirements include:

- Establishing and training for the key creative elements in the system. This might include developing a partnership with university and educators to teach elements of next gen strategic innovation like learning and embed them in operating rhythms and/or re-pointing learning and development resources at these outcomes.
- Reviewing reward mechanisms and aligning them to long term outcomes.
- Color mapping - understanding the enablers, decision makers and impediments in the organizational hierarchy and clarifying their roles and decision-making requirements.

ESTABLISHING THE NEW PRACTICE

How can we set this up? What are the steps we envisage? There are different paths but first, we could focus on Learning Loop 3 with the creation of a Studio, bringing together new talent from within our organization. These studios are running twice yearly and tackling business problems. Then, we can extend Customer Testing Panels to broader ecosystem players and developed new delivery model for key initiatives which removes hierarchy and designs a cross functional squad pointed at continuous delivery.

REFLECTIONS, LESSONS LEARNED

"The difference between what we do and what we are capable of doing would suffice to solve most of the world's problems."

- Mahatma Gandhi

The challenge in a legacy organization is that all the history, the systems, processes, and people have been designed, structured, and maintained to keep the status quo, to eliminate risk on the basis that this maximizes the change of survival. There has not been enough challenge to the status quo. We have been more interested in maintaining the status quo, believing that will maximize the chance of survival and that has been a disincentive to change and challenge. For the last 100 years this has been a stable set of assumptions and with the accompanying scale has come disproportionate power. It's this power that has kept systems in place.

Today though, power structures are being disrupted everywhere. Technological power that gives us the ability to compute at rapid speeds, also opens our access to knowledge, and insight is changing everything.
As our awareness expands so must our methods and actions for dealing with change. Accepting existing structures, working with rather than fighting them, by injecting new collaborative learning practices that drive broad, diverse insights into decision making, setting organizations up for brighter futures.

Coding, but not as we know it

We interact with an incredible amount of data, numbers mainly, and generally with numbers there is a pathway to a number. Coding has opened access to a new way of looking at qualitative information and quickly cutting through content to find meaning. Coding works on almost any data set by drawing out information and organizing it in a way that provides rapid insight but is open to find pathways to new more abstract insights that cannot be mathematically derived. A blend of the quantitative with this qualitative analysis could provide a far richer view of cause and effect or of lead versus lag indicators and help shape our business.

3.17

MENTAL SKILLNESS

Bo Ellery

Complex problems feature a myriad of interconnections and a high degree of ambiguity, particularly when addressing vital societal issues such as the interplay between mental health, employment and participation. It was this nexus of challenges and opportunities that inspired a diverse group of stakeholders from across community, government, academia and private enterprise to use the Frame Creation methodology to collaboratively address local priorities and improve the health and wellbeing of people living with a mental illness in Northern Sydney.

Specifically following a process of data collection, survey and lively discussion we decided to work on the following opportunity statement, "Creating safe workplaces and opportunities for inclusion and participation in the Hornsby area for young people between the ages of 16-35 living with or at risk of serious illness". We moved tentatively at first, creating trust by setting aside traditional rivalries and declaring our reasons for wanting meaningful change rather than the usual closed thinking rehash of yesterday's programs. We scanned the literature on the subject and confirmed what we had all felt and heard; that a job brings opportunities for social inclusion and financial independence. We also identified several paradoxes that appeared to exacerbate the problem of increasing employment participation for people with mental illness, not least that employers need to be involved in the solution yet do not see it as their responsibility. Most work has previously been on the job seeker side of the equation not on the employer side, while issues of stigma persist and hamper the efforts of traditional job placement.

Stakeholder identification was extensive on this project with consumers, employers, mental health, clinical and employment services and the wider community all involved at different stages of the design. We spoke with everyone we could and asked, "what's important to you" this is where the magic really happened as people cut straight to what the fundamental truth is for them. The collaboration hit dizzying heights when we began theming the various answers and work-shopping how they related to each other, this is where the project turned from traditional approaches to a higher plain of thought and reason, discussing elemental human values and needs. We kept at it, digging deeper, playing with the relationship between the concepts and ultimately, with the help of many responses, landed on three values that framed the issue and could guide our work,

Confidence - the knowledge and assurance of mutual benefit that employers and consumers can have. For employers' confidence means having certainty in their ability to hire, retain and support staff with a mental illness, for consumers it is the confidence in their ability to get and keep a job thereby contributing to their own recovery.

Belief - this is more personal than confidence and came through loud and clear in the research. It refers to self-belief and self-worth for the consumer and can be applied to the employer regarding their organizational values and vision. Belief is created, influenced and fostered by the stories we tell ourselves and each other.

Permission - This derives from the context of stigma that surrounds mental illness and constrains belief and confidence. Societal stigma often makes the consumer feel they should not disclose their condition, and they do not have "permission" to apply for the position. Likewise, employers may feel that they lack society's permission to employ someone with a mental illness.

Without this thorough exploration of human values and what they mean for each stakeholder the multifaceted approach at a solution could not have happened, the practicable nature of the project design was a direct result of the honest philosophical and lived experience discussion of all stakeholders.

We had discussed multiple values but the imaginative leap to a conceptual frame was missing until we started exploring the unique abilities and strengths that people living with a mental illness possess. The re-frame tackled the stigma head on and what slowly emerged from our series of workshops was a move from the loaded term Mental Illness to the opportunity of Mental Skillness, smart word play but an even smarter reappraisal of what skills different lived experiences can teach us.

The solution took the form of several nested projects relating not just to people with a mental illness but all stakeholders.

EMPLOYER SUPPORT

Best practice - Employers need to be empowered to amend processes, practices and policies to be more inclusive of people with a mental illness.

Mental Health Training - The benefits of mental health training are many, individual resilience is enhanced, stigma can be dispelled, early warning signs spotted, and early intervention sought out.

Charter - A voluntary agreement by an employer to set out a broad set of principles that the organization adheres to, in creating a mentally healthy workplace.

SOCIAL SUPPORT

Research strongly suggests that promoting connection, preventing disconnection and restoring connection within the workplace and relevant community supports are effective strategies to enable resilience.

CONSUMER READINESS

Skill building, access to job opportunities, advice and support in gaining and retaining employment are vital to the consumer

COMMUNITY AWARENESS

Most stakeholders professed a need for strategies to work in tandem with a concerted effort at educating the wider community. An emphasis on the value people with a mental illness can bring to an organization was a key feature.

This is usually where designers and their project's part ways but the design work and recommendations for implementation did not get caught in the wheels of bureaucracy but found solid purchase in the local area it was intended for. A series of mentally healthy workplace employer breakfasts were organized to kick off implementation and what followed was a remarkable community program. All aspects of the plan were delivered in a local pilot including a design award winning advertising campaign focusing on the skills people with a mental illness possess on prominent billboards throughout the area. Primary Care and Community Services, a founding member of the collaborative design team, has since taken the concept and adapted it to create a wonderful suite of programs and services for people with a mental illness in both NSW and Queensland.

So, what was different about this project?

For me it was both the methodology, which allowed for a structured, yet creative flow of discussion and exploration of all insights and the trust created in the room, which removed old rivalries and fear and replaced them with respect and understanding.

One sentence was repeated ad nauseum throughout this project and I feel it gets to the heart of Frame Creation and life itself...What is Important to YOU?

3.18

CATALYZING MULTI-MODAL LEADERSHIP: TRANSFORMING LEADERSHIP DEVELOPMENT EXPERIENCES

Nick Ellem

INTRODUCTION: LEADERSHIP IN CRISIS

'Those who practice leadership must confront, disappoint and dismantle and at the same time energize, inspire and empower".

- Sharon Daloz Parks (2014)

As a practitioner embedded in a public sector context, my vantage point allows me to see how enterprise efforts meet (or miss) the messy realities of leadership. This case does not seek to prescribe a solution, but rather illuminate an evolving practice shaped in real time. I have worked in the field of leadership development and learning development for 15+ years, and in that time, I have developed a growing frustration and sometimes a dull ache, for the failure of the leadership development field in achieving individual, team, and organizational outcomes. I often find myself thinking, "here we go again" "I've seen this before, and it's ineffective without x, y and z." Often I find myself in the middle of designing and delivering a leadership experience and realize it's happening again. These sub-optimal results have led me to believe leadership development is broken. This is concerning given the leadership development industry is worth a massive $14 billion per annum. In 2019, the Center for Creative Leadership (CCL), benchmarked leadership development in a global study. They found the median leadership development budget is $346,200 in organizations with more than 1,000 staff. Yet we still see ineffective leadership when it comes to achieving our organization's outcomes. This is despite the imperative and urgency placed on leadership development by executives.

Over the last two years, the focus within my professional context has been on understanding the current state of leadership and building the future strategy and road map that is going to get the organization where it needs to go. I sit within a large complex public sector organization, within the people and culture function. The team's primary focus is about creating great people experiences for today and tomorrow; one of the key functions of our team is to deliver a defined leadership strategy and road map as well as embed our leadership model across all parts of the organization. This model, like any such artifact, is a social construction–partial, provisional, and inevitably shaped by the biases and preferences of those who co-created it. Still, it offered a useful starting point to begin challenging inherited norms. My team is focused on designing and delivering a leadership development program of work to support senior leaders in building their leadership capability and therefore create a high-performing organization.

WHY LEADERSHIP DEVELOPMENT? WHAT LEADERSHIP DEVELOPMENT?

Independent research by Bersin Deloitte and others consistently shows that "Leadership development is one the most pressing issues facing organizations today". CCL conducted a survey of 5,000 participants across the world and 8,765 of their colleagues, and close to 100% of those surveyed said they achieved their development goals relating to "communication, self-awareness, implementing change and other areas". CCL identified 4 reasons to invest in developing leaders: (1) to improve financial results, (2) to attract, develop, and retain talent, (3) to drive strategy execution and (4), to increase success in navigating change.

The situation I was unearthing in my organization confirmed what we already knew we needed to do, and came out in the form of a question; if the alignment and capability of the leadership group are approached as if it is a problem of one-and-done experiences, then how do we create differentiated experiences that are continuous and multi-modal for leaders? We would need to create a clear pathway with differentiated experiences regardless of the context, business objectives, individual needs, cohort size, and learning preferences.

We started with a few discovery workshops bringing everyone from across the team together to ask ourselves what is really going on here, and what we are trying to solve? What follows is not a solution, but a set of working hypotheses. We began to explore what might happen if we treated leadership development not as an event, but as a continuous inquiry into self, system, and situation. How might we use best practice approaches, and what might we test and experiment with?

The discovery phase involved extensive stakeholder engagement to understand their needs and the collection and theming of various data sources to prioritize leadership themes. Our aim was to propose a program of work with a focus on creating differentiated experiences for our leaders to create a leadership ecosystem and deliver leadership initiatives that lift capability.

Key aims:

- Leaders understand the organization's strategic priorities and their role
- Leaders operate together to deliver shared value
- Leaders' behaviors enable our operating model
- Leaders know where to go to support themselves and their teams
- Leaders have access to the development that enables the right leadership skills to deliver in their role.

Differences to be realized:

- A clear leadership development pathway that supports them to be effective in their role today and in future roles
- Complete leadership program pathway for our people.

Historically, the organization has overly relied on external delivery partners catering for a senior and small cohort.

We realized that it would take too long with the current model to deliver the organization's strategic ambitions and transformation that was needed. Current programs focus on models, tools, and resources rather than focus on leadership as a practice or connecting people across organizations to learn with others, there were:

- Multiple entry points to leadership programs generating confusion
- Sub-optimal delivery of a consistent leadership development experience
- No clear way of accessing leadership resources, tools, content, or programs making it hard for the end user to access development anytime or anywhere
- Ad-hoc and local leadership solutions are developed in response to the needs of today rather than focusing on the strategic outcomes we aim to achieve in the medium and long term.

There were differing levels of maturity, requiring going back to a foundational level for some cohorts and no one central source of data on; talent reviews, benchmarking, staff engagement results, conversations with senior leaders, program evaluation and reviews. Quality data was elusive, and the greatest challenge is cultivating the will and capability to act on good-enough insight. Strategic knowledge emerges not from more metrics, but from using what we already know.

It was clear that there was a need for alignment and consistency across leadership content across the program. We needed to rethink and create new ways to address the challenges and create differentiated leadership experiences that met individual needs in their current role and future roles.

There was a clear need for one distinct leadership pathway for all leaders, regardless of where they sit in the organization, and other variables like workload commitment and level of capability. To develop this we could not use a programmatic approach; we didn't yet have a defined suite of programs by level, and this led to people feeling unsupported by the organization when it came to development. The rapid development of both enterprise and local options created competition between programs with a need to create scope and sequence between leadership levels and program content, along with alignment and consistency of key messages for leaders. We felt that there was an over-emphasis on courses and programs to deliver leadership capability outcomes.

How to navigate this?

We took the decision to focus on rethink our leadership program and pilot the idea of including reflection and action moments into the program, what we call 'temple and podium' moments to interweave into the program planning - we aim to ground leadership development in collective, public action. These moments matter, not because they are dramatic, but because they change the music others dance to. Leadership shifts the rhythm of work–often imperceptibly–through what leaders do differently in the presence of others.

My course of action:

1. I set up two workshops, the first, with my peers and followed by one with my leadership team to get some 'outside system perspective' and corroborate from a workshop with my team.
2. After synthesizing initial findings, I ran a perspective workshop series with three different levels of leaders; Executive, middle management, and front-line.
3. I collated and analyzed the findings to see a rich picture of the direction to take with executive leadership development planning.
4. I utilized the thinking tool activity as well as the systemic toolkit process to understand the issue from a systems perspective.

The rationale was to understand the system better and understand the leverage points from within the system itself by bringing together key stakeholders as well as end-users. I had a workshop with my colleagues, and we explored the problem from each of our perspectives. It provided the opportunity to "Jam" on the straw model proposal provided as part of the strategic delivery road map outcomes work. Through this we built an understanding of what's important for senior leaders were able to formulate recommendations to share with our people and culture leadership team, seeking their endorsement.

We needed to understand where people stand without assuming or forcing our perspective on people - we needed to give people autonomy in the system and give up some control of the final solution. At the same time, we needed to share our perspectives through the intervention approach we co-design and delivered together.

Using the straw model workshop as a thinking tool we disrupted people's thinking of the future of leadership programming and development with all stakeholders. The intervention approach had congruence with the values, agency and legacy principles that underpin the leadership strategy, which are (1) Leadership for all (2) Connected leadership (3) Context matters and (4) the realization that leadership is a practice.

Even though these principles were co-designed and validated by people in the business, some key stakeholders do not necessarily align with these principles in practice - particularly leadership for all and connected leadership. They have asked for a cohort-based approach to leadership development because they prefer to train together as a closed team. The intervention approach accommodated the agency of stakeholders and was integrated into the approach as co-designed together - it was interesting to think about what the partnership would look like from a business partnering and learning and development perspective as we see them not playing a significant role, but they really want to play a pivotal role.

It has been a worthwhile exercise as part of the workshops to map stakeholders and their values to elicit what is getting in the way of momentum, particularly as work ideation is happening in parallel with what values are not so explicit that we are considering as part of the executive development planning. Integrating the Studio model and Heifetz's (2009) iterative leadership cycle/ process has been fruitful as it allowed us to explain to stakeholders what is different about this proposed program and how it will create differentiated experiences for individuals and teams.

We want to create an adult learning balance between instructor-led and experiential learning, as well as a micro cycle of learning within a leadership moment underpinned by Heifetz's observation-intervention cycle. It's about bringing it together into an overarching macro view of an individual's leadership journey - their micro-learning cycle forming together as part of the macro learning cycle (the leadership program). This has yet to be fully tested and scaled to an organizational/ field level, rather, we are letting go of viewing leadership development as a process to be mapped. Instead, we're experimenting with principles that serve as a compass—orienting, not dictating, the path. Through our further testing we will learn and have opportunities to change the organization and potentially the field of leadership development within the organization.

STEPPING INTO TRANSDISCIPLINARY INNOVATION

Our approach does not discard management or command models. We recognize the limits of binary thinking—leadership is not a better screwdriver to replace the hammer. Different challenges require different tools. The real skill lies in discernment.

The Studio Model (§2.7) is a Transdisciplinary innovation cycle to support deep change. It provides an opening to explore new ways of learning from the metaphorical domains of - academy, lab, temple, and podium. It is relevant to the study of a learning organization as it is a change model for shaping learning design differently and where and how people learn- particularly the focus on the podium and temple. I started to apply this model in my discovery workshops with colleagues to how we can change the learning experience we deliver.

The co-evolution of a new model of leadership development aligned to create a learning ecosystem. When we started on this path we had no working principle on how to create leadership development programs from the beginning, but co-evolved as we went.

It is important along the way to step back and see with fresh eyes what is the ultimate opportunity of the intervention to move the system. There are four focus areas in the organization's leadership strategy, two of these seed a change in people's demonstration of leadership. Drawing on Carolyn Taylor's (1989) work "Walking the talk" focusing on systems, symbols, and behaviors versus just rolling out another training program. We had planned initiatives and utilized leverage points across our employee life-cycle moments to nudge a shift in leadership to be more humanistic - for example, if we take recruitment and selection as a moment in the life cycle of employees, we will embed our behaviors into position descriptions, job ads, interview guides, and processes. We are also integrating into performance, goal setting and recognition.

After the discovery phase, we experimented with differentiated leadership experiences outlining what each experience could look like. We have presented the below as a proposed concept that we have been iterating on with stakeholders and our team, and we have received an endorsement to move forward to co-design. This is an amazing outcome.

There are numerous activities to be undertaken now, but success is clearer and more achievable as we elicit leverage points from stakeholders through co-design. To see the challenges as they see them rather than assuming what the leverage points are, we will test and experiment with the intervention approach. Rather than trying to bite off too many needs of stakeholders, we homed in on experiments we could run within our spans of control and build credibility through ongoing stakeholder feedback and iteration of our proposed program of work. We would meet regularly with the project steering group and key stakeholders to provide updates and try small experiments to meet people where they are when it comes to the challenge and proposed solution.

What will it take?

We have proposed a leadership journey that addresses the context, leadership and challenges and hyper-complexity that leaders experience every day.

We are intending to pilot experiences over the next few years to diversify a leader's development portfolio. We are shifting our philosophy to act our way into new ways of thinking, rather than think our way into new ways of acting. Rather than assuming awareness precedes action, we are designing leadership moments that catalyze new awareness through practice in motion. It will be interesting to explore how we might discern the quality of what happens. Once we have final approval for the proposed program of work, our first task is determining our resourcing plan, as we will need to reallocate activities and let go of other pieces of work.

We will need our own lab, academy, podium and temple throughout the market research and procurement phase, as well as during the co-design and implementation phase. Rather than setting up labs and academies as standalone environments, we are designing in-situ experiences where learning happens live—within a leader's real work, real team, and real pressures. The lab becomes a mindset, not a place. The podium and temple emerge through real time reflection and public performance—not simulated episodes. We must embed the learning infrastructure into the live work environment—supporting leaders to learn in real-time, with their real teams, and on actual work.

Development must be integrated into the day job, not removed from it, We will need to build an academy and a lab, but also a place to share and a temple to reflect on lessons learned. Starting with the Academy, we will need to understand what we will deliver and how we will partner with external providers. We will need an academy between the vendor and us to share their expertize and for us to bring the context and leadership data to the fore.

Taking these steps sparks a whole raft of questions for my organization and for the future of the field of leadership development:

- *What infrastructure will you need/ should be built to support the above going forward? What are key elements in the Studio? (Is there a Lab, Academy, Podium, Temple?). Which element would you build first?*
- *How can we shift from using leadership development in its pure form and de-frame development to more reflect the conditions and contexts, challenges and politics of change, and the leadership capacities needed?*
- *How might we accelerate the learning cycle, and expand people at a rate they can absorb that is relevant for the organization? (timely and at scale?)*
- *How do we transform leadership development itself to be more inclusive of different disciplines, practices, and fields of thought? The leadership development field is often spoken of as a must, but rarely do people see what its blind spots and biases are. How might they be overcome?*
- *What does it really mean to be a leadership developer?*

Leadership development has traditionally been a one-off event, just as no one learns to surf by reading a manual, leadership is learned in the doing. The knowing-doing gap is closed not by theory, but by real-world application–observing, adjusting, and doing again, in context. Rather than a sustained and continuous leader-led experience that brings together labs, and instructor-led training, but also rounds their experience aligned to our leadership development framework which we call 'temple' and 'podium' moments. The 'Temple' and 'Podium' metaphors were not instructional modes, but invitations–ways to shift from pedagogy to practice. Temple moments allowed leaders to ask, 'Who am I, and what do I stand for?' Podium moments asked, 'What will I stand up for, and with whom?

The Executive leadership program of work will (1) Enable outcomes by connecting leaders' challenges to showing leadership in everyday moments (2) Grow leadership capability across senior service levels to drive enablers: step changes and building blocks, (3) Strengthen leadership effectiveness at scale to maximize behavioral change to enable people strategy drivers.

We began to treat the organization as a living lab, where leadership development is less about transmission of knowledge and more about testing hypotheses in the field; acknowledging that systems push back, people resist, and meaning is made in motion.

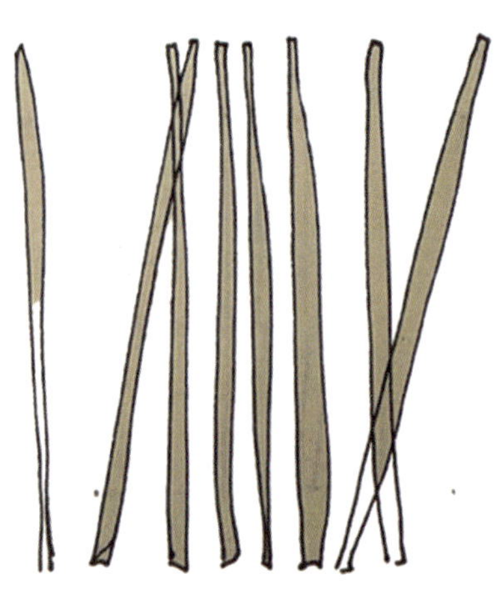

3.19

FUTURE HUNTER: FROM PERSEVERE TO PROSPER

Simon Byrnes

INTRODUCTION: MOVING BEYOND COAL

Australia has long been the 'lucky country' which has relied on its abundant natural resources to drive economic prosperity along the roller coaster of global commodity markets. Economic outcomes have driven decision making, with economic prosperity considered a proxy for a thriving community. The global challenge of climate change is an opportunity to implement the ecosystem infrastructure required to both change the economic model in Australia and drive vitality in our life-world across a broader range of outcomes that deliver lasting real value.

The Port of Newcastle (PON) provides physical, market and personal connections between our Hunter Valley community and the world. PON is seeking to develop the infrastructure across those connections to enable a more diverse, equitable and inclusive community both today and for future generations.

Australia is a resource led economy. The state of NSW comprises the third largest export market for Australia and coal is the largest contributor with circa 90% of coal exported through PON. Royalties payable on the sale of coal comprise about 4% (or AU$3.5B in 2022) of total revenue for the NSW Government. Coal royalties go into consolidated revenue and are applied by the NSW Government across the annual budget process, rather than being reinvested in the community that generated the revenue. Tempo-centralism governs not only the extraction and consumption of natural resources developed over millennia, but also the application of the profits. The NSW Government has modeled the financial impact that falling coal export volumes (or values) may have on NSW Government revenue. The figure shows coal volumes (and value) falling to zero around 2040 in the most conservative scenario.

Beyond the economic impact, the NSW and Australian Governments are committed to de-carbonization achieving net zero by 2050. Simply leveraging the resilience inherent in the Hunter community to move from the fossil fuel energy industry into the adjacent clean energy industry will create value (in clean energy) but not capture that value (exporting clean energy to buy back value added products from Asia). So de-carbonization is necessary, but not sufficient, to create a thriving future Hunter community.

This section outlines why we need:

- To innovate from a position of strength;
- Transformational innovation underpinned by a strategic vision that re-imagines what is possible to dare to dream and to demand that we not bravely persevere, but pursue prosperity through the open and curious pursuit of prosperity.

THE SITUATION

PON's journey towards curating the diversification of trade in our region began in 2019. The Hunter community was not ready to talk about "transition" during 2019. The situation is hyper-complex, playing out in layers across policy, systems, life-world and the biosphere. During 2021, the situation was being portrayed as the need to 'transition' (re replace) the Hunter economy, and success was defined by economic metrics. The narrative placed an emphasis on things 'needing to be fixed' and a reductive view on the community which undermined its agency and fractured its identity.

A review of the themes arising from the literature and narrative arising from the systems world at that time:

PON undertook a range of individual interviews seeking to uncover the themes playing out in the life-world of people in Newcastle and the Hunter valley. The striking finding from that exercise was that the Hunter community was extremely knowledgeable on climate issues living at the interface between strong economic, environmental and social forces; and viewed its community culture, not the physical minerals, as the key resource for our region.

The Hunter community was aware of its value, needed to talk about issues to dislodge the paradox, wanted leadership from within and wanted to navigate issues together (acknowledging that sustainability is not a destination but a journey). Narratives that are divisive were to be avoided as we sought to leverage diversity of the Hunter community to drive transformational innovation. Some paradoxes became visible.

THEMES FROM THE LIFE-WORLD:

PON found itself at the center of the situation, as an energy port as it facilitates part of the world's most efficient coal export supply chain. Communities at both ends of that supply chain rely on that energy trade for security and economic prosperity. The current situation was locked in place by a range of paradoxes;

The resources and expertize of the existing energy supply chain were required to create a new clean energy industry,

yet

the participants in that supply chain were identified as the problem and not part of the solution.

We needed to be able to openly and authentically talk about the need for change (and the real value that could realize) to unite the Hunter community,

yet

talking about change polarized the discourse and led to isolation and silos.

We needed to contemplate the complex situation as part of a global ecosystem,

yet

issues around sovereign interest and control prevented a collaborative approach.

INTERVENTIONS AND EXPERIMENTS

Sessions: prototyping a creative culture harnessing a transdisciplinary approach

The infrastructure and resources industry is typified by a risk adverse approach with a long term investment horizon. Practices are shaped by engineering, legal and commercial norms and relationships are typically conducted through what Argyris (2000) terms the 'Model 1' approach. Precedence (i.e. good or best practice) is revered and held in place by an industry culture developed over centuries. Parking 'Model 1' approaches and activating 'Model 2' requires mindfulness, practice and trust. This can be cultivated both through dedicated 'experiment sessions', quarantined from our normal business programs which allowed participants to hold outcomes more lightly. Developing a common way of communicating on elements of practice was integral. We sought to develop a 'rain forest' nourished with trust and held outcomes loosely as a 'buds' team. Acknowledging that complexity can only be navigated (not resolved) provided some comfort to team members whose practices preferred a 'best practice' approach to problem solving. The goal of these sessions was to enable stronger connections between people.

Creating time and space to be specific about our practices, our preferences in 'colors of change', Soros' concepts of fallibility, reflexivity and self-reference and maintaining a 'yes and...' approach to discussions allowed for a playfulness that assisted the mobility of issues. The existing culture kept drawing participants back to problem solving mode and gentle reminders to sit within the complexity and hold outcomes lightly were required.

Sessions: Frame creation and practices

The frame creation process opened up what can be considered as 'real value' which led to a more ambitious (blue sky) collective vision. Taking time to acknowledge how the situation was currently playing out gave participants the opportunity to 'place concerns on the table'. Only once concerns were spoken and validated, could we move past them onto more fruitful frames. This step was augmented with the practices tool and were very specific about our values, principles (strategy), methods (systems) and actions (tactics).

Openness to adjusting each level of thinking takes time, as this can (often) be viewed as 'flip-flopping' and a failure by leadership to stick to a plan. A useful addition in this space would be an exercise that highlights the issues associated with fixing assumptions when seeking to navigate complexity. Working through who is currently, and who should be, involved provided useful focus on the importance of diversity, equity and inclusion. This is a particularly important concept in the emotionally charged subject of climate change. Bracketing and re-framing intentionally through the eyes of that group allowed us to open up the frame and think about a completely new future where we have agency and are united through an identity that embraces more than one thing. If replicating this approach, we recommend the application of some futuring exercises at this point to expand the sense of what may be possible.

By exploring different metaphors and myths around growth, underdog triumphs, transformation, celebration and inclusiveness, we landed on the preferred frame of 'what if we sought to inspire a thriving Hunter community as if it were a Year 12 formal/Prom'. There is a strong cultural tie to the frame in that a high proportion of school leavers also leave the Hunter community, in search of learning, growth and celebration opportunities elsewhere.

Many of these people return to the Hunter community when it is time to 'settle down' (within the myth that true growth can only occur outside the community and one can return once that is no longer a requirement). The power of this frame was to provoke discussions around why the Hunter community cannot be a place of growth and celebration rather than just a place to settle (as a second city).

Team members enjoyed the framing exercise, but the question of 'what does this mean for PON?' always quickly followed. Drawing on the fruitful re-frame, we looked at PON's role in leveraging the broader, more optimistic vision and have picked up some of the concepts below (e.g. 'Your Port, Our Community' and PON as a window for the Hunter community to and from the world). The figure provides a summary of PON's characteristics under the old and new frames.

In hyper-complex situations, it is hard to know how to involve everyone that 'should' be involved. We facilitated separate sessions across different stakeholder groups and seek to find a way to develop a narrative that highlights (rather than suppresses) the nuances. An important point is that each individual can only speak to their individual experience as a community member, nobody can speak on behalf of a whole community. We are interested in whether we can develop a process that allows thousands of people to participate in frame creation without losing its vitality (e.g. mimicking an open source technology development platform for an open source frame creation platform).

Sessions: A preferred future vision

Futures Literacy (Dorst, 2025) facilitated a shift in focus from the most accurate current prediction to entirely new future scenarios (what type of future would you want your children to live in). Future value and impact created space for discussions about sustainability, vitality and real value. Whilst re-framing allowed us to be more ambitious about what we could collectively try to achieve, futures allowed us to glimpse what truly transformational innovation may require (e.g. explicit acknowledgment of a single global climate ecosystem and a shift away from sovereign ownership of resources and people). Causal layer analysis is an easily approachable tool that assists to open up future scenarios for a preferable and truly sustainable vision for the future with specific litany, systems, worldviews and myths. Taking the time to define the preferred future, and the opportunity cost of not striving for that vision, helps implement a culture of experimentation, where we proactively sense, probe and respond to navigate a hyper-complex challenge.

That future vision seems incredibly difficult to achieve, but relaxing the immediate goal to focus on small experiments that can grow via learning loops is a fertile field to begin. Scans of the environment identify early indicators of possibly powerful themes and we have small teams experiment to test their strategic importance. We then amplify more important themes to engage external networks and increase awareness. Highlighting potential drivers of sector wide change and creating links to individual strategies. The table (on he next page) provides an example of a preferred vision for sustainability (rather than just more sustainable versions of our current systems).

We found the three horizons framework extremely useful; in particular the alignment of the broader PON business around a specific aspirational future, upfront acknowledgment of existing issues and problems that must be overcome (or moved past) and the concept of essential features to maintain. Each of these items assisted a balance across the business with value being attributed to the great work done today

Based on Hemingway's Iceberg Model.

	Current Vision	Preferred Vision
Litany	Green/Clean Energy	Net Zero and Total Life-cycle Costs
Systems	Capitalism and Sovereign Nations	Sustainability and Global World Order
Worldview	Tempocentrism and Individualism	Single Ecosystem
Myths	Human right of unfettered consumption	Balance between humans, all other living things and the environment

(the most efficient coal export port in he world) and gave legitimacy in investment in trends for the future (e.g. enabling the nascent clean energy industry). This helps galvanize the 'why' across front-line workers to Board members.

A challenge here is identifying the most productive early indicators where technology is emerging together with the new field. Strict role definition where relevant experts assess potential impact would be assisted by the practice map and peer-to-peer engagement. Done correctly, we could establish a loop between technology developers, executive leadership, Government departments responsible for industry development and skills and training institutions to generate a virtuous cycle for meaningful change.

Sessions: Creative practices

We utilize the Creative Reboot (2021) book and tool kit on a regular basis. Our creative fitness is exercised and we develop new ways of thinking and communicating within our team. We set aside an hour or two each fortnight as a purely creative space. This is useful as a reminder that playfulness assists creativity and navigation of complexity needs to be done lightly with an open and curious disposition.

Infrastructure to support the innovation ecosystem

Establishing an effective infrastructure and rhythm to drive the dynamics of change has been difficult. There is significant conflict between our need to achieve pressing goals in a resource constrained environment and taking the time for quality conversations and maintaining an open and curious approach. The method cards from §1.7 and our own creations provide a playful way to engage with establishing the infrastructure required to support the Studio Model (§2.7).

Below we describe how we have sought to implement the studio model across the ecosystem.

The temple provides a leveler through which any individual can contribute to what constitutes real value, the labs are industry led experiments which define what we need to learn, the academy is led by the curious, Academics and other knowledge institutions who develop initiatives to the issues arising from the labs, the podium provides space for participants across the process to communicate what value may be delivered before the temple closes the loop determining how that value should be delivered.

Temple: What is real value? Establishing a clear and inclusive set of values is integral to uniting a community behind a cause. Convening groups to explore what individuals see as real value (providing significant benefit in their lived experience) has been both challenging and rewarding. Our hypothesis is that articulating real value allows a logical entry point for a diverse range of individuals to participate in driving lasting change. This needs to include those who are most impacted by the change (e.g. existing fossil fuel workers) who will otherwise resist the change (or no longer feel part of the community). Lastly, as the cycle completes and podiums are held, the values arising from the temple are again tested as we ask 'how should we create value'.

Labs: What needs to be investigated? There are many challenges that need to be overcome to realize a truly sustainable, clean energy future. Our labs are configured around specific aspects of those challenges and led by the industry players that require the challenges to be overcome. A key benefit here has been hat the deliverables arising from the labs are tailored to the needs of the companies that must seek their own approvals to progress the process.

Academy: What have we learned (or what do we need to learn)? The academies play two integral roles: 1. Developing the solutions to the challenges posed by the industry led labs and, 2. Developing the skills and training pathways that will allow education to be a lead (rather than a lag) indicator. Coordination of these roles has proved challenging and the area would benefit from greater collaboration, support and funding from government. Involvement of the next generation of workers in the temple process is essential to the scoping of new skills pathways.

Podium: How should we create value? Podiums provide stakeholders involved across the temple, labs and academy with the opportunity to showcase outputs from each stream and the interconnected nature of the work. For example, PON convenes an event where participants in the power solution streams from the labs, and the academy, co-present on the challenges that need to be overcome and what we have learned (and are yet to learn) so far. The key output from the podiums is communicating what value may be created. Whether this is real value, and how that value should be created, will be the subject of the following temple meetings which will in-turn inform the labs on what needs to be investigated through experimentation.

REFLECTIONS

PON has been effective in seeking to enable a new clean energy industry. A key part has been identifying the new initiatives that may add real value whilst acknowledging the parts of the existing systems that could be retained or re-purposed.

PON does not have the resources to scale up to develop the initiatives and replace the existing systems. PON has established an ecosystem with around 30+ participants who are each devoting resources to the challenge in their own context. We are continuing to work on creating the connections necessary to allow outcomes to be shared and collaboration on transformational innovation to be commenced. If successful, PON's role will change as its shifts to focus on curation of opportunities and allows better resourced entities to step into delivery.

Driving a rhythm for the process is a key challenge. A threshold issue here is agency, where there is a conflict between individuals' personal values and the extent to which the work can be pursued within that individual's current professional context. A mixture of top down engagement at the corporate level (e.g. through MOUs) and bottom up engagement at the personal level (e.g. Hunter Innovation Action Group temple sessions) has been partially effective in addressing this issue. Generating buy-in through reference to case studies, and continued quality discussions on a 'trustworthy' process, will further assist.

Ultimately, clear leadership from socially principled members of the Hunter community is required. The vision is for a community that does not have to simply persevere through resilience but can prosper through vitality.

The tools in this book give a voice to an approach many of us have always felt to be necessary to enable a more caring and collaborative world.

Complex challenges can seem completely overwhelming. The tools allow entry points to start coming to terms with the (real) issues, expansion points that allow us to consider what real value might be realized (or at least sought after) and leveling points that allow the people that should be involved to be involved.

The challenge is then moving through the mid-term towards sustainable, and lasting change that drives real value over the long term. Lasting change cannot be driven by any one person. In our context, it requires a community united around a shared vision of a preferable future.

And the frame-creation process may even allow us to have a bit of fun on the way.

3.20

RELATIONOMICS: CREATING THE SOCIAL INFRASTRUCTURE FOR SOCIAL INNOVATION & COHESION

Lee Cooper

CONTEXT

Society tends to approach wicked problems as complex puzzles requiring professional, scalable, and organizational solutions. Communities are expected to adapt to these models, bending to fit systems not built for them. But what we need is to scale place-based, relationship-driven innovation, connecting individuals and networks that share knowledge across boundaries.

In 2022, I joined ThinkPlace, a social innovation and design agency. It was my first role in consulting after 25 years in the nonprofit sector. I made the shift because I wanted to explore and apply new ways of thinking and working, things I'd struggled to do within the constraints of the nonprofit world. That's not a critique of the sector but a reflection of the conditions in which it operates.

This chapter explores what becomes possible when we view societal challenges through a relational lens.

Social sector organizations are built on relational missions. They aim to disrupt the very causes that make them necessary by:

- *By respecting and valuing everyone exactly as they are, by listening to them, by recognizing that the adversity people face doesn't define them.*
- *We seek to strengthen social links.*
- *Build an inclusive, resilient, self-reliant and creative community.*

But funding structures push these organizations to deliver services that treat people as problems to be fixed.

Growth and scale bring demands for standardization, control, and efficiency, shaping organizations more like businesses than communities (Argyris, 2000).

As scale increases, language shifts: people become customers, care becomes a commodity (Butcher, Gilchrist, & Wanna, 2019), and policy and procedure start to overshadow purpose.

In Radical Help, Hilary Cottam writes that experimenting with new ideas is a reputational and financial risk–making any genuine innovation feel heroic (Cottam, 2018).

This case study looks at a small, place-based experiment that stuck to relational principles while allowing plans to remain flexible. What emerged was a new kind of social innovation ecosystem–one that helped us learn by doing and move forward through connection, not control.

THE SITUATION (HIDDEN RULES)

If we truly embrace the social value of innovation, we're not following a codified, step-by-step process; we're embracing relationships, networks, and shared human qualities. In this context, innovation is about creating the conditions for vitality, allowing individuals, communities, and organizations to respond to their challenges with creativity.

In his TED Talk *Why Innovation is Like a Rain forest*, Victor Hwang (2017) highlights seven values and relational elements that underpin thriving innovation systems and give credence to innovations' relational value:

- Openness
- Diversity
- Serendipity
- Fairness
- Experimentation
- Play
- Giving

These values rest on three core relational elements:

- **Low fear** - a sense of psychological safety
- **Trust** - especially across diverse groups
- **Love** - a deep sense of belonging and shared purpose

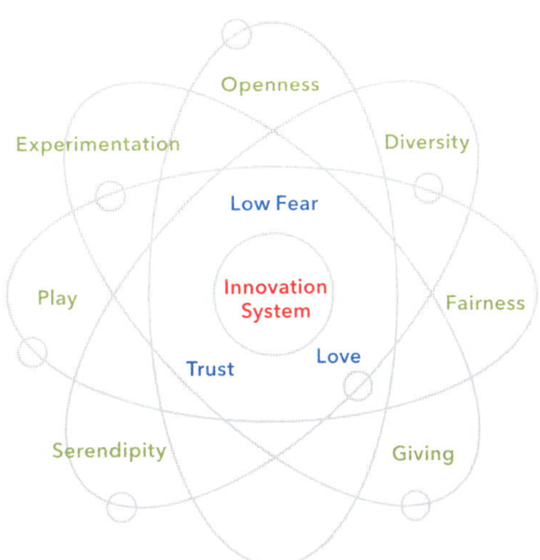

Figure 3.20a Innovation system represented as basic building blocks.

These characteristics aren't controversial, but they are hard to find in much of the social sector. To move from "what is" to "what if," we need to confront some uncomfortable truths:

1. People are framed as problems to be solved.

We often reduce complex social challenges to individual deficits, blaming people for lacking motivation or resilience. Our language reflects this: terms like dole-bludgers or lifter and leaners imply that people are at fault, reinforcing systems of punishment and compliance as the creative means to support and motivate change.

2. People need more programs.

The sector often assumes that new or scaled-up programs are the answer. Evaluations are used to validate models, even when the core issues remain unchanged. We rarely ask whether these programs are actually responding to the real, local context–or if they simply replicate what's familiar and fundable.

3. We keep building market models.

"Person-centered" approaches are increasingly framed through market logic. People become customers, services become products, and relationships are flattened into transactions. This logic has crept inside organizations too–where performance reviews, KPIs, and workforce management speak more to economic value than human value (Sandel, 2013; Stacey & Griffin, 2005).

4. We protect the system more than the people in it.

Ironically, organizations are treated as more human than the people within them. We worry about brand, culture, and values as if the organization itself has feelings. But, structures are only as human as the people inside them. And if those people don't feel safe, trusted, or like they belong, the structure doesn't serve its purpose (Argyris, 2000).

When we compare the qualities of an innovation system to the characteristics of many organizational systems, the contrast is stark.

Innovation System	Organizational System
Openness	Closed
Diversity	Uniformed
Serendipity	Predictable
Fairness	Plainness
Experimentation	Procedure
Play	Policy
Giving	Removing

Figure 3.20b

If we want to build systems capable of real social change, we can't just add new programs or scale existing models. We need to re-imagine how we work; structuring around people and relationships, not just processes. This means nurturing environments where safety, trust, and belonging aren't aspirational–they're the norm.

PARADOXES

"Societal challenges are systemic,

yet

our responses remain programmatic."

"Governments, funders, and organizations call for innovation

but

offer little support or tolerance for failure."

"We aim to build more caring, effective, and productive organizations,

yet

burden them with increasingly complex policies and procedures."

"We design person-centered services

but

rarely give people real power or decision-making authority."

"Relationships are core to care,

yet

services are becoming more transactional."

INTERVENTION/EXPERIMENTS

Introduction

Explaining the project alone doesn't fully capture the relational dynamics that made it work. The experiments we ran weren't just about delivering outcomes; they were about creating the conditions for people to connect. Through those connections, we uncovered what was needed to support our clients.

This case study is part of a broader initiative to co-design a place-based employment and vocational strategy for Walgett, commissioned by Regional NSW. It focuses on the Walgett Cultural & Community Pop-up Hub (The Hub), a central element of the project. The Hub was recognized with a Good Design Award in Social Impact (Good Design Australia, 2024). The jury described it as:

"A transformational design that shows great potential to boost social cohesion, spark economic growth, and challenge negative yet unfounded assumptions of the community." (ThinkPlace, 2024).

Traditional project plans tend to be linear, a method that works for assembling furniture but not for tackling complex social challenges. While The Hub was the most visible feature of the work, this case study explores three interconnected experiments that reflect the non-linear, adaptive nature of relational social design:

1. Living Lab - co-location
2. The Hub - social lab
3. Activities - interacting with the life world

Principles & Methodology

Two key principles and methods served as our compass for this project, one drawing on the work of Susan Fournier and Lara Lee on brand communities and the other from Christopher Alexander's pattern language. These shaped our approach, extending beyond standard co-design practices and grounding it in a transdisciplinary mindset.

1. Pools, Hubs & Webs

Based on the work of Susan Fournier and Lara Lee (Fournier & Lee, 2009), this model explores how people form connections in relation to brands. I've been adapting these concepts over time to apply them in new contexts, including this project.

Here's how the model played out in Walgett:

Pools	Hub	Web
Individuals share beliefs but lack social connection.	A central figure or space maintains connections.	Strong interpersonal connections shape the group.
Everyone wanted a better future for Walgett, but visions varied and people were disconnected.	The Walgett Cultural & Community Pop-up Hub became a space "owned by no one and shared by everyone."	Collaborative projects created trust and shared understanding that outlasted the project.
Risk of distrust and social fragmentation.	Could the project also build lasting social infrastructure?	Emerging networks formed the foundation for future collaboration.

Figure 3.20c Pools, Hubs & Webs.

2. Pattern Language - Quality Without a Name (§5.4)

This second approach draws from the late Christopher Alexander's design philosophy, particularly the idea that certain forms and patterns give life to spaces not by direct intention but as a by-product of how things are done.

Through this, the "quality without a name" emerged. This isn't something you design outright it emerges when you lead with care and trust. In Walgett, that meant moving with the community's pace and allowing that quality to surface naturally, shaped by shared experience (Ketcham, 2009).

Instead of structured workshops or sticky-note sessions, we co-created a space with the Walgett Community Working Group. We let that space do the work of forming relationships. From those relationships, we were able to re-frame and explore the problem/solution space together.

Project Context

The Aboriginal meaning of "Walgett" is "meeting of two waters". It also described the aspiration to combine traditional and western knowledge and cultures into a shared Walgett culture.

Images were essential artifacts and boundary objects for this project, communicating insights and meaning and opening new avenues of thinking about the problem solutions space (Star, 2010).

Take the image below the logo of the Walgett Community Working Party (WCWP), a local Aboriginal group representing their community and the many meanings it holds:

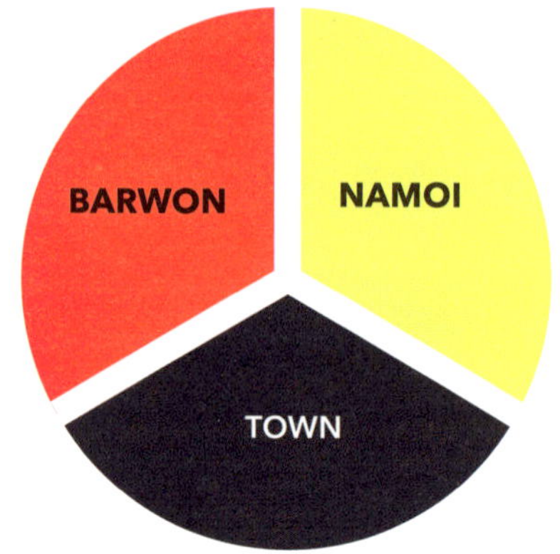

- Describes three different groups within the community
- Walgett is located at the junction of two rivers (Namoi and Barwon) meeting of two waters
- Peace symbol.

Figure 3.20d Walgett Community Working Party.

Figure 3.20e helps us understand the three experiments and their relationships.

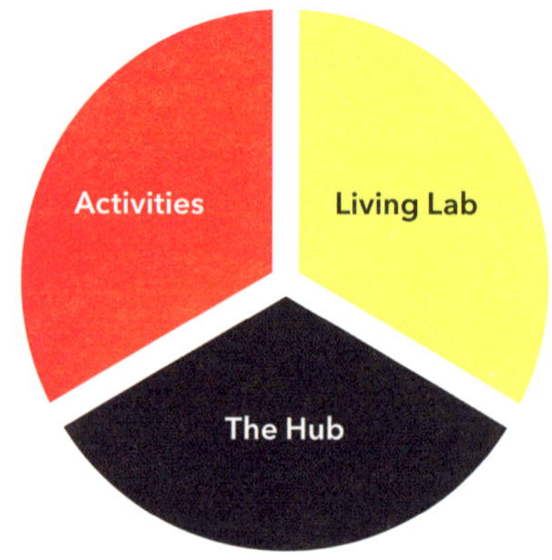

- They are separate but connected
- There is no specific start and finish order
- Each informs the other
- Equal importance
- Unique in their value

Figure 3.20e

Arriving in Walgett, you're met with striking contrasts. The natural and cultural beauty invites you to linger, yet the main street is lined with buildings behind metal bars, shutters, and wire mesh. Too often, this visual contrast is used as a shorthand for the town's racial, cultural, and economic divides. Those divisions exist, often perpetuated by single narrative, but to define Walgett only by them overlooks the strength and beauty of the community within.

EXPERIMENTS

Renowned architect and design theorist Christopher Alexander argues that rigid master plans often fail to adapt to local context, creating new problems instead of solving existing ones. We saw this firsthand during our initial engagement, where we were met with hostility – a reaction shaped by the media narrative and, more importantly, a long history of outside intervention.

To be clear, that response was not only understandable, it was earned. Like many disadvantaged communities, Walgett has been picked apart by outsiders. People arrive, diagnose, report, and leave. We were part of that pattern.

With our client's backing, we dropped the plan but held onto the principles and methodology. That pivot helped us find a new way forward.

We drew on another of Alexander's (§5.4) ideas 'quality without a name' calling for an 'activated populace': people shaping their environment through shared traditions, a common language, and open, democratic participation. In short, we could not achieve this if we were unwilling to be part of the community, we decided to make Walgett home.

Our new base made it easier to connect and build real relationships. In partnership with the WCWP, we co-developed, launched, and ran the Cultural & Community Pop-Up Hub (the Hub). Rather than relying on planned workshops or sticky-note sessions to meet the design brief, we leaned into the 'quality without a name' choosing creative experimentation over traditional activities. The idea was simple: do something meaningful, and let the by-product meet the project goals.

The Hub became our social lab a space for diverse groups (social), experimental methods (process), and systemic exploration (place) (Hassan, 2015).

Experiment One: The Living Lab

Most experiments, researchers want to remove themselves and become non-judgmental independent observers. In dynamic social systems built around relating and relationships, this is not possible; researchers and designers are participants in the experiment (Soros, 2013) .

This living within experience provided insights no workshop could and provided several critical frames for the project.

Framing

Kees Dorst's book "Notes on Design" outlines a core principle of framing as "a process of thinking around the problem rather than confronting it head-on" (Dorst, 2017).

By being within Walgett, we experienced how Walgett was framed. Drawing from our own experiences of the town and importantly validating this with our community.

The first frame was important as it set the scene for the project providing the support rational for the Hub. This was informed through the experience that there were no spaces considered neutral that we could base ourselves in.

Yarning with our new partners from WCWP and our local project sponsor, a new frame emerged that would go on to be a foundation principle for the project and the idea of the Hub was borne.

Frame	Re-frame
There is no shared space	Owned by no one, shared by everyone

EXPERIMENT TWO: WALGETT CULTURAL & COMMUNITY POP-UP HUB

We didn't plan to create a Pop-up Hub; it emerged through the relational approach of listening and connecting.

WCWP had been exploring the idea of a cultural center, and we saw a chance to align with that interest and proposed a working prototype to test key elements and generate insights.

No one wanted to re-diagnose the problem or fall back on vague solutions like "more collaboration." Instead, the Hub became a space to trial real ideas and, in doing so, a way to better understand both the problem and the solution together.

This reflected our commitment to a sociological approach to social design (Koskine & Hush, 2016) defined by:

- **Shared space** - The Hub
- **Method of investigation and experimentation** - A prototype for the cultural center
- **Focus on relationships** Capturing new perspectives through everyday encounters
- **Local and global understanding** Place-based insights with policy relevance

The site we used had been a former social enterprise – many locals called it "the heart of the town" and this became our second guiding frame.

Frame	Re-frame
Heart of the town	Getting Walgett's social heart beating again

This beating heart would begin with a small pulse and build from here.

Transforming this space began with clean up and introducing local Aboriginal artifacts kindly donated Outback Arts and the Trindall family. From here it started with a few visitors, followed by a request for a workshop and then into something more special.

This took shape most clearly in our third experiment.

EXPERIMENT THREE: ACTIVITIES – COMMUNITY DINNER

This activity was a semi-structured social event and a reminder that moments of magic can't be planned. But when the right conditions are created and people are given space to connect, transformation can and do happen.

Returning to the core challenge: Walgett was often described as divided along economic, racial, cultural lines. We set out to counter that narrative by hosting a shared dinner.

Organized in just a few days, the event relied on volunteers cooking a home-style meal, alongside cultural activities and conversations focused on imagining a brighter future for Walgett.

We set modest expectations: if 10-15 people showed up and stayed for 15-20 minutes, we'd consider it a success.

What unfolded instead was something deeper the 'quality without a name' revealed itself throughout the night.

The results can be broken down into three stories:

1. The Community
2. The Cultural Story
3. The Song

The Community

More than 30 people attended the event, most staying for over two hours exceeding expectations. The diversity of guest from young and old, locals and visitors, Indigenous and non-Indigenous, farmers, town workers, teachers, and social workers was harmonious, where instead of dividing into "us and them," they connected as a community.

This moment validated our early methodology – and it wouldn't have happened if we hadn't been embedded locally. Our engagement was grounded in a social affiliation model adapted from Pools, Hubs, and Webs (Fournier & Lee, 2009):

- **Pools:** In Walgett, people broadly agreed they wanted a better future, but connections between groups were thin, marked by mistrust.
- **Hubs:** Our physical Hub created space to strengthen those ties.
- **Webs:** the experience of cohesion would demonstrate what is possible.

Through daily interaction, we saw those webs forming. This event made them visible.

The Cultural Story

Mistrust between groups in Walgett runs deep, shaped by past conflicts and long-standing divisions.

A group of teachers arrived unsure of how they'd be received. Instead, they were welcomed, not just socially, but culturally.

They were guided through a story that didn't end with an Indigenous perspective alone, but offered something more: a shared cultural identity. Their guide described Walgett not as a place of separate stories, but as a place where "two waters meet", where Indigenous and non-Indigenous people learn from one another and flow forward together. A culture shared by all and owned by none

The Song

One of the most powerful moments came from a 19-year-old woman who attended at her mother's suggestion. She hoped to rehearse a speech and song she was preparing for RUOK Day. In front of 30 people, she opened up about her mental health journey and the pain of losing her brother to suicide. She ended with a song.

The room fell silent. She held everyone in that moment – through her courage, vulnerability, and authenticity. For the first time, she was seen, heard, and embraced by her community.

A local Indigenous resident captured the feeling of the night:

"This is the first time Walgett has had something like this where no one was excluded, and everyone felt welcome." (ThinkPlace, 2024) .

This created the frame that helped shape the final report.

Frame	Re-frame
Divided Community	Headlines hide the true story of a town with Heart

Deliverables

You might ask, what does this have to do with an employment and vocation strategy? And we would suggest it depends on how you think about commerce.

We often think of commerce as the exchange of goods and services, the engine of a market economy. But an earlier meaning of commerce refers to the exchange of ideas, views, and attitudes. This older definition points to the social foundations of commerce, and a crucial insight for this project.

To engage people in meaningful employment and vocation, we needed more than economic transactions. We needed trust, relationships, and connection.

This provided the frame for the report.

Frame	Re-frame
Commerce - market economy	Trusting Commerce - social infrastructure for a market economy

These experiments didn't just re-diagnose the problems, they gave the community lived experiences of the conditions needed for transformation. And through them, we discovered what mattered most for the strategy ahead.

ARCHITECTURE OF INFRASTRUCTURE

First Nations people are the original researchers and designers. Their deep knowledge is built through relationships – with Country, culture, and community – and it informed the infrastructure needed to support this work into the future.

Relational Infrastructure, made up of Backbone, Social, and Network Infrastructure, was identified as the "missing beginning" – the foundational element required to create the conditions for trusting commerce.

This form of infrastructure offers the scaffolding for communities to work in partnership with organizations, businesses, and governments on shared-value initiatives.

It consists of:

- **Backbone Infrastructure** - supports and scales connection, collaboration, innovation, and knowledge sharing.
- **Social Infrastructur**e - fosters relational ways of understanding, exploring, and working.
- **Network Infrastructure** - links resources across social, organizational, sector, and institutional boundaries.

Throughout the project, we looked to the Indigenous meaning of Walgett and its geography for guidance. This became the basis for a central artifact within the strategy – ensuring that future applications would be shaped by the design process itself.

This approach was influenced by Indigenous academic Tyson Yunkaporta, who describes a dynamic interface where different knowledge systems meet and interact (Yunkaporta & McGinty, 2009). In this project, the Hub became that interface.

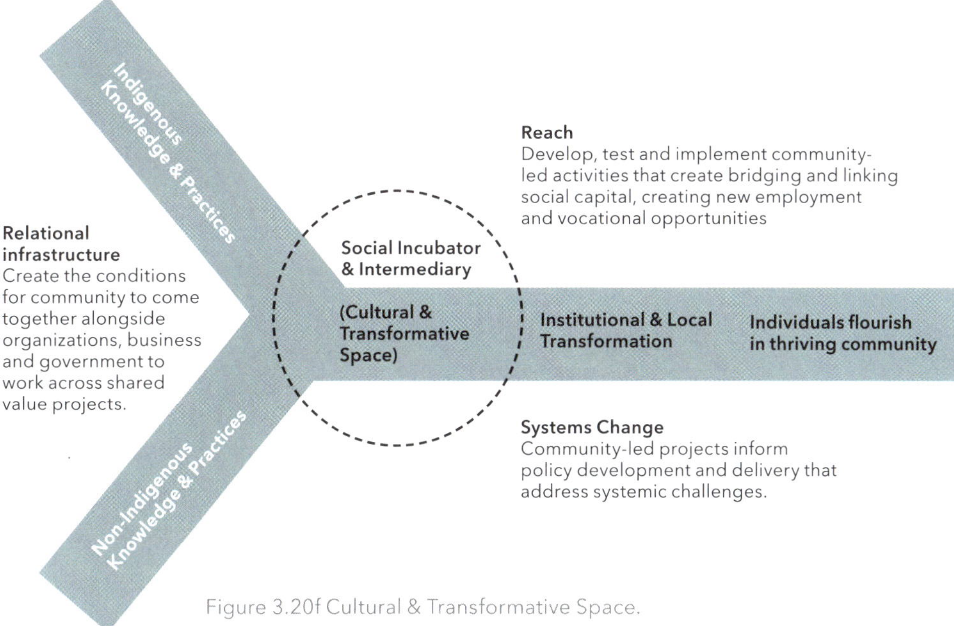

Figure 3.20f Cultural & Transformative Space.

The Hub is critical in providing space and place where new practices, experiments, conversations and connections are formed and shaped. This space became the Lab, Academy, Podium and Temple:

Elements	Meaning	Project Example
Lab	For experimentation.	We have designed and implemented prototypes to gain insights and develop new practices.
Academy	Where knowledge and insights can be synthesized.	Sharing ideas, insights, and outcomes with community, groups, and stakeholders.
Podium	Where new practices are acknowledged.	Activities and prototypes provided an experience of collaboration and cooperation; people became witnesses to their new narratives.
Temple	Reflect on what is essential and what is not.	Holding tight to processes, not activities, the space demonstrated the value of a 'healing space' and the benefits it brings.

REFLECTIONS, LESSONS LEARNED

This section narrates my experience, highlighting the hurdles I navigated and the lessons I learned and connecting these to the course content.

Organic Order

Encountering resistance required a re-evaluation of the approach.

This led to the realization of the fallacy of a rigid master plan. Our initial proposal, with detailed activities and a timeline, had to be re-imagined once we engaged directly with the community. This demonstrates the importance of flexibility and adaptability in respecting the 'lifeworld' and the importance of holding tight to design principles rather than activities.

Relational Leadership

Leadership is not a position of authority; it is a phenomenon that only occurs between people (Ladkin, 2020).

A pivotal moment was connecting with the Walgett Community Working Party Chair, spending time with them and their community, and openly requesting their guidance, knowledge, and understanding of their aspirations. This underscored the value of genuine engagement and participation, which paved the way for the Hub.

Pattern Language

Deciding to immerse ourselves in Walgett without a structured agenda or traditional workshop allowed us to create a shared language and frames that created an understanding.

This highlighted the necessity of embracing the time to build support, trust and insights into the way forward.

Social Labs

This adaptive and open approach aligned with community interests, leading to emergent workshops and mini-experiments that explored innovative ways of working together and provided insights for the final deliverable.

The strategy of incremental engagement facilitated cooperation and produced immediate, tangible benefits, proving that small-scale initiatives could have a significant community impact, helping us learn our way forward.

Balancing Risk & Reward

Despite the project's success, it is crucial to acknowledge that success is not a given. My experiences have taught me that trusting the process often reveals essential learnings, though it does not guarantee readiness or receptiveness from clients, project sponsors, or organizations.

Organizations

The original meaning of organization dates to the 15th century and means "structure of body parts" and "process of organizing, the arrangement of parts in an organic whole." The organic part of the meaning is lost in how we currently experience structure, but it is within our reach.

This design-led consulting project reflected more characteristics and activities of community centers where I worked. If we consider organic ways of working, we could imagine a future where the unconventional consulting practice, enabled by the government and embedded with community sector organizations, works in an open, collaborative and networked way, creating new innovative ecosystems to reshape systems to be fairer for all. Moreover, the risk involved in trying something new may be distributed across the network, reducing it for all and opening new innovative practices to emerge.

3.21

IT TAKES A VILLAGE

Kate Clugston

The cases in this chapter show a variety of examples from across sectors. They illustrate how applying the tools and methods from the book can unlock suck situations time and time again. In this final example, we spoke with Kate about her experience in applying Frame Creation to her organization.

"When I first joined the organization (a not-for-profit social enterprise), there were 6 of us; four years later, there were 26. We grew so rapidly that our processes and ways of working together were continually evolving. It was COVID lock-down times too, which made it extra complex - we were building the plane while flying it."

"One of our funders needed us to create an organization chart, but all the templates I found were hierarchical pyramid-shaped ones, which didn't look right, based on the living experience of working inside our social enterprise. I read about the history of organizational charts, which revealed origins in command and control systems of leadership/ management. But being driven by a social mission, and the values of community and collaboration, to improve the lives of migrants through first Australian jobs, we aspired to be the antithesis of commanding. A new way of visualizing workflows and relationships was needed that better reflected our team and values"

This feeling of unease with how things are and what the orthodox approach would be is a key milestone in unlearning how we have been educated. For Kate, a useful structure wouldn't be found through applying standard organizational chart tools to her organization. What's more, Kate realized that mapping an organization creates little value. This should be about meaning-making, not simply holding up a mirror.

"In applying the frame creation methodology, I interviewed a dozen people who worked either in a similar organization to ours or were stakeholders in the field; aligned civil society organizations, philanthropy and government agencies working to support refugees and new migrants in Australia. The themes that emerged from these conversations included: equity, social justice, inclusion, connection, community, security, freedom, belonging, identity and pride. I clustered the themes together and used them to make creative leaps into new frames. The one that felt most fit for purpose was inspired by the counter-cultural festival, Burning Man. This new frame generated rich insights and possibilities for interventions that would work at the values level to re-frame organizational culture, including how we mapped relationships and workflows - the organizational chart"

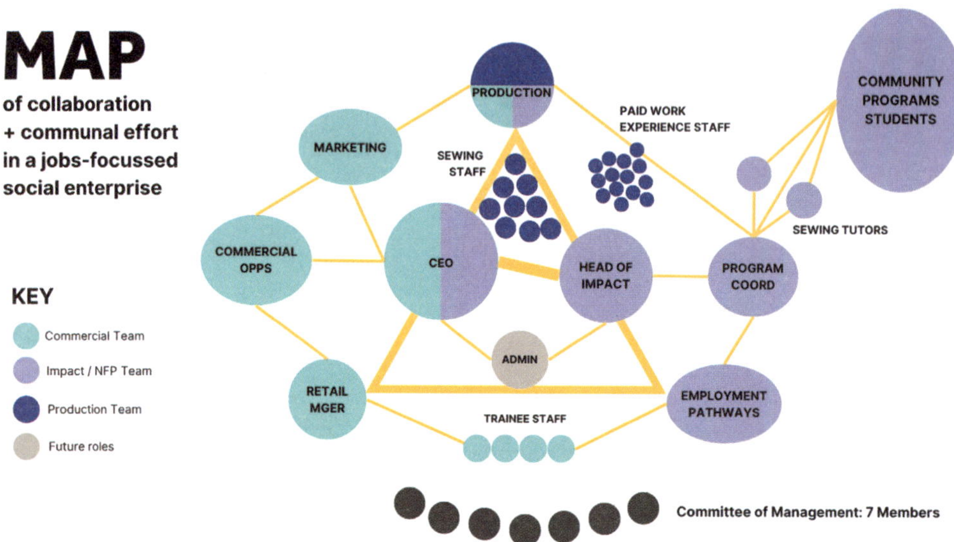

Figure 3.21

"The question for me then became: What if we saw our organization as Burning Man and adopted its working principle of a village?

"It's worth highlighting for the readers who have not experienced Burning Man that for all the hype around this counter-cultural festival, it's also one of the most unique civic experiences on earth - an experiment in temporal community, boundless creativity and a catalyst for values-based cultural change. The Burning Man Project's mission is: 'to produce the annual event known as Burning Man and to guide, nurture and protect the more permanent community created by its culture. Our intention is to generate a society that connects each individual to his or her creative powers, to participation in community, to the larger realm of civic life, and to the even greater world of nature that exists beyond society.'

"Our social enterprise's purpose - to support migrant and refugee women - was all about creating the conditions for belonging. Contemplating how our mission intersected with that of Burning Man, I imagined a future workplace for people who've been on the move; where their talents are developed, they have the opportunity to make a meaningful contribution to, and participate in a supportive community."

"Inspired by the Burning Man civic map, I re-imagined our organizational chart which I called: Map of Collaboration and Communal Effort. In sharing it with the board, they responded positively and have taken inspiration from it as they go through staffing changes and a mini restructure, to set the organization up for future growth and impact."

Kate's intervention gave her organization an opportunity for radically rethinking how they structure themselves, and to what end. Putting the aspired values of identity, community, inclusion, diversity, pride, belonging and participation gave Kate all the ingredients she needed to reconstitute the company around collaboration and communal effort. Once seen in this way, it is hard to unsee it. The elegance of the re-frame becomes an energy that is contagious.

CLOSING REMARKS

In this day and age, the pace of change needs to be quicker than we can muster through normal evolution in a sector; all sectors and disciplines are ripe for re-invention. The case studies show that there is no simple solution to the creation of these deep changes - and it is interesting to see several cases land in one domain, with innovation coming from all directions.

The projects together then close the net around the existing ways of thinking and working. To do this deliberately requires a different level of strategy. In the next chapter we will introduce some cases that show how a sector shifts when innovation projects are initiated strategically and implemented over time.

1c
6a

CHAPTER 4

CREATING DEEP CHANGE: STRATEGIC INNOVATION JOURNEYS

INTRODUCTION

The art of abstraction is bringing everything together in deceptively simple and elegant models - but in applying these models to the real world, all of the complexity and muddle of the everyday comes back in. Hence there are many ways we can create paths to impact - this takes many forms that can also change over time. Yet there is a basic structure, some principles that these processes have in common and a general 'movement' that seems to hold. And the models are helpful, not so much to point towards a single way of progressing, but by highlighting what elements of the situation most likely need to be heeded as you move forward. A good model provides this sense of completeness, an infrastructure for thinking and acting.

In Chapter 3 we have seen how all of the different objectives and starting points the proponents of these case studies did lead to very different outcomes. And that is a good sign. Strategic innovation can never be about following a straight line to a pre-ordained result. A truly strategic journey is more like a thoughtful wander.

Even the starting point is not as clear as you may think: setting out from a specific position, you quickly realize you need to revisit the assumptions that are embedded in it.

It sometimes takes a long time, going backwards before moving forwards from where you thought you were. And if that is needed, well then it is what it is.

For instance; all real innovation is a stepping-away-from current ways of thinking. That requires a safe environment for all involved, and a high level of trust in an organization. If the Trust isn't there, it needs to be worked on first. Just do it.... Resistance is futile... This type of brutal honesty is vital, because flawed assumptions create risk for later.

Such crucial navigation skills have not come to the fore so much in the strategic innovation cases of Chapter 3. These were all early stage explorations of what is needed as an infrastructure for change (the furnishing of the Studio, if you want). The strategic innovation case studies that follow are much more progressed. As with the earlier cases, they are widely different in problem domain, sector, timelines, and scale (from finding ways around local misdemeanors to revolutionizing the agriculture in a whole country). We hope that they do give a good sense of the Modus Operandi and show what can be achieved when strategic innovation is approached differently.

4.1

CASE: THE DEATH OF THE CRIMINOLOGIST

Rodger Watson

My Creative Intelligence and Strategic Innovation journey was introduced in §1.3 in the form of an epiphany, under the ominous title 'The Death of the Criminologist'. Here, I go more deeply into the underlying factors behind this moment of insight, questioning the assumptions behind my home discipline of criminology. As I share my perspective and ask probing questions along the way, please apply those questions to your own discipline as you read along.

We are educated and trained to think in certain ways. Our practices and disciplines (§1.2) are grounded in assumptions that may have been once true, but then tend to largely unquestioned - the vast majority of education, training and scientific inquiry is not critical. It does not really engage critically at the conceptual and theoretical levels.

In scientific inquiry there are schools of thought (or paradigms) that build knowledge which is then disseminated through education (knowledge) and training (skills). It is only at the highest degree levels (Masters and PhD) that students are expected to demonstrate critical engagement at the conceptual and theoretical levels. This is not to say that people who aren't studying at these high levels can't or don't engage, it is just to say that they are not explicitly taught how to or encouraged to.

When we enter a discipline we enter a doctrine that has certain ways of looking and acting within the world. These doctrines can be seen as a combination of mythos (belief) and logos (logic) that holds together the discipline.

Thinking pragmatically, a doctrine is something that seems to be true. This is fine until we start to recognize that the doctrine is not giving us the outcomes it promises. When the goalposts have shifted and things aren't going well, doing more of the same is just plain madness.

Then it is useful to apply a set of probing questions to your own practices and discipline. How do our disciplines think? What are the historical origins of our disciplines, and what assumptions were made? We'll continue this using myself (and the field of Situational Crime Prevention) as a Guinea Pig, in a deeper exploration of 'The Death of the Criminologist'.

QUESTION 1: WHERE DOES YOUR DISCIPLINE COME FROM?

The present-day field of Criminology is underpinned by two predominant paradigms, or schools of thought;

(1) In the Classical School - it is held that people have free will and choose to commit crime based on a rational choice between the risk of getting caught and the benefit gained by doing the crime. Classical Criminology takes a deterrence approach to preventing crime.

(2) In the Positivist School - it is held that people don't have free will, rather their behavior is the result of an interaction between their own biology, psychology and their social environment. Positivist Criminology seeks to prevent crime by addressing contributing factors.

Cesare Beccaria was a law and economics graduate who, as part of a philosophical society published an essay in 1764 titled "On Crime and Punishments". Based on Enlightenment philosophical discourse, this piece put forward a new paradigm which hinged on several central principles.

Principles adapted from Bernard, et. al. (2010)

Crimes and their punishments should be clearly defined

Judges should determine guilt and assign the predetermined punishment to the guilty

The harm done by the crime determines the seriousness of the crime

Punishments are to deter and should be proportionate to the seriousness of the crime

The severity should not exceed the harm done and the loss of the good which the crime may have taken away, to do so can create a perverse incentive to commit more crime

Punishment should be prompt to avoid 'the useless and cruel torments of uncertainty'

Punishments should be certain

Crimes and their punishments should be known by citizens

This thinking was picked up after the French Revolution and the American Revolutionary War when France and the United States of America were establishing their democracies. Despite the Roman Catholic Church placing the publication on the Index of Forbidden Books in 1766, the principles are still evident in many justice systems across the world (Bernard, et. al, 2010). Beccaria's principles provide a rational underpinning for criminal justice with a core assumption; that people have free-will and choose to/or not to commit crime based on a rational choice. Situational Crime Prevention emanates from this Classical Criminology paradigm.

More than 250 years of crime policy and reform have been heavily influenced by this theory. As a teacher of criminology to undergraduate criminology students, I was astounded to read this passage in their set text;

These ... "approaches are modeled on the relatively simple classical model of human choice, as originally proposed by Beccaria. In general, none of this research has directly attempted to test that model. Rather, each approach has developed policies that should reduce crime if its model is correct." (Barnard, et. al. 2010)

Evidence of the success of the approaches, is then taken as evidence that the model of human choice is valid. Thinking critically, this raises concerns that Classical Criminology and whole institutions within criminal justice systems are based on assumptions that 'seem to be true' but have not really been tested. Ever.

QUESTION 2: HOW DOES YOUR DISCIPLINE MAKE SENSE?

Myths have helped us to make sense of the world, filling in knowledge gaps (like how our world was formed) and providing a template for cultural practices and rituals. In this context they are to be respected and celebrated as part of our rich and diverse cultural histories. If we look a little closer however, we can start to see how some myths perpetuate mistruths and prejudices and how myths can be weaponized. When paired with logical fallacies they can become a potent element that maintains the status quo or even worse, can be used to perpetrate great harm.

"I don't see the myth itself, just as I don't see the lenses in my glasses" (Ford, 2007).

In early Roman culture myths were communicated through stories of the gods. Countless gods and goddesses helped to make sense of any conceivable situation (both in the natural world, but also in the cultural lifeworld). Stories of natural events (like the sun making its path across the sky), or cultural practices and expectations (such as the expectation of hospitality) helped the Romans to navigate their complex lives. The gods and goddesses were invoked up to the end of paganism but not in a way that those of the monotheistic religions (Judaism, Christianity, and Islam) would recognize.

The Roman myths were not doctrinal, they didn't represent ordained holy truths but were more a dynamic constellation of opposing forces, explained in stories. Belief and practice was fluid (Perowne1986). We might describe Roman mythology as situated, a collective of myths that inform cultural practices, explain natural phenomena, and help citizens to navigate the complexity and tensions of their lives.

Why is this important? In the Western world many of our civil institutions have their roots in the Greek and Roman civilizations. This is important because the Greek and Roman civilizations were not static and fully formed, they were fluid works in progress that didn't assume there was a determined way of doing things written into the universe.

"Render therefore unto Caesar the things that are Caesar's"

(King James Bible, 1769/2017, Matthew 22:21)

At the time Beccaria wrote On Crime and Punishments, 'justice' was a very local matter, and judgments were meted out by the ruler. In Christian Europe, crime was seen as an act against God's law. Some believed that it was the result of demonic possession (not an act of free will). The ruler, (who governed by the grace of God) would then determine guilt sometimes using trial by ordeal; such as burning/drowning an accused witch to test if she were a witch, other times making a decision based on the evidence presented (and many other factors, such as local politics) and would decide on the punishment. Beccaria was writing his piece in response to what he saw as unjust, irrational, and ineffective justice practices.

His rationale was along the lines of - if we want less crime, then we should create a system that is tuned to deter people from committing crime. In drawing on enlightenment thinking he was attempting to remove spirituality and mythical thinking as the underpinning assumptions behind crime and punishment, in search of a more just doctrine.

Going back to the meaning of the word doctrine, 'that which seems to be true', there are many ways something can seem to be true. Something can make rational sense and seem to be true, but when we start talking about rationality we have to educate ourselves and be literate in how rationality can be used to persuade.

QUESTION 3: HOW DOES YOUR DISCIPLINE ESTABLISH TRUTH?

Writing in the context of academic thought, Thomas Kuhn describes a paradigm (literally, 'example') as a shared way of thinking and acting within a scientific community that has a common contextual focus and principles. He notes that it can be made up of 100 producers and validators of scientific knowledge, occasionally significantly fewer. According to Kuhn, most scientists spend their careers working within the accepted paradigm, and engage in puzzle solving that deepens the knowledge within the paradigm. They do so using the inductive method.

At first applied to the natural world, the scientific method was formalized in the Scientific Revolution as a move away from spiritual and mythical ways of seeing truth and making sense of the natural world. In this method the natural scientist (think astronomy, chemistry, geoscience, biology, physics) objectively, firstly observes and diligently records facts about a natural phenomena, and then infers a causal or explanatory theory. The Inductive method has brought centuries of scientific progress and was useful in so many ways. But has also been misused - by applying a way of investigating that is created for understanding the natural world, to the life world of people.

Beccaria completely disrupted a mythically inspired paradigm of crime and punishment - but if this new paradigm can then go untested, informing policy and practice for more than 250 years, then what can science bring? Adhering to the Inductive scientific method, Cesare Lombroso studied criminals and began to observe patterns. He proposed that physical attributes, like the shape of fingers, noses, necks, hairlines, etc. all correlated with the type of criminal he was observing. It all pointed towards a theory of anthropological criminology. It proposes that if these criminals have these attributes, then anyone with those attributes are likely criminally inclined.

Lombroso founded the Positivist School of Criminology with his 'evidence-based' body of work (with publications spanning 1859-1909). He demonstrated with measurements, observation, and statistical analysis that criminality is innate and hereditary.

Prominent from 1887 up until the first world war, this paradigm was influential in sentencing reform in many jurisdictions. If we accept that criminality is innate, then it is rational for those who are innately criminal to be sentenced more harshly than an offender who offended due to circumstance.

There are some clear flaws with Lombroso's method. His theory was based on a study of convicted criminals (no control group) and claimed correlation between physical features and criminality, he went further and claimed that criminality (as with physical features) is innate and hereditary.

Using Lombroso's original data, Seven Jay Gould in his book The Mismeasure of Man (1996), went over Lombroso's data with contemporary statistical methods and found that there was no evidence that there was a correlation between physical attributes and criminality. He further found that images used in Lombroso's book were altered to make certain people look 'more devious'. Lombroso was thoroughly discredited (about 70 years after his death), and to their credit the scientific community of the days of his prominence poked enough holes in his science that by the time of his death he had stepped back his truth claims, though not to the extent of withdrawing them.

The thing is, it was too late for so many, and for so many still to come, his truth claim of innate and hereditary criminality built a foundation that would allow the weaponization of science in the humanities that would help set the conditions for the holocaust in Europe and the mass sterilization of women deemed of low intelligence.

It is harsh to apply rules retrospectively. Lombroso applied the scientific method of the day (Induction), and in doing so is an excellent case study of the vulnerability of Induction to prejudice and fallacy. Lombroso attributed secondary qualities (physical features) as being correlated with innate criminality and built up his case to prove his point.

That's the dark bit of the criminology story. It gets better, because now we offer that the mythos of humanity can't be understood through the same ways we understand the stars, planets, and how the earth relates to them (astronomy), the interaction of the elements and how that plays out (chemistry), the structure of the earth and how we can interact with it (geology), the plants and creatures we live with and how it all works (biology), and mass, motion, acceleration, gravity (physics). It would have been tempting to take a proven scientific method that had been so useful in establishing a sophisticated understanding of the physical world and to apply it to the lifeworld. But when it comes to humans and how we interact, the world is more complex than that.

QUESTION 4: HOW DOES YOUR DISCIPLINE GET TO USEFUL OUTCOMES?

In some cases there is nothing further from the truth than Inductively constructed theories made into practice 200+ years ago. The theories probably weren't true then, and yet they impact our civic society to this day. It is a case of doing things as they have been done for centuries, JUST BECAUSE we have been doing it that way for centuries.

The human sciences have had moments of 'physics envy', where they coveted the ability of the natural sciences to make and establish theories. Yet while Inductive science has worked well for understanding the natural world, it has created much harm when applied to the human

sciences. In the late 1890s a new scientific method was articulated by the American Pragmatist C.S Pierce and developed by other 'Pragmatists'.

John Dewey's 1910 articulation in How We Think is credited as a seminal piece in the development of the hypothetico-deductive model of science:

> Thinking productively starts with;
>
> A feeling that something is amiss, or out of place that needs to be addressed
>
> The formulation of the thing that is amiss, perhaps as a problem statement
>
> The construction of a hypothesis that can be tested
>
> A thinking through, or unpacking of the elements of the hypothesis
>
> Testing and evaluating the hypothesis
>
> Repeat

Later Dewey articulated how important it is to approach "human predicaments" (as distinct from hard sciences) and "problematical situations", with this approach (in Analysis of Reflective Thinking (1933)). Donald Schön went on to study Dewey's work and Schön's work is heavily influential to the thinking behind this book.

Thinking back to the death of my inner criminologist, I can locate it to a specific moment in time. Some time in 2013 I was walking home from the bus stop, across a park and I was reflecting on the theory of abductive logic, thinking back from the desired outcome to the open variables of how and what.

My usual path was blocked by a flooded fountain. I had to find another way, I had to go around the fountain. It was at this precise moment that I had an epiphany.

Suddenly I was able to think differently, pragmatism had hit. After spending my whole education being taught facts about the world, and how to do things in certain situations: to diagnose and prescribe the right treatment/intervention. I had never understood the benefit of, or even how to concentrate on thinking about the desired outcome first, I had never understood how to question 'why' and then move to creating or choosing a 'how' before deciding on a 'what to do'.

This epiphany moment came after working at the Designing Out Crime research center for three-years, and being immersed in way of working that was deeply pragmatic and abductive (see §4.2 for case studies that illustrate this body of work). The core practice of the Designing Out Crime team was to engage with a complex social issue, to obtain a deep understanding of how the situation was playing out and to work with multiple stakeholders to frame the problem around desired outcomes, and to imagine alternative interventions that would impact on the situation as it was initially framed.

Reinvention

To draw this dark chapter to a close, a chapter that has invoked many existential crises, it is important to tell of a movement that had great positive impact and who were an active part of the American Pragmatist movement, the establishment of the Chicago School of Criminology, and created deep change. Their story is not widely known.

It is now 15 years since I first saw how people could take on the very crime challenges I had been responsible for in vastly different ways. They weren't trained in the doctrine as I was. They had their own ways of seeing the world. Together, over time, we created a way of approaching the complex briefs that came to us. We created impact, won awards and accolades. It was good work, done by hard working people, and created a foundation from which to reflect on and build many of the models in this book.

Recently I came upon a journal paper that surprised me. It was a paper that talked about the American Pragmatists, but from an angle I wasn't aware of. Danielle Lake and Judy Whipps (2023) published a paper in a design journal, and they gave an overview of a body of work that I was completely unaware of. I took a Masters in Criminology, one of the subjects was Feminist Criminology, and yet, I completely missed the most extraordinary example of deep change makers in criminology in the modern era.

Jane Addams established Hull House in Chicago in 1892. Hull House was many things; childcare for working parents, cafeteria for workers, school for adults, and a think-tank. As a think-tank it was a place where citizens could come for a residency and engage the Hull House community to participate. Together they took out people smuggling and prostitution rackets, founded the first youth justice court in the USA, and had a vibrant community of active citizens navigating the challenges they saw in their daily life world, and in the systems world.

To 'discover' that a laudable person (Addams was awarded a Nobel Prize) had established a way of approaching complex societal issues more than 100 years before I took on the task, using basically the same approaches that I had been part of developing was at first exasperating. Surely I should know about this!

In Criminology the whole American Pragmatist contribution of Addams has been deliberately scrubbed from history . This has only recently come to light, and so we have a fresh opportunity to engage with a sophisticated body of work that emerged alongside the emergence of the hypothetico-deductive model of scientific inquiry.

This historical exploration of my own discipline got me thinking. By scratching away at the surface of classical and positivist criminology I've seen that they are based on assumptions that have not been tested (the classical school is based on the theory of human choice), or that have been debunked (in the case of Positivist Criminology, the founding father of the School was found to be using false science). Both schools of thought are a product of the Inductive Scientific method, which was superseded by Pragmatism in the human sciences more than 100 years ago, and yet they are still the dominant paradigms.

The extracts from Designing for the common good (Dorst, Kaldor, Klippan, Watson, 2016) in the next section are chosen to give a snapshot of how a pragmatic approach to criminology created positive impact and provided an environment where the models from Ch2 could be developed and refined whilst also taking on complex societal issues. The way of working developed by the Designing Out Crime team was developed under unique conditions. We had a mandate to engage with crime and complex societal issues from outside the doctrines of classical and positivist criminology.

We were tasked with coming up with and sharing this new practice.

4.2

CASE: DESIGNING OUT CRIME

Rodger Watson and Kees Dorst

In Australia, the New South Wales Government's Department of Justice and Attorney General established a Designing Out Crime research center together with the University of Technology Sydney (operational 2008-2022). The center's remit was to use design practices to revolutionize the way we achieve safety and security in society. Prevalent problem-solving strategies in the area of safety and security are focused on the creation of countermeasures, through erecting defenses, introducing CCTV camera systems, and using strong-arm tactics to force people's behavior away from unwanted, illegal or otherwise unfortunate patterns.

These principles generally make sense, but as is often the case with conventional problem-solving, they suffer from the twin sins of oversimplification and over-generalization. Central to the Designing Out Crime approach is the pledge to avoid the creation of countermeasures to crime, as these countermeasures create a climate of weariness and fear that destroys the social fabric of our public spaces and our society.

In its projects, the Designing Out Crime center was careful to avoid this pitfall, seeing crime as a symptom of things that go wrong in society, and taking aim at 'upstream' causes. This requires a re-framing, right from the start. The initial briefs or questions formulated by the project partners were often a direct result of their earlier problem-solving attempts, and these questions are almost always aimed at symptoms, rather than core problems. Re-framing these questions is the key to achieving innovative interventions.

The Designing Out Crime body of work was supported by the Assistant Director General at the time, Brendan Thomas, as part of his mission to reform the criminal justice system - working closely with people throughout the organization, and providing top-down support. The Designing Out Crime projects didn't just create new approaches to problems in society, internally they served as exemplars of what is possible when issues are re-framed.

GROWING UP IN PUBLIC

For the best part of a century, Sydney's Kings Cross has been an entertainment district of legendary status.

Bars, cafes, restaurants, fast-food joints and theaters sit alongside grand art deco apartments, backpacker hostels and the Wayside Chapel, which supports the area's large homeless population. Strip clubs, brothels, a supervised drug injecting center, a police station, lots of neon and an iconic Coca-Cola billboard complete the physical setting. Edgy, illicit and anonymous, Kings Cross is a place of disadvantage, risk, delight and opportunity.

> "Where the night is full of dangers/
> And the darkness full of fear
> And eleven hundred strangers/
> Live on aspirin and beer."
>
> – Kenneth Slessor, Darlinghurst Nights (1933)

Tens of thousands of young people come from across the city, the country and the world to let loose on a Friday or Saturday night (or both). The streets are abuzz with people going from bar to bar, and queues for the popular places spill onto the footpath. A trip to 'The Cross' is a rite of passage for eighteen-year-olds celebrating their milestone birthday with large groups of friends. Young men and women, sartorially resplendent, go there to try and meet other young men and women while pretending to be there for other reasons. And, with around 100 entertainment venues crammed into two streets, Kings Cross seems ideally built for having fun.

Yet statistics suggest otherwise. Each weekend night, Kings Cross suffers some of highest rates of antisocial behavior and violence anywhere in Australia. It was the site of the tragic deaths of two young men who were assaulted by strangers on a night out. The violent loss of young lives heightened political and public awareness of some of the problems in Kings Cross, fueling the resourcing of government interventions, as well as panic.

Government responses have included stopping the sale of strong alcohol after midnight, introducing identity scanners for use in 'high-risk' bars and clubs, banning drunks from all venues for 48 hours, establishing a sobering-up center, replacing glassware with plastic after midnight (so that glasses can't be used as weapons), and introducing strict lock-out laws where entry to bars was forbidden after 1:30am.

All of these interventions aim to reduce the risk of young, drunk people getting more drunk, fighting and using whatever is at hand to hurt each other. It sounds logical enough, but there are considerable limitations in this response. Many of the restrictions punitively target the physical environment of the clubs and bars, when much of the violence happens out on the streets. Additionally, they penalize everyone who goes to Kings Cross, rather than targeting the small number of people who either start out or end up as troublemakers.

At the same time as the state government was working on this risk management response, Designing Out Crime was working on a project with the City of Sydney Council to rethink the overall approach to managing King Cross at night.

The team did 'field research' and what they saw wasn't 30,000 delinquents looking for a fight in a cesspool of antisocial and illegal activity, but a very large number of young people trying (and often failing) to enjoy themselves in a fairly unique and exciting place.

The team reformulated the problem from an issue of violence, to a question of how to grow up, have fun, explore and form identity – in public. This reformulation led to a new approach to the problems of Kings Cross.

Thousands of young people converging in one place to have a good time is well-trodden ground; it is the core business of music festivals, dozens of which are held in Sydney each year. Like Kings Cross, music festivals are also at risk of alcohol and crowd-fueled problems, but festival organizers have evolved a sophisticated discipline of event management that aims to anticipate problems and manage them in a positive, non-antagonistic way.

The team investigated the tried and tested practices of music festival organizers and found a great many that could be applied to Kings Cross, including introducing precinct ambassadors (friendly young people in branded t-shirts); bringing in temporary public toilets and a managed taxi stand; converting lane-ways into lounge and recreation areas to take pressure off the main streets; installing bright and graphic transport and way-finding signs; programming cultural attractions such as public art and urban sports; and creating a 'safe space' where people can go for information, first aid and general help on a night out.

These ideas were well received and many were implemented. But beyond these interventions and the great number of yet-unexplored possibilities, the project helped the City of Sydney to re-imagine its own role at Kings Cross. In the words of Suzie Matthews, who was at this time manager of the Safe City team at council: "We stopped asking how we could prevent alcohol-fueled violence and started asking: how can we create a vibrant night-time economy?"

The response to this radical re-framing was the establishment of the 'Late Night Economy' team at the City of Sydney, and the formulation of a comprehensive strategy document, Open Sydney, which aims to create a diverse nightlife throughout the city.

The NSW Government now has a 24-hour Economy Commissioner who is responsible for creating a vibrant night-time economy across the state, and joins what has become a global movement with more than 40 cities across the world adopting this thinking.

In all, the Designing Out Crime project portfolio has grown to hundreds of interventions, big and small. They have helped convene a broad array of stakeholders around sophisticated approaches to safety in society. Many of the project outputs have been implemented, creating real-life impact and showing everybody involved how the field of criminal justice can be shifted towards practices that better serve society.

LICENSE TO DRIVE

Every year in Australia, a number of people go to prison for being caught driving without a license, and not paying the ensuing fines. At first glance this may seem fair enough -after all, driving without a license implies driving without ability or skill, which sounds like a dangerous thing to do. But scratch the surface, just a little, and it becomes clear that people are going to prison not because they can't drive (they can!), but because getting a license is prohibitively expensive and requires navigating what could be experienced as an impenetrable and hostile bureaucracy.

In the remote areas of Australia it is possible to drive for hours without seeing another vehicle. These are places where public transport is non-existent and essential services (food, health) can be hundreds of kilometers away. The people who live here - mostly Aboriginal people - learn to drive however they can, in whatever vehicle is available, because they just have no alternative.

In 2013 this issue was selected as a case study for a government educational program to re-frame a societal problem. The challenge was

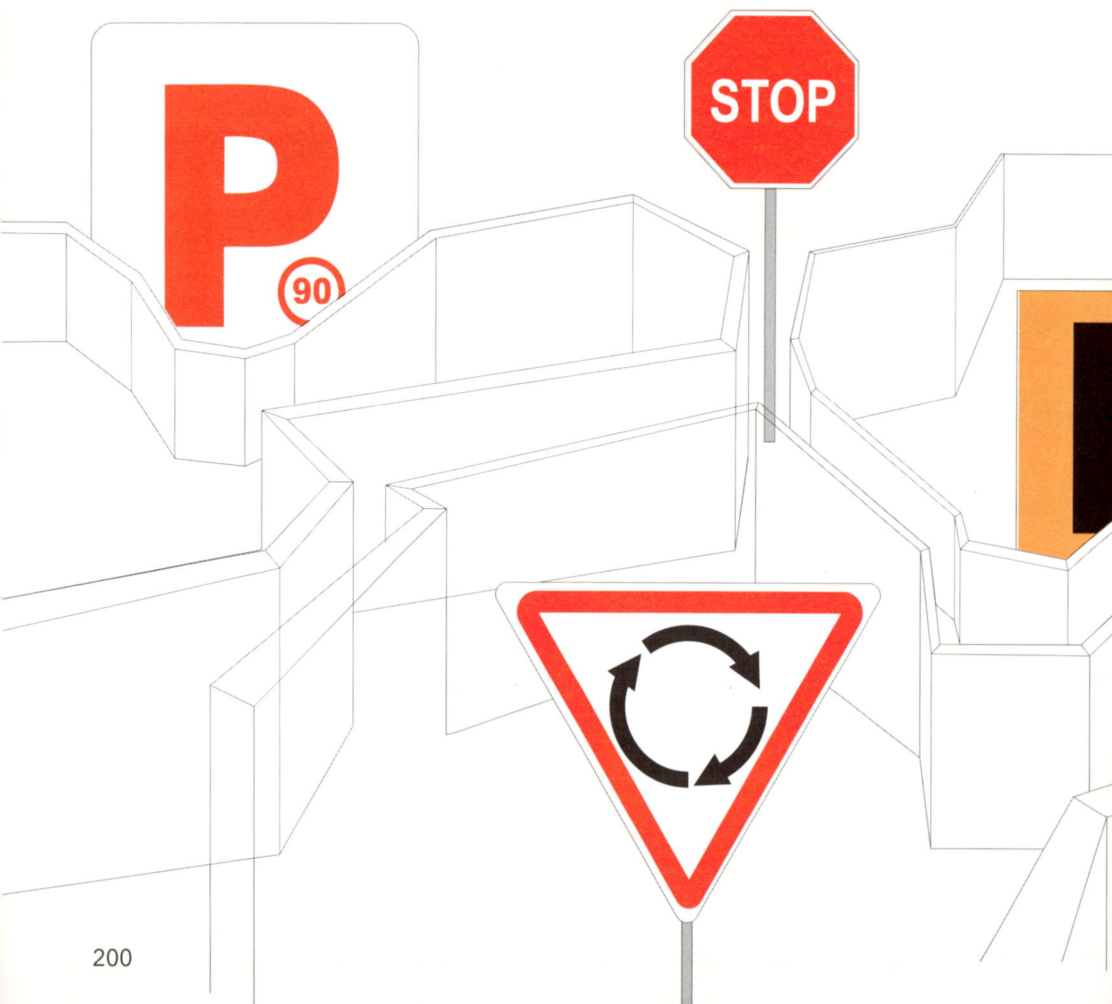

to reduce the significant number of Aboriginal people going to prison for unlicensed driving. The Designing Out Crime team began by mapping the process that a person must follow to obtain a driver's license. Major milestones were identified, as were the assets and skills required to pass each milestone, such as money, access to a registered car, a licensed adult to be a teacher in the first stage of supervised driving, English literacy to take the tests, and so on. Many of these hurdles are clearly insurmountable obstacles in these remote contexts. Next, interview data - anecdotes from Aboriginal people with experience in driving without a license and the ensuing court processes - were overlaid onto a large process map, highlighting the obstacles and pain points for the students to gather around and talk. This revealed that the licensing process is incredibly long and costly, and while it is well engineered to test compliance with administrative procedures, it is poorly designed to test a person's true driving skill. What's more, the perverse situation where a parent is consistently fined for unlicensed driving while bringing her children to school, or bringing an elderly community member to the doctor, is intolerable.

The stream of intervention ideas that followed moved away from focusing on improving the bureaucratic procedures in favor of helping these communities to meet their transport needs (a car and driver sharing system, for example). Small but significant projects like this - in which a government designs for people - will help to create a more equal society where people aren't unnecessarily imprisoned.

GETTING A LICENSE

BARRIER:

Unlicensed driving is the norm: feel they can avoid detection

'Yeah, I just take the back roads, plus the cops are like clockwork. I drive when I think they aren't patrolling'

female, 22 years, regional

BARRIER:

Feeling uncomfortable at RTA motor registry

'Having a black fella coming out would make it a lot easier and that and they explain it good'

male, 52 years, remote

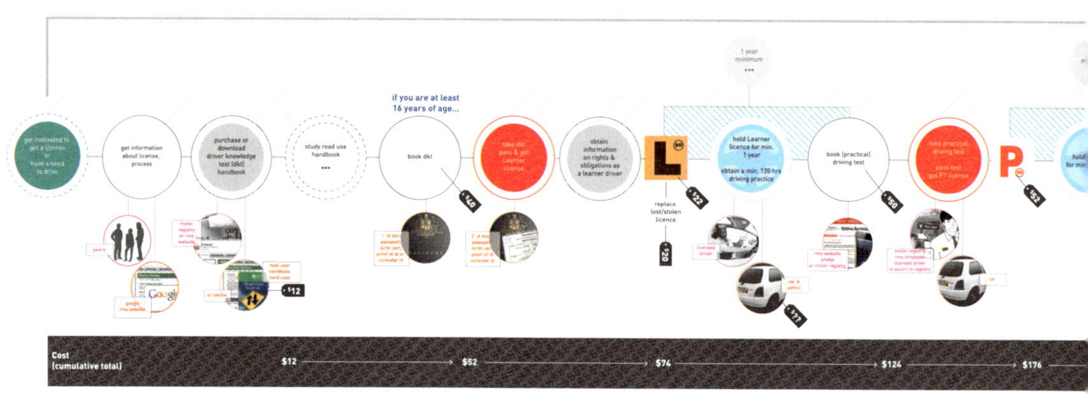

BARRIER:

Financial barrier to afford multiple tests

'They used to have a program on that RTA computer for people to test their knowledge and stuff. But no-one uses it because they think it's a waste of time and money because they can't afford to go through the L's and green P's and red P's'

male, 39 years, urban

BARRIER:

Literacy difficulties

'I'd get one [a license] but I can't read. I can drive good but that test is shit.'

male, 17 years, urban

BARRIER:

Lack of registered vehicles for practice

'I'd say there's only three people with a license here in this community. And two of them are on their P's'

female, 36 years, remote

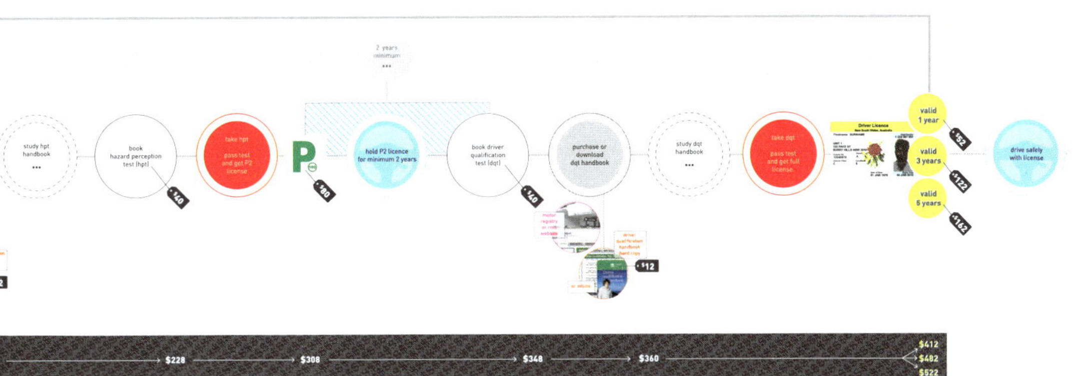

BARRIER:

Lack of registered vehicles for practice

'Yeah right! How many Kooris you know who got a license and will let you drive it. Unless you drive them home when they're pissed you never get a run'

male, 17 years, urban

THINKING INSIDE THE BOX

Based on a text and a project led by Rohan Lulham.

Prisons make prisoners. It's alarming, but true: the single biggest risk factor for ending up in jail is having been to jail in the first place. Rates of recidivism (re-offending) among prisoners are estimated at around 80%; that is, as many as four in five prisoners can be expected to re-offend upon release.

Another significant predictor of criminal behavior and subsequent incarceration is a lack of educational and employment opportunities. The overwhelming majority of assessed (male) inmates in Australian prisons have reading, writing and numeracy skills well below expected adult levels. Put differently, educational attainment among the prison population falls drastically short of the minimum standard required for opportunity, self-determination and meaningful participation in society.

These statistics alone predict a fairly bleak trajectory for prisoners, not to mention the broader society that suffers when further crimes are committed. Preventing offending in the first instance and re-offending in the second has therefore been a priority for government in recent years.

In 2012 the NSW Government wrote an inspired brief to build an 'Intensive Learning Center' in a maximum-security prison. The brief envisioned a place where educators and up to 40 inmate learners would engage in project-based learning, using twenty-first century technology within a supportive, therapeutic environment. The intention was to provide high-risk inmates with an opportunity to gain new knowledge and skills and greater confidence in their abilities, making them more employable upon release as well as better prepared to complete prison programs that treat the causes of their offending. In this way, the government aims to break the cycle of recidivism.

Typical prison architecture and design seeks to separate, contain and restrict. The government knew this to be incompatible with effective learning, but did not have the internal expertise to design an environment that would transcend the prison walls and promote interaction, transformation and aspiration. Designing Out Crime was approached for the job.

The research process, which was immediately recognized by participants as unusually (and pleasantly) inclusive, included talking extensively with prison staff, management and inmates to understand the needs and harvest the experience, skills and knowledge of each. The resulting program space and philosophy reflected this diversity of input and the freedom inherent to this process.

Interpretive and visioning devices such as themes and metaphors were widely used in the project, both to design and to communicate ideas. A defining value was 'connection', which referenced the aspiration for inmates to (re) connect with family, friends, workplaces and society more broadly through education, work experience and personal growth. A powerful metaphor for connection was the 'cloud' metaphor, which referred to the way in which clouds traverse the territory of the sky, and how the same cloud that is seen by inmates can, moments or minutes later, be seen by people 'on the outside'. This metaphor also referenced cloud technology and the idea of universal and ubiquitous knowledge that is not place-bound.

The cloud metaphor was expressed in the design of the classroom roof, which is curved and slopes gently upwards at one end, to give learners a view to the clouds. The metaphor and its manifestation in the physical design was particularly appreciated by the inmates, one of whom subsequently declared that he wanted to become an architect.

The final designs were constructed by inmates and hoisted over the fence at the maximum-security facility. The first cohort of inmate learners graduated in December 2014, following an official opening by the Attorney General. It was a celebration of achievement and the promise of opportunity, aspiration and transformation that is rarely seen within a prison environment. In this learning environment, the inmates are given the chance to imagine the new and different life they might lead when they are back in society.

4.3

THE ART OF CARING: CREATIVITY AT THE HEART OF HEALTHCARE TRANSFORMATION

Barbara Doran

Most healthcare systems, with best-intentions, are built for clinical encounters. But people spend most of their time outside that frame, navigating, managing, and coping with their conditions in everyday spaces. That's where creative knowledge translation comes in. A quiet transformation is unfolding in healthcare, one that draws on the power of art, story, and community to connect, inform, and transform. It's not about adding another layer to an overstretched system; it's about working differently, creatively, and with care. These approaches center lived experience and shared meaning, bringing together artists, researchers, clinicians, and community members to co-design responses that can be practically and meaningfully grounded.

A group of practitioners have created a vehicle to embody this ethos in the SPHERE Knowledge Translation Platform, part of the Sydney Partnership for Health Education Research and Enterprise, also known by its Aboriginal name, Maridulu Budyari Gamul, meaning "working together for overall wellbeing." SPHERE's vision is reach beyond systemic dis-juncture and to build health networks where knowledge flows in many directions, between clinical expertise, lived experience, cultural insight, and creative expression.

One such example began with a question: what happens after the appointment ends?

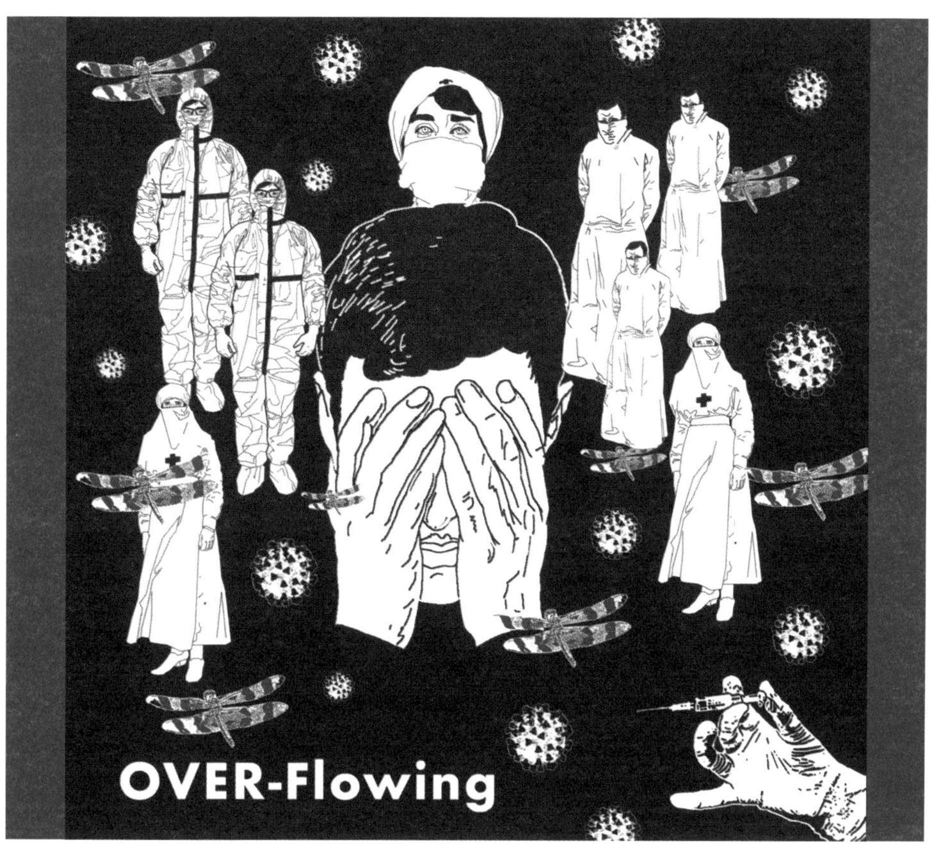

A family finds themselves with a tiny baby who struggles to feed. Weeks turn into months of uncertainty. There are specialists, check-ups, and clinical charts, no clear diagnosis and the child isn't thriving. Finally, a paediatrician introduces tube feeding. It's life-saving and requires carers to learn this mechanical skill. But it's also the beginning of another story: one of home bounded routines, two-hour feeds, and social and emotional isolation. Another world beyond the hospital door opens up, and it's one that healthcare isn't often equipped to navigate.

Paediatrician Dr. Chris Elliot recognized this space not as a failure of medicine, but as an opportunity for care. He created a support network for families navigating tube feeding and complex care. Beyond clinical coordination, he sought ways to honor the often invisible labor of carers. Through collaboration with the SPHERE artist-in-residence program and a photographer, a portrait exhibition of mothers and their children was created, shining a light beyond policy documents and research papers. These images offer a different form of connection, reaching others on similar journeys and acknowledging the stoic commitment of carers with a quiet affirmation; "We see you."

This scenario is one of many that catalyzed what would become known as Succeed - a co-designed project that extended this work further. It recognized that for many families, technical instructions alone are not enough. Succeed brought together healthcare providers, families, and artists to create resources that were not only went beyond the clinical encounters, fostering emotionally attuned communities.

The artist-in-residence program is one way this vision takes form. Artists are embedded in research projects as collaborators helping to surface unseen stories and co-creating new ways of seeing, doing, and understanding. They work across diverse art mediums and communities, listen deeply, and translate complex narratives into forms that resonate emotionally and relationally. These collaborations have sparked a series of transformative projects, each grounded in the SPHERE's wider commitment to working creatively within health contexts. Topsy Turvey and Stitch it for Dementia are other examples that span health care continuum.

TOPSY TURVY

During the early days of the COVID-19 pandemic, the program was invited to collaborate with healthcare leaders to help surface their experiences. What emerged was a powerful blend of vulnerability and expertise, revealing leaders as people with families, navigating the same uncertainties as those they served. These insights were translated into an interactive exhibition "Topsy Turvy", that reached clinicians, patients, and families alike, becoming a living space for shared storytelling. Audiences engaged in exploring the disorientation, resilience, and intimacy of crisis. The resulting installation became both archive and sanctuary, holding the dual tensions of care and loss, creativity and anxiety, community and uncertainty.

STITCH IT FOR DEMENTIA: CRAFTING CONNECTION

In Stitch It for Dementia, people with dementia, their families, and community members came together to create textile works that held memory, identity, and presence. Interestingly, most people didn't come with sewing or textile skills but the medium was collectively agreed as somehow accessible. The act of stitching became a form of expression, advocacy, community and visibility. Displayed in hospitals and public spaces, the works sparked new conversations about aging, care, and what it means to remember.

Each project shares a common thread: care as a relational, creative act.

These initiatives are indicators of a broader shift. As Professor Catherine Boydell notes;

"The time is ripe for thinking about how we bring arts and science together in meaningful ways. There is now a robust evidence base for this work, with measurable improvements in mental health, physical outcomes, and health system responsiveness. But the most enduring impact may be cultural".

These projects foster trust, dismantle stigma, and build communities of action.

They also move knowledge. Research no longer stays locked in journals or echo chambers, it circulates. It travels across hospital walls, into family kitchens, community halls, and waiting rooms. Feedback loops shorten. Practices shift. People feel seen, heard, and supported. And importantly, the notorious 17-year gap between research and implementation begins to shrink.

This is what transformation can look like - not necessarily grand restructures, but quiet, consistent shifts in how we value knowledge, creativity, and connection. The arts bring nuance to complexity. They help us sit with contradiction, explore ambiguity, and name what data alone cannot. They offer a language for what we feel and often struggle to express, inviting diverse voices to join the conversation.

As healthcare systems face increasing challenges, from chronic disease and aging populations to mental health crises and widening inequities, the case for creative approaches is clear. They aren't "add-ons" or soft options. They are cost-effective, human-centered strategies rooted in ethics and care.

SO WHAT'S DIFFERENT?

Silent stories have been shared. New relationships have formed. Research has been shaped by the people it seeks to serve. Public health messages have become more human, more relatable. Creative practice is moving from the edges to the center. This work is growing. But it still needs champions, people who will hold the line, nurture connection, and protect these spaces when the system has erased the person and personal. This is the work of culture change, of reclaiming creativity, ethics, and care as fundamentals in reshaping healthcare one story, one stitch, one movement at a time.

4.4

CASE: THE NITROGEN CRISIS

Kees Dorst and André Schaminée

In the late 2010's the Dutch government was involved in a lengthy court battle about Nitrogen Pollution. The Netherlands is a signatory to the Paris Climate Agreement, and the lawyers from an activist NGO took the state to court over failing to protect designated nature reserves (designated as such under the EU Natura 2000 rules) from Nitrogen pollution. Nitrogen oxide emissions mostly come from transport, building works and agriculture (about 45%).

Nitrogen acts as a powerful fertilizer, dramatically altering the soil, and thereby also the flora and fauna in nature reserves - which, the lawyers argued, is not allowed. In the end, the protracted legal process came before the country's High Court, and in March 2019 the court ruled in favor of the NGO, rendering the government in breach of the law. This ruling came into force immediately, and had huge repercussions all through society: (1) to reduce the emissions from transport, the Dutch government reduced the maximum speed on the highways from 130 to 100 km/h. (2) About 18,000 ongoing building works (close to the nature reserves) were ruled in breach of regulations and had to be stopped, immediately. (3) The ruling impacted agriculture more than any other sector: many farms would now have to stop or radically change their practices to cut their Nitrogen emissions. Farmers were up in arms, and marched to The Hague to protest in front of the Dutch parliament - and they came on thousands of tractors, effectively blocking traffic in the whole country for days, week after week.

The Dutch ministry that was at the center of this crisis, the Department of Agriculture, Nature and Food Safety (LNV), enlisted André Schaminée and his team from the consultancy TwynstraGudde to look into this matter. Their approach to both understanding the problem situation and creating proposals for ways forward was largely based on the methodologies in this book.

They started out by doing about 60 interviews with various stakeholders from across the problem arena. This led to the identification of 4 main paradoxes: (1) It is a zero-sum game, (2) It is not clear who we are listening to (3) The farmers are the victim of government policy failures (4) the value-models and value discussion are not sufficient, (there were more paradoxes, but these four cover the problem arena well enough for the purposes of this book). To elaborate:

1 - It is a zero-sum game

The discussion is stuck in an either-or-pattern (a piece of land is either 'nature' or 'agriculture'), there is only conflict, and no room for dialogue. This lack of a basis for dialogue is exacerbated by the fact that Nature and Agriculture both have their own value and meaning, but that these are of a very different kind. A possible solution lies in transitioning to a new type of nature-inclusive agriculture. This is not a small step either, adopting such a different paradigm requires new practices and a reconsidering of deeply held values (what it is to be a 'good' farmer). It is much easier for both parties to stick to their positions and not move.

2 - It is not clear who we are listening to

There is a suggestion that the farmers are united, as they have organized themselves in cooperatives. Some of these organizations represent 'the farmer' in government committees. But do they represent 'the farmer'? This uncertainty leads to extreme standpoints and political posturing to reassure their members that they are fighting the good fight. Yet the crisis at hand will only be resolved when all parties are ready to offer considerable compromises.

3 - The farmers are the victim of government policy failures

While the farmers blame 'the Greens' for the Nitrogen crisis (despite the Green Party never having been in power), the more farmer-friendly political parties whose policies over the years have actually led to this crisis are not questioned. While the sector 'wants clarity from the government' and complains about 'going from crisis to crisis', there is very little appetite to look forward.

4 - The value-models and value discussion are not sufficient

While a change in agricultural practices is the only viable option, there is no clear path of action for the farmer - economically, this could only work if there is a structurally higher price level for high-quality food. Because there is no economic value to nature, the only thing that gets counted in economic terms is 'a loss of food production', not what everybody would gain from biodiversity in a natural landscape.

These four paradoxes on the relationship between Nature and Agriculture have been exacerbated by the lack of connection between the layers of the problem arena (spanning the world of policy, the systems world, the lifeworld of citizens and the biosphere - see Figure 4.4.

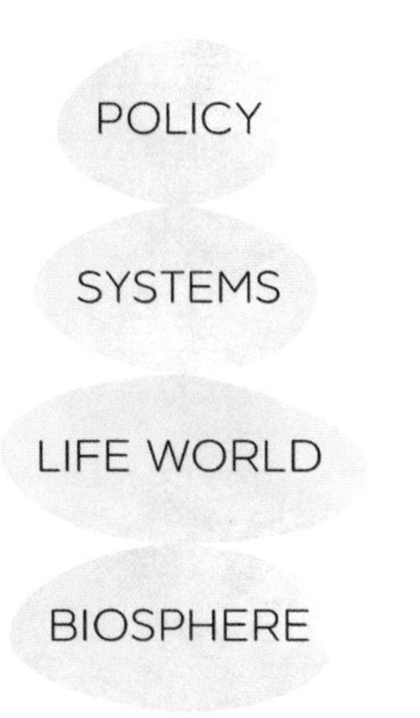

Figure 4.4 Layers of the problem arena

These layers all have their own scale, dynamics, timelines, history and way of addressing the future. And they are mostly disconnected, as 'worlds to themselves'. For example: the timeline for substantially changing the Biosphere (have plants change the soil) takes about 50-70 years. In the lifeworld of the farmers, generations are important hence the relevant timeline is 20-30 years. In the world of systems and organizations, the horizon is often not more than 2-5 years, often substantially less. And in the world of Policy, there have been continuous changes in the rules of the game as the government is struggling to influence the sector. The system is badly out of sync.

Underlying themes that emerged in the frame creation sessions centered around notions of Mastery (relationship with the world), Identity (relationship with self and your peers) and Vitality (relationship with the future). These led to a very rich collection of possible Frames. Just one example here: one could create 'Fields of Freedom', pieces of land that are given in shared stewardship to farmers and nature conservationist to run together. In complete freedom, but it has to be productive, and have nature value. In doing so, the two parties will have to sit together and learn from one another, creating new mastery in their professional fields. This is crucial: in the long run, the field will only change once the education of farmers and biologists will also move towards this new, hybrid sense of mastery (for more frames see [Dorst, 2025] and [Dorst and Schaminée, 2024]).

Such frames are not separate projects or experiments; the trick (art) is to position these frames along the learning cycle. This creates a structure for an ongoing change process, rather than a single activity (a 'project' or 'a pilot'). In adopting this common learning cycle we have moved away from doing a project to 'fix' the nitrogen crisis to laying the foundations for an innovation infrastructure. This infrastructure in itself is the key outcome of the whole program - it can be harnessed to approach current challenge (Nitrogen), but it is needed to deal with upcoming issues like (1) drought in the east of the country, (2) salination of the soil in the west of the country, (3) the long-term viability of low-lying areas (4) and the surface water quality crisis, just to name four of the main crises that are going to become reality in the foreseeable future.

4.5

CASE: BIODIVERSITY AND THE CITY

Kees Dorst

Cities were always built for people, very much as the antithesis to nature - the very essence of a city was to take people away from nature. Now we are at the point where the growth and growing density of cities is a threat to biodiversity worldwide. The challenge is to re-create a city as a biosphere, an ecosystem of people, plants and animals - could a city be re-imagined as a thriving ecosystem, a source of biodiversity, even of food?

Taken seriously, this requires a complete rethink of what a city is. Pioneering municipalities are leading the way, developing plans for execution and monitoring of the greening of the city, but often there is not much enthusiasm or support from the citizens. The abstract nature of the notion of 'biodiversity' doesn't help, it doesn't really conjure up much of an image (let alone an attractive one) and the timescales for change are much longer than what people are used to dealing with in their everyday lives. Yet of the outdoor spaces in a city, about 60% is privately owned. And if we then add balconies, roofs - there is a lot to gain in making these less barren and turn them into a fertile environment for people, plants, bees and other insects, the neighborhood.

If we really want to make a difference in biodiversity and climate adaptation, getting the people on board is absolutely crucial. This provides a classic 'top-down AND bottom-up' problem arena (see §2.4); both these movements should happen in parallel and be synchronized. But how can we support people to take initiatives that increase the biodiversity and livability of the city? And how can we then show that small bottom-up initiatives actually do contribute to the bigger (often quite abstract) goals?

This is where technology might be helpful, in two ways: (1) technology can help people by providing information and advice in shaping their initiatives, helping them decide on what to do, and (2) a network of small and cheap sensors can provide real-time data to show progress on the large-scale goals (this helps provide the rationale for the municipality to support small-scale local initiatives).

In the City of Rotterdam, a startup called Bioto has developed a sensor technology (a 'plant listener') that measures the quality of the soil, air, etc. as well as an accompanying database that provides the know how to create clever combinations of plants that help each other grow, attract insects and protection against pests. Crucially, the collective data from these sensors is used to inform local and city-wide policy-development, creating feedback loops that tracks the impact of all interventions, big and small (e.g. on micro-climates) as a contribution to climate adaptation. The 'technical' learning loop of the sensors and database of observations needs to be in sync with people coming together in the social learning loop - the overall city biosphere can only thrive when these are in balance.

A great opportunity to prototype and experiment with this new approach presents itself in Oud Mathenesse, a typical late nineteenth century neighborhood in the city of Rotterdam - in the coming years, all drains will have to be renewed, and to stay dry the whole area needs to be raised by adding soil. This creates pretty much a blank slate as far as the public spaces and private gardens are concerned; everything will have to be redone. And it creates an urgency to think this through now. Social designers from Bioto used a mobile tea-stall to get into contact with the people of the neighborhood, creating with them an 'energy and opportunity map' that pinpoints areas where there is local commitment and a good opportunity to create a bio-diverse environment. And then build from there.

To re-create our cities, from the stone deserts we have today to an oasis for the next generation, we need to move far beyond isolated initiatives, think in timelines that go beyond the policy cycle. All of this is hard, but it can be done as long as we decide that the current cities are not fit for purpose anymore, and that it ends with us.

The strategic focus then shifts from convincing the incumbents to looking to the future, envisioning where the vitality of our cities is going to come from. Then it is only a small logical step to realize that biodiversity should permeate everything. As Riel Miller (UNESCO) argues; all decisions taken now should be seen in the light of the future they lead to.

We need to take charge of future challenges.

4.6

TAKING CHARGE OF FUTURE CHALLENGES

Kees Dorst and Rodger Watson

We are facing huge (and parallel) transitions in the coming years. Overwhelming changes are coming to the way we deal with resources like energy and water, and how we approach care, mobility, education, healthcare and economic thriving. These transitions require us to go beyond fixing a sector or system, they require a complete reinvention of how we live. We have no choice. But what does that mean?

Three key points:

1. These transitions are truly complex because they all combine several developments: technological, economic, organizational, social, cultural and personal. For a transition to be successful, all of these developments need to happen at once, and in concert with one another. So these very different spheres of human endeavor have to be brought together and connected in a process of co-evolution. In practice, this means we need to ensure the human/social side of transitions doesn't get overshadowed by the technical and economic drivers.
2. This is doubly important because transitions are not happening one-by-one, they are all occurring simultaneously over the next decade. There is a real risk that in all of these transitions, the same people will be left out. This could lead to increasing vulnerability and deepening schisms in society (while we are all as vulnerable as the most vulnerable people in our community). We cannot allow this to happen. Inclusivity is not a luxury, or a nice word to use in a policy document, it is key.
3. Transitions are happening at speed. They are fast, outpacing the normal rate in which our organizations and institutions evolve. When they do this, they become revolutions. In particular, the breakneck speed of technological developments and the urgent need for sustainability outpace the social (economical), organizational, cultural and personal development needed.

Transitions should be dealt with in a connected way, and their shifting goalposts require a flexible, co-evolutionary approach - whether they are originally sustainability driven, technology driven, socially driven or economically driven, they will need to be all at the same time. Traditionally, industrial transitions (like in Newcastle, see §3.19) would be driven by technological and economic development, and people's lives and society would be left to deal with the impact (with the City of Detroit as an example that comes to mind). This will not do. If a transition doesn't work for society, in the lifeworld of people, it doesn't work at all.

The Taking Charge of Future Challenges program is set up from a University environment to create balanced transitions. It takes an 'Open-Innovation' approach, working with communities, enterprise and institutions to navigate societal transitions towards broad prosperity: to create transitions that are balanced, open, just, and fair.

With four distinct functions, the program provides a platform for focused impact through end to end integration of research, teaching and learning:

1. Deliberate and purposeful exploration of the societal transitions that are coming through wide-ranging discussions, drawing on international partners, identifying and prioritizing areas of collective focus.

   Activities include: convening strategic partners and knowledge and expertise, engagement in public narrative, (current) paradigm mapping.

2. Framing Future Research curates and convenes multiple Strategic Partners and leading expertise to collaboratively frame a portfolio of research and action.

   Activities include: multiple stakeholder framing workshops, insights reports including re-framing of initial challenge, pilot concepts, research questions/ opportunities.

3. A portfolio of action and research is developed and implemented by program participants (Partners and University faculties). Taking Charge of Future Challenges creates a space for reflection in and on action for the Research and Probes. Fostering a community of practice where research projects and probes are part of a community of mutual learning and cultivating teams of teams.

   Activities include: development of research questions and probes, support in accessing resources, quarterly workshops to share insights across research projects and probes, annual report.

4. Capability building based on new knowledge. Insights drawn from the research and probes are then disseminated into capability frameworks. Sectors build new capabilities, and the cycle continues.

   Activities include: Short Forms of Learning, Special Issue Journals, Edited sector focused books, media, hosted industry conferences highlighting impact. This step is a crucial one, it is where the new vocabulary within the sector flips the paradigm.

This is one of those things that is harder to do small. Key to the Taking Charge of Future Challenges program is to have these running in several sectors/ societal domains in parallel, so that the pioneers involved can actually become fellow travelers. For instance; it is crucial for people planning the physical infrastructure (roads etc. - with a long lead time to design and build, and a use time of decades) not to concentrate on the current needs, but have a keen idea of the future needs of society in a region. Who will be the people that will be populating a certain region (say, the Hunter Valley) in 20 years time? What will their needs be? And how do the pioneers in sectors like Education and Care think their sectors will operate by then? What repercussions will that have for infrastructure decisions we are taking now?

CHAPTER 5

NEXT GENERATION STRATEGIC INNOVATION LEADERS

5.1

THE HUMANITY OF IT ALL

The models we have introduced earlier in the book look quite skeletal - and that is not surprising; they are very much the backbone of the new strategic innovation practices. With the methods, tools and the practices that are embedded in the cases we have started to put some flesh on the bones. We hope the reader finds these useful in their own work. But this is all about 'doing' - what we haven't touched upon yet is possibly the most important point of all; the underlying mentality. People make change by 'being' inspirational, by bringing their personal magic to the problem situation.

In that sense, this book has perhaps been too technocratic; if change isn't personal, it isn't real. We need to give the floor to the personal stories of commitment, growth and transformation. Something powerful can happen when people really start to deframe the problem situations they find themselves in. They find a new freedom of thought, coupled with a deep realism - knowing 'what this is really about' is both liberating and comes with the undeniable responsibility to then act upon that knowledge. This sets them on a path to fearless action and a special kind of leadership. You come to it, because you have to.

The following vignettes are small snapshots of fellow travelers who have also embraced the challenge.

ANDREW TRIEU

Andrew works as a change manager across a range of sectors. He has been developing his thinking on the use of metaphor and building that into his practice. By framing an organization, or sector through metaphor, Andrew creates a space for opening up assumptions that have become set in the sector. While at first the metaphors can feel abstract, it is through looking at an organization, or a sector "as if it was" that concrete insights begin to emerge.

"The Circle of life symbolizes the universe being sacred and divine. It represents the infinite nature of energy. If something dies it gives new life to another. This spiritual meaning of the circle represents a divine life form, or spirit that keeps our reality in motion.

It is symbolic of vitality, wholeness, completion and perfection. The meaning of shapes and symbols meet us when we are ready to listen and learn. The circle at its core is about relationships, harmony and unity."

Within organizational change management there is a constant tension of managing different perspectives, while building capability and capacity towards desired futures. Within Andrew's practice, the use of metaphor has become increasingly fruitful, and central to his practice. Reflecting on his work in the care sector, Andrew brought together the Circle of Life and the Waterhole metaphors to create space for creative discussion within his organization.

"The Circle of Life and the Waterhole make a creative conceptual space to reflect on how our sector creates 'vitality' and 'relationships'. In the lived world situation of an African Waterhole, diverse species have come to learn to migrate to the waterhole at a particular moment. Natural predators and symbiotic animals transcend to this special place for various significant rituals; to quench their thirst, to mate, to prepare for end of life.

Take for example a herd of elephants, the act of migrating to the waterhole is part of developing memory loops to the baby elephant. A flock of birds is able to travel significant distances, sometimes across continents to congregate to a specific waterhole.

If we flip this context of the waterhole back to an organizational change management context, we begin to ask: Why are we here? What is our purpose? What is the change, and why are we changing?

This may be representative of the 'water' as a boundary object in the waterhole landscape. Who are the stakeholders? What relationships do they hold? What tensions exist? How can they collaborate? What can they contribute?

This may be representative of the 'different species'. What are the behaviors that we want to sustain and embed? What is the culture we want to shape and form? This may be representative of the invisible forces that signal the activation of migration to the waterhole and how we behave at the waterhole and the rituals that take place along and during the journey.

Does the waterhole represent and symbolize Care? Care for self, the herd and the offspring? If so, who are we caring for? How do we care? Why do we care?"

CARL HEISE

Business architecture can be a relatively abstract concept. For Carl, a leader within a large transport agency, helping people to understand business architecture so that they could then engage in the process was an important first challenge. Carl drew on his history as a High-school drama teacher, where he worked with students to stage many live performances. He also drew on framing tools, to create a space where people in his team, and in his organization could collaboratively build the business architecture function.

Carl playfully framed business architecture as if it were the film score of Star Wars. In creating this conceptual space, people in the organization were invited to see the various functions within the organization as elements of the film score. "We wanted to create something to bring the pieces together and make music. Music can help lift us to an aspirational state. The metaphor helped people see the organizational 'jigsaw' pieces as a 'musical score'. This helped us to facilitate the conversations, starting with a shared language to bring the 'musical score' to life."

The abstraction of the business architecture function into a film score opened the space for people to see themselves as being part of a complex system. "If we look at ourselves as a cross-functional musical team we can see that the connected parts of the systems are formed for a particular purpose. In a film score there is a vision and a purpose, with various viewpoints of this vision. There are many parts to the score, and not every instrument plays the same notes, or at the same time."

Looking at a large organization as if it is a film score then invites people to see the performance of the score, as the running of the organization. There are many roles within a film score, and within the performance of the score. "The score gives us a method to communicate the when, how, and why, conducting the purpose through the system. The conductor needs to work with experts, and make the whole bigger and better."

Having created the space for discussion Carl and his team then used the space to collaboratively build and position their function within the organization.

"Architecture is the building plan. This plan then shows us what we need to see, from each of the relevant viewpoints. It articulates the purposes and perspectives across the organization. It also creates business assets that can be used, reused and scaled. The architecture can then also be seen as building blocks." Having created this conversation Carl and his team then set about building a shared understand how quality is defined within the organization. This then provides the opportunity to have important discussions like "how do we know if a change is an improvement?"

"We want to build a culture that engages people in the process of continuous improvement and models and maintains business knowledge."

LEE WALLACE

"Rape and sexualized assault are under-reported." These seven words, put together in this certain way make a statement that is as undeniable as it is complex. We've become accustomed to crime being solved. Our prisons have never been fuller. So why are we worried about rape? Lee took her decades of experience in policy and innovation and focused on this question. Victim-survivors are often silenced by perpetrators, or the systems that are meant to protect them. Silence comes from a real fear that they will not be believed or will be victim-blamed further adding to barriers to engage with the system. They're described as wearing the wrong clothes, or drinking too much and so the blame is on them. Silence is normalized in the community as it is an uncomfortable conversation that most would rather ignore. This silence allows for the emergence of a cultural acceptance of rape and violence."

Lee used some new tools to make sense of this and in so doing re-framed the issue. "I used Movement Mapping to visually represent the national reporting and conviction rates of rape and sexualized assault. I took time to think about it and make a graph. I put rates on the Y-axis and reporting and convictions on the X-axis. I was using colored pencils that are soft and a little crumbly, which allowed 'broad' marks to fill the space in each column quickly choosing different colors to differentiate columns made it easier to read and understand with a glance. Pondering what this last column might be, I quickly realized the common theme was trauma. And trauma was pervasive, reported or not, and whether there was a conviction. As I started to color, imagining an entire column of trauma representing 100 per cent, my coloring did not stop. The pervasiveness of trauma spread as I colored above reporting, unreported and convictions columns. It did not stop there. I colored above and below, completing every uncolored space, driving home that trauma was pervasive of the whole civic and justice ecosystems. The act of coloring revealed the extent of the trauma. My physical body did the work, and I saw the result on the page in front of me."

What difference did it make?

If the system can't deal with it, then we need a new system. The current system is failing. It's not just that it isn't working to achieve justice, it is perpetuating the trauma and contributing to its own failure to uphold justice.

In reaching this insight Lee has shifted her thinking from being bounded within the current system. The current criminal justice systems weren't made with rape and sexualized violence in mind, or at least, not front of mind. We have many different types of courts that are purpose specific (Industrial, Children, Family, Criminal, Civil, etc.) what if we had a purpose made system for rape and sexualized violence? What kind of system would we need to shift from rape and sexualized violence being rarely reported, to making them rare?

JUSTINE HAUSER

Justine serves in the defense force and is accustomed to working in highly structured environments. In her profession, actions become like muscle memory. The actions all hang together in a broader process that achieves the tactical objectives of her team, her unit, and the broader defense force. Each action must be done right. It can be a life and death environment where precision is key.

As a parent Justine has been navigating a complex situation with her 6-year-old son G. G had fallen behind his peer group at school. He undertook a benchmarking test at the beginning of the year and scored 9%. He had become disengaged and had lost his curiosity. The test score helped the system jump into action. G took a number of medical tests and they helped explain why he was struggling to engage with school activities.

"G's ear drum is not moving to sound, he can hear but; it is like hearing under water and certain sounds are not heard correctly, mainly sh, ch, ish, ff sounds. He is also unable to track with his eyes without moving his head, this means that he physically exhausted by mid-morning after attempting his tasks." G was given glasses to help reduce the exhaustion, and Justine began working with him to reengage with his schoolwork. Justine drew on the thinking from §1.5.

"The first step was creating flow and play. I liked the idea of John Cleese's 'space for play' that will allow the 'open' mode mindset. I used toilet humor and gave G colored pencils and asked him to draw the toilet and what we might find in the toilet. It was hilarious and it got him to use pencils and draw. He also started telling me stories about how things end up in the toilet. I think when that happened we reached that space for play and an open mindset. Each week we came up a new environment and what we may find in it."

Justine used six types of exercises in engaging with G:

- Embracing creativity and playfulness.
- Probing - the art of exploring.
- Visualizing - tapping into the senses and how we communicate.
- Scale - traveling with time, space and materials.
- Conversations - becoming fluent with the obvious and not so obvious.
- Stories - the biology and magic of making sense together.

In the last week of the school term G scored 89% in the same benchmark test.

"I am not sure which interventions were the main driver of the dramatic change, but I would like to think that they all contributed - like vitamins in a system they have given G the health holistically to unlocking the written word.

All the teachers had noticed a dramatic change not just in his ability in reading and writing but in other areas, art and even sport. Also his willingness to participate and engage has increased as his confidence has grown. His curiosity is back, and we now have new tools to explore the world with."

DANIELLE HANDLEY

For the last 7 years, Dan has been a senior leader in the General Insurance and Healthcare sectors. Dan reflects on her journey and the models and tools in this book that have been useful in successfully navigating complex change.

"In the last 3 years I've moved from a leadership role in general insurance, to an executive role in a global health care company. My role has been focused on leading a major transition for the organization to shift from primarily being a health insurer to being a health carer with a wider range of services to meet our customers needs.

The thinking required to be a successful health insurer is different to the thinking required to be a successful healthcare provider. The organization has been a successful insurance business, and so recognizing a different approach would be needed to translate that same success into a new field required a significant shift. I found I could draw on the tools and models referenced in this book to help my peers and colleagues' step into a creative space and shift paradigm."

As we have seen in many of the cases, good leadership isn't about changing people, it is about helping them to draw on their own creativity to engage with the complexity that they and their organizations are facing. Dan's leadership was acknowledged in 2024 when she was named in the Australian Financial Review's Women in Leadership series as the Leader of the year in the Health Category.

"The key three developments of my practice that I've taken from the models and tools in the book are;

1. Navigating complexity: you could assume that general insurance and financial services have enough similarities to Health Insurance and thus shifting to Healthcare would be an obvious extension of the other. But healthcare is more complex. It is more fragmented, it's more personal, and definitely more emotional.

2. Taking a Systems View: Health is driven by so many elements, some of them genetic, some of them behavioral, some of them environmental, but caring for people is a whole of system challenge. There's public policy, private companies, pharma, education and a massive network of providers. Thinking about access, affordability, quality of care, and sustainable models requires collaboration and partnership across the sector from all the players.

3. Framing and re-framing: I've used this at a personal, corporate and systems level to understand how things are framed and to be able to bring people into the problem solving. As an executive around the leadership table and influencing change across the enterprise, it is about being reflective and learning how to observe, appreciate different perspectives, and facilitate peers and colleagues through the difficult process of re-framing.

I've found it useful to share the models and tools with my colleagues and teams as a way of creating space to invite in and welcome different perspectives to the complex challenges we are facing, and navigate pathways forward in a coherent and structured way."

5.2

LEADERSHIP

Who is (or who should be) the driver(s) of a systems change process? Who should take the lead, and what does leadership actually look like in this case? What is strategic innovation leadership?

The really big issues we are facing cross the boundaries we have set up between our organizations and professions... hence they can severely suffer from a lack of clear ownership, falling between the cracks of different institutions and organizations. If nobody feels enough responsibility to get to action, nothing happens. Societal shifts require a "societal midfield" between the domains of the Government, Public Sector, Private Enterprise and the Citizen. Strategic projects connecting the practices of these four societal domains in this Societal Midfield (Figure 5.2) will lead to the deep insights needed to create more open, dynamic and networked 'new world' practices between them, to tackle the big societal challenges.

This model is a useful lens to situate the case studies. We can conceive of projects that connect two or three of these domains but often there is a worrying gap in the middle, where a lot of the issues are so much everybody's problem ('common good') that they become nobody's problem in particular. Workshops that end in statements like: 'this is very important, somebody should really do this' have failed. The four societal domains need to engage in constructive dialogues with each other and change the way they operate. All four domains need to learn from one another in order to move to 'the middle'; (1) citizens need to organize themselves, (2) governments need to engage with less formal processes and rules to further experimentation with new approaches, (3) the public sector needs to open up its knowledge and its professionals and make those available to the other three, and (4) private enterprises need to engage with these developments, not only through providing tools and infrastructures, but also through accepting a more responsible role in society.

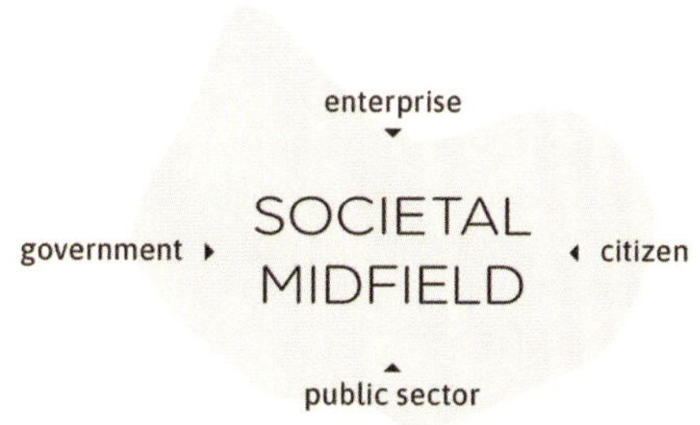

Figure 5.2 The societal midfield.

We have seen this is the case studies, in each of them strategic innovation leadership comes from stepping out of the 'standard' role of the organization in society and taking on a broader responsibility.

And this is not a closed ('blue' - planning and control) approach to leadership, but it is all about creating a space for supporting 'Open Innovation'. 'Open Innovation' is here interpreted as an attitude that seeks to expand the horizon of an organization by learning from other organizations, sectors, disciplines, and being generous in return. As we said before, this the natural (and ONLY) valid response to the open, complex, dynamic and networked problem situations we are facing.

Still, the idea of this radical openness, deliberately paying it forward with unsure returns, does go against the grain for many people - especially in times of change. In truly open innovation, there is very little basis for second-guessing what an eventual return might even look like: we will need to keep our expectations open for a long-term give and take cycle.

People in an organization need to feel the license and support from their leadership to explore and bring in practices that are further afield. In the Studio model, the Podium gives shape to open innovation by creating an open dialogue about the work that is being done, as seen through many perspectives. It is the locus where other disciplinary practices can be brought in, and transdisciplinarity can start to happen.

The hyper-complex nature of transitions demands this open, dynamic and flexible approach to navigate all the unknowns as the future unfolds.

This takes us away from more conventional/traditional views of leadership and management. This could be the start of a new profession, in its own right. What would the name be? A 'strategic innovation studio conductor'? A Strategic innovator? If this is a new profession, what would be the job ad for this role? (See Appendix 3)

How would you educate people in Creative Intelligence and Strategic Innovation?

5.3

EDUCATING STRATEGIC INNOVATORS

More than ten years ago together with colleagues, we designed a Creative Intelligence curriculum for the University of Technology Sydney, as a Bachelor degree. It is based on the model of Transdisciplinarity that is also used in this book: the learning in this degree is not about combining disciplines but becoming nimble in exchanging practices between them. After all, every discipline has a way to deal with complexity, create newness, etc that are all equally interesting. That is why the curriculum is presented as a double degree across all 27 disciplines of the University.

Students study in a regular faculty (Engineering, Business, Nursing, Design, etc.) and in summer schools and winter schools plus one year full-time at the end, they can add a second Bachelor degree. The curriculum included summer/winter school subjects like; Problems to Possibilities, Creative Practice and Methods, Past Present and Future of Innovation, Creativity and Complexity, Leading Innovation, Initiatives and Entrepreneurship, Envisioning Futures. Their final year is studio-based, in which students work together on long projects for partner organizations in subjects like Professional practice at the cutting edge, New knowledge making lab and Speculative startup. This undergraduate program was designed with Tanja Golja and Louise McWhinnie.

When this Bachelor program became a great success for the University, the inevitable question came to devise a Masters program in this same space. But Masters programs here are for mid-career professionals, so there was no way that a Masters could mirror the Bachelor curriculum.

We started from scratch, and in doing workshops with fifteen organizations we landed on a new model for the Master of Creative Intelligence and Strategic Innovation. This degree program for professionals is a flexible suite of on-line subjects, studios and labs.

While the degree is suitable for individuals, ideally organizations should enroll groups of staff to strategically build innovation capability across their existing departments and disciplines - effectively building a Studio. Some people will take the full Masters to become the core innovation leaders, others can take separate subjects to build capability and support the innovation network.

Masters Curriculum

Masterclass

The key concepts and through a short project, creating strategic advice for an industry partner. This gives a sense of how the creation of deep change can be approached in practice.

Transdisciplinarity

Participants are challenged to think about their own discipline and work environment in terms of practices; interrogating patterns and assumptions guiding what is the 'normal'.

Fields of Thought

We explore concepts, principles, practices and methods from various disciplinary fields. These lenses/ this depth of thought is then used to examine your own professional practice from different philosophical and pragmatic perspectives.

Complexity

How do we better recognize, think, communicate, and act within complex systems, moving beyond problem-solving approaches.

Frame Creation and Co-evolution

The Frame Creation model is explored and the participants are challenged to explore a complex problem situation from within their own organization.

Futures

This subject starts by questioning the assumptions that underpin the approaches to futuring and innovation in your discipline, and then moves on to articulating multiple alternative future landscapes for your professional field.

Future value and impact

This is a hands-on subject introducing a very wide range of futuring methods from different fields. The participants experiment with these in creating possible future scenarios for their own sector and society more broadly, and explore how these can be used to drive positive change on a world scale (Sustainable Development Goals).

Networks & ecosystems

In this subject we introduce methods and tools for creating networks of committed people: what does it take to create a Studio and/or Innovation Ecosystem?

Changing Minds

Various theories and models to detect elusive patterns of practice that can inhibit change, and examines a range of practices to overcome these.

Theory of Change

Here we examine the various theories, principles and methods of organizational change, devise speculative strategies for creating change and critically assess the applicability of these approaches in your own work. Then the challenge is to create your own theory of change.

Creative Practices and Methods

Participants explore creative practices and tools from across many professional domains to generate, discover and explore new ideas, insights and solutions.

Context Challenges

Participants come together to collectively take on a complex real-world challenge for a partner organization and apply, trial and experiment with the concrete methods and tools you have gained through other subjects within the Studio environment.

Bespoke Labs

Detailed in §2.8.

This program was designed by the first author, Kees Dorst, with Rodger Watson (second author, and also founding course director) and Katrina Moore with many industry partners.

As the practice of a Next Generation Strategic Innovator is a very fluid new role, responding to very fluid and changing environments, a curriculum like this is, and has to be, forever unfinished. The third co-author of this book, Barbara Doran, has picked up the challenge to develop the offering further in response to developing insights.

5.4

THE MOVEMENT

The models and structures in this book are meaningless unless they are acted upon by inspired people. In his book *The Timeless Way of Building*, the architect and philosopher Christopher Alexander (1979) ponders what it is we strive for in life - what he calls the 'quality without a name'.

"The search which we make for this quality [the quality without a name], in our own lives, is the central search of any person and the crux of any individual person's story. It is the search for these moments and situations when we are most alive."

This notion of 'feeling alive' then is never defined in his book. That may seem problematic, but in fact it is not. Because 'feeling alive' is so closely tied to our human nature, we can recognize it by intuition - we just know.

This is a great help in navigating the complex world of projects and jobs. Whatever we chose to do should create these moments of aliveness in us. This is doubly important for innovators.

Innovation requires working with others, to get people along, take them on the journey with you and to inspire them with approaches, ideas, findings, insights. For this, inspiration is our secret weapon. But you can only authentically inspire people when you are inspired yourself.

We hope that this book has inspired you.

There is no need to try this alone, you have now met a collection of pioneers reinventing strategic innovation, each in their own way.

APPENDICES

APPENDIX 1 - FRAME CREATION STEPS

APPENDIX 2 - PRINCIPLES

APPENDIX 3 - NEXT GENERATION STRATEGIC INNOVATOR

APPENDIX 1 - FRAME CREATION STEPS

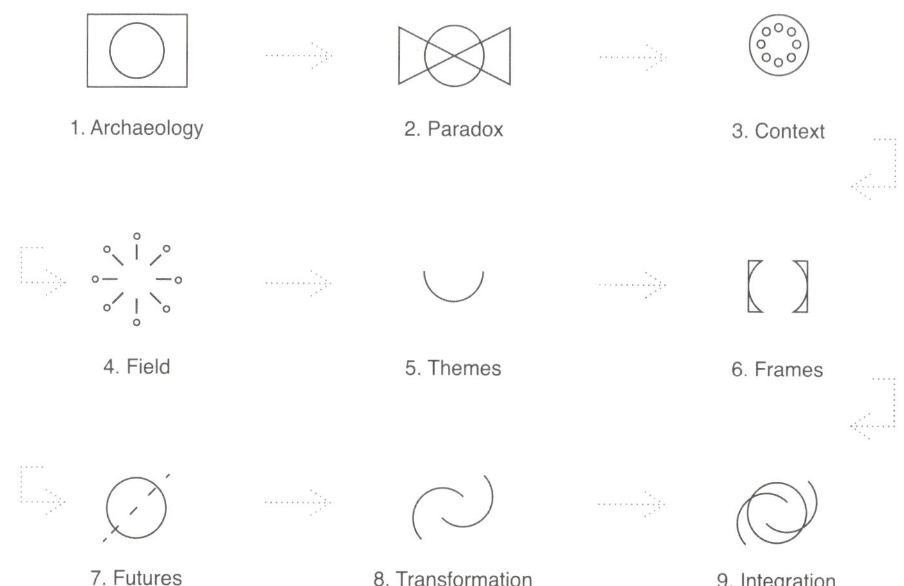

FRAME CREATION

The frame creation workshop is a definitive moment in our process. This workshop provides an opportunity for people from the stakeholder network to come together and think afresh, using their combined knowledge; to take a long walk around the problem, suspend judgment about how to solve it, and create frames that provides new ideas. The workshop also helps generate the momentum that is required in the long term, to carry solutions to fruition.

Several versions of the frame creation workshop have been developed, ranging from a rapid two-hour version, to a five-day-long 'deep dive'. The latter leads to better results, but for the purposes of this book, we offer here the one-day version of the workshop. The methods that follow should be completed in the sequence they are presented, since each tool builds on the previous one. The first two methods are done with the 'plenary' group; if there are more than, say, eight workshop participants, later methods are done in smaller sub-groups, while others are done in pairs.

When planning a frame creation workshop, foundational research into the problem context is important to identify potential participants (stakeholders) and provide sufficient grounding in the subject matter to ensure that facilitators feel comfortable leading a group of people that will include content experts. (As a side note, facilitators do not need to become experts in content to run the workshop effectively.) Irrespective of the total number of participants, try and get as broad a spread of stakeholders as you can.

The methods shown here have been developed by Designing Out Crime and tested on many 'real' projects as well as in 'lab'-style conditions. Some have been inspired the work of collaborators from our network, and all of them have been refined through practice.

Here we use the Kings Cross case from §4.2 as a running example for the different steps of the Frame Creation workshop.

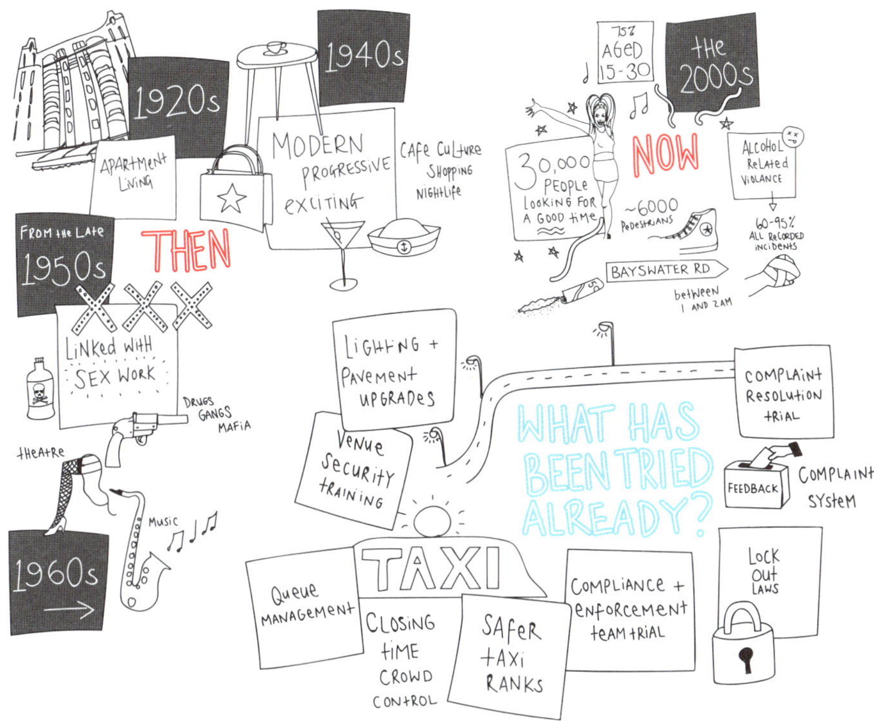

ARCHAEOLOGY

Organizations operate at several levels, and problems manifest in many ways. Consequently, problem-solving efforts can take many shapes and forms. They may be political, strategic, or tactical; they may involve few people or many; and they will vary in success and impact.

This tool - the first in the frame creation workshop - is used to map out all and any past actions that could be considered as attempts to solve the problem as it presents. The aim is to create an exhaustive list that provides background, but also to allow participants to 'purge' or park their thoughts about the problem, and not to fixate on what has already been attempted. This exercise can be done with all workshop participants in a 'plenary' session, or in smaller sub-groups of participants.

DURATION: 20 minutes to list, 10 minutes to discuss.

QUESTIONS: What has been tried before, and to what extent have these efforts been successful?

ACTIONS: Ask the question and list the responses on a whiteboard or flip-charts. Encourage everyone to participate - there are no wrong answers - but gently dissuade participants from debating the merits or pitfalls of problem-solving efforts while the list is being made. When there is a natural pause in the room, read over the list and give participants the opportunity to comment or discuss.

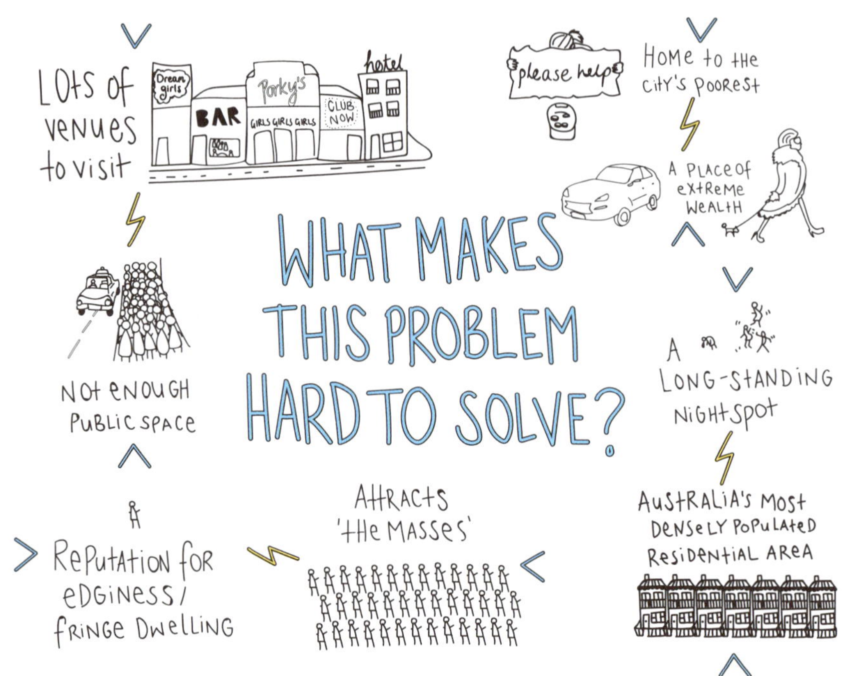

PARADOX

In a complex problem, there are usually many pairs of oppositional forces that confound attempts to solve it. In the frame creation workshop we refer to these oppositional forces as 'paradoxes'. Identifying the paradoxes, then setting them aside, is an important early step in the workshop process and is done with the plenary group of participants.

Duration: 15 minutes

QUESTIONS: What makes this problem so hard to solve? What are the opposing forces in the problem context?

ACTIONS: One facilitator asks the questions, while another writes the responses on a whiteboard or flip-chart. Responses to the first question (what makes this hard to solve?) should be noted down and discussed, and when the responses begin to flow, facilitators can guide participants to reformulate their answers into statements of opposing forces.

Some examples of these pairs of opposing forces are described below using the example of Kings Cross in the project 'Growing Up In Public':

For a place to be vibrant, there needs to be a critical mass of people

vs.

If a place is vibrant and popular, and attracts large numbers of people, it can become unpredictable and hard to manage

and

Young people get in trouble when they go to Kings Cross

vs.

Kings Cross's reputation for edginess and danger makes it attractive to young people

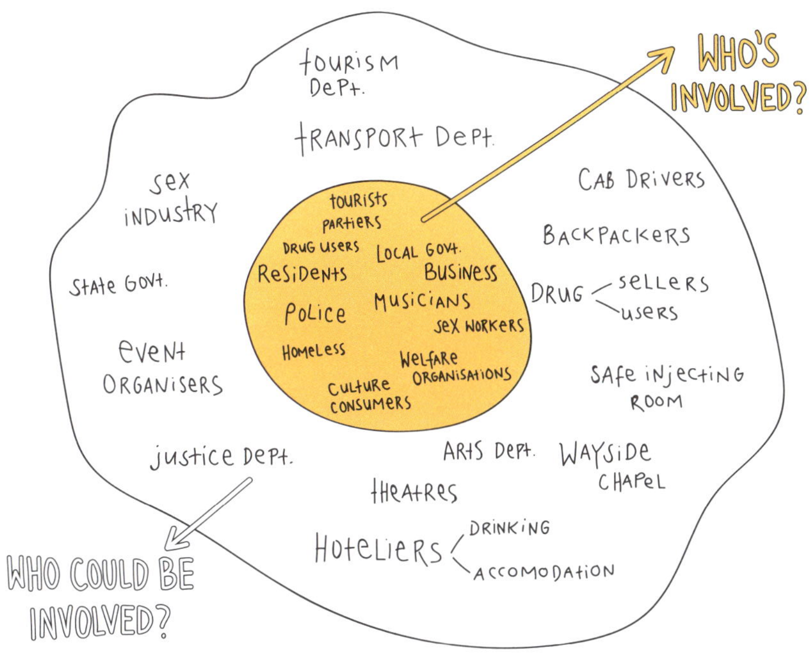

CONTEXT AND FIELD

People are accustomed to seeing thing through their own individual or organizational lens. This necessarily narrow viewpoint is important - it helps us get on with lives and jobs, day to day. But an essential part of exploring a problem through frame creation is expansion - making a situation more complex, adding rather than subtracting.

In this exercise, we aim to widen our view of who is involved in a problem situation. We use a specific terminology to categorize stakeholders according to how 'close' they are to a problem. In the frame creation workshop, stakeholders who are closely connected to a problem - having either been affected by it, or involved in previous attempts at solutions - are described as the 'context' stakeholders. The wider group of stakeholders - those who could conceivably be involved in a future solution - are those in the 'field'. Note that stakeholders can be specific individuals, generic groups or organizations.

This exercise - and several that follow - is generally done in sub-groups of around six people, since participants need to be able to gather around a shared writing/reading surface (whiteboard, paper, wall) and discuss what is written on it. Allow for one facilitator per group.

Duration: 10 minutes.

QUESTIONS:

Context: Which stakeholders have been a) directly impacted by the issue in question, or b) had direct influence in this problem situation?

Field: Which stakeholders could be involved in, or interested in a solution?

ACTIONS: This is a generative exercise - more is better. Write the 'context' stakeholders in the center, and the 'field' stakeholders in the outer circle.

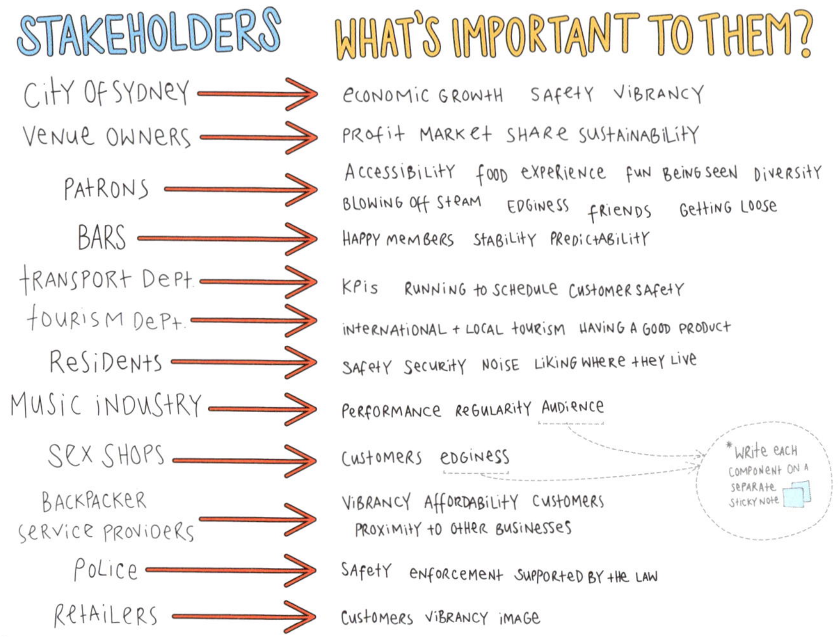

THEMES

By analyzing what our stakeholders value, we can better understand the complexities of the problem context. This exercise is done in the same small sub-group as the previous tool.

Duration: 30 minutes

QUESTIONS: What is important to the stakeholders? (and creative variations, e.g. 'What gets X out of bed in the morning?)

ACTIONS: Have the participants take a selection of the stakeholders identified in the previous tool (eight, or more if time permits). Write the name of each stakeholder down the left-hand side of a piece of paper or whiteboard and ask participants 'What is important to them?' Think about each stakeholder in succession, and have participants write their responses next to the stakeholder. (We recommend writing each response on a separate sticky note as this will be used as data in the next method.)

Encourage participants to think, and answer, in terms of 'human' (rather than organizational or bureaucratic) values or concerns. For example, if the stakeholder were a company, one response to the question 'What is important to the company?' would be 'money'. We can expand this idea into more empathetic concepts by asking why money is important, and to think in terms of the employees (organizations don't really have 'values', people do). Money is important because it gives a company a future, affords a lifestyle for individuals, is a reward for hard work... and so on. There are no wrong answers but resist the temptation to be sarcastic - empathy is one of the goals in this exercise. Aim for 'positive' values. Note that there will be much repetition, which is an inherent consequence of the exercise and, indeed, an important point to hammer home: different people value the same basic things in spite of appearances, and this realization is crucial to designing something that will satisfy the majority.

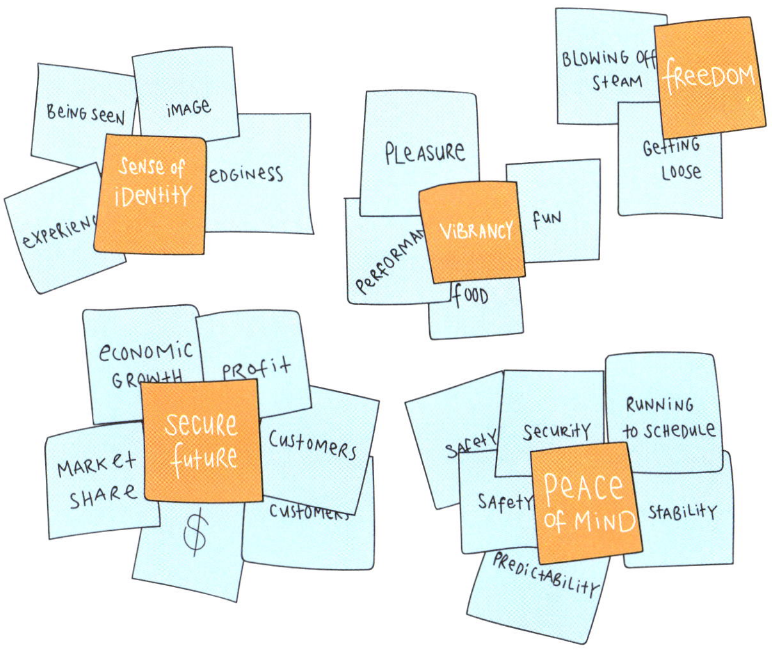

THEMES

In this part of the frame creation workshop we move away from concrete analysis of the situation and into abstraction. The exercise helps participants to form an understanding of the shared interests or values of the stakeholders connected to the problem. These shared values we call 'themes', and arriving at themes is the goal of this exercise.

Duration: 20 minutes

ACTIONS: As a group, and on a separate worksheet, cluster the responses from the previous method (which are, ideally, written on sticky notes) into groups of similar concepts. Encourage everyone to participate. Remember that there will be repetition among the responses in the previous exercise, so some clusters may contain virtually a single idea, written many times.

Do this roughly and rapidly until every response from the previous method has been put into a cluster. Once this is done, discuss and analyze each cluster, and regroup clusters if necessary, by asking questions like 'What is this cluster about?' and 'Are these concepts really related, or does this idea perhaps belong in another cluster?'

Next, give each cluster a definitive name. Ask participants to drill down to the deep, shared human needs represented in each cluster. For example, of a group of words relating to financial security, ask 'what core needs drive the desire for financial security? What does financial security give us?' Personal experience can guide this exercise. Explore synonyms until the group settles on a satisfactory word or phrase that sums cluster up (and note that, as a result of this step you may need to shuffle the clusters around yet again).

Finally, place a name in the center of each cluster. From this point in the workshop, each cluster. From this point in the workshop, each cluster name is now referred to as a "theme".

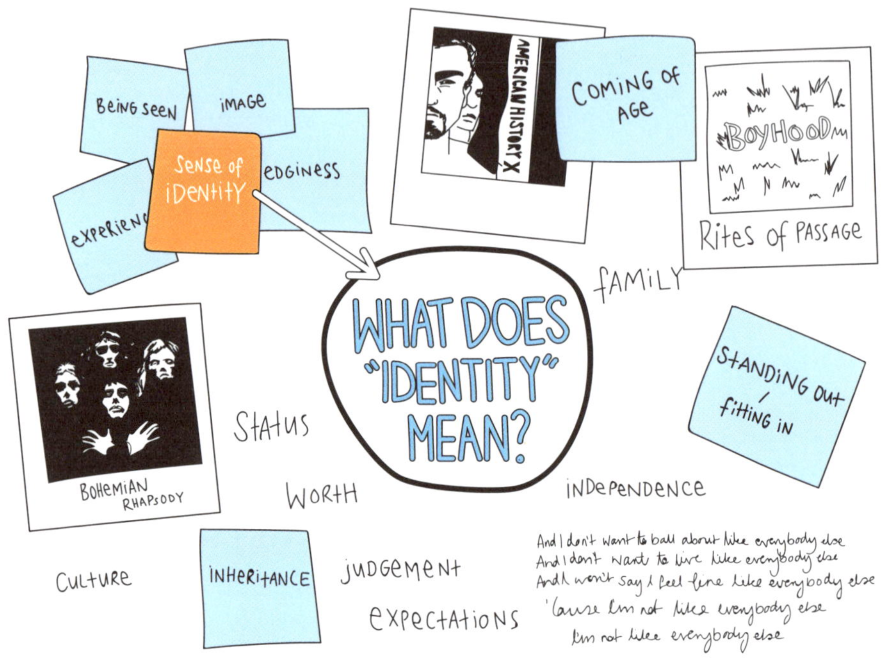

THEMES

Poets, authors, songwriters, visual artists and movie-makers are adept at communicating thematic meaning, showing us how themes play out on a human level. We can also understand themes by exploring experiences from our own lives. This method asks participants to analyze deeply the themes that they identified in the previous exercise.

Duration: 30 minutes

QUESTIONS: Describe a personal experience of the (theme). What novels, songs, movies, etc. convey the meaning of the theme, as you understand it?

ACTIONS: Ask participants to form pairs. Depending on the size of each subgroup and the number of pairs and themes, each pair will discuss and analyze one or more themes. Use the questions above as prompts.

To explore the theme 'sense of identity', for example, participants can think of how people (themselves, others) acquire a sense of identity or a sense of self.

Participants can ask their partners 'What identity-forming experiences have you had? When do you feel most like yourself? When and where do you feel able to express your identity?'

Personal stories are interesting and valuable, as everyone's experience will be different. The pairs then share and discuss their findings with their subgroup.

FRAMES

A 'frame' is a viewpoint that gives a different perspective on a situation. There are many ways of constructing frames and many ways in which a frame can be overlaid onto a problem context. In a workshop setting, metaphors and analogies make effective frames. To use, again, the example from 'Growing Up in Public': in exploring the theme 'sense of identity', we asked the question 'what other experiences give young people the opportunity to find/develop/ express their identity in a positive way?' One answer was 'a music festival'. We then mapped out the main characteristics and operating principles of the 'ideal' music festival (i.e. the music festival we would aspire to create), and found in this context both an approach (event management) and many ideas that could be transposed from the music festival environment to Kings Cross at night.

As a rule of thumb, a 'fruitful' frame is one that makes sense to all the stakeholders and helps them envision a new approach to the problem.

Duration: 1 hour

QUESTIONS: Consider one or more of the themes (values) you have identified in previous methods. Is there a discipline area or profession that is especially known for creating these values? Is there another context or situation where these values are very keenly expressed?

Next, examine the working principles used in these alternative disciplines or situations. What activities do actors in these contexts do that could be adapted to the current problem?

ACTIONS: In subgroups, create alternative frames. Test each for fruitfulness: if a frame is not fruitful (e.g. if discussion stagnates, if no new ideas emerge) discard it and try another, or start the exercise again.

FUTURES

In the previous method, multiple frames were created. In this method, we aim to articulate the fruitful frames in more depth and extrapolate the new approach, goals and scenarios that arise from these new frames. We also use this method as a way of seeing the current ('old') approach in a critical light, and to understand how existing solutions are underpinned by a particular viewpoint (as shown at left).

For instance, from the new frame of the music festival, and the new approach of event management, the City of Sydney reformulated their original goal of trying to prevent alcohol related violence into the creation of a thriving late night economy. From this new goal, new scenarios and solutions could be expressed.

Duration: 5 minutes to explore each frame, 20 minutes to discuss and decide which solutions to develop further.

QUESTIONS: What organizational goals should be set to achieve the desired values? What scenarios need to be created to enable this (i.e. what roles can different stakeholders play)? What actions will need to be taken to achieve the solutions arising from the frame?

ACTIONS: Use the diagram below as a template. Start with the most fruitful frame from the previous method, and populate headings 1-3 with the data from the previous method. As an optional extra step, forensically analyze current ('old') solutions to understand the scenarios, goals and values that underpin them.

PROBLEM FRAME
ALCOHOL RELATED CRIME
SOLUTION FRAME
CRIME PREVENTION

PROBLEM FRAME
A MUSIC FESTIVAL
SOLUTION FRAME
EVENT MANAGEMENT

OLD		NEW	
More police / security "drunk tanks" tougher laws	**ACTIONS**	Crowd control managed taxi ranks public toilets diverse businesses	3.
Crime prevention partnership	**METHODS**	City council as event manager	2.
Reduce opportunities for crime	**PRINCIPLES**	Create a thriving late night economy	1.
Security, safety	**VALUES**	Vibrancy Identity	

APPENDIX 2 - PRINCIPLES

The following are rules and principles established to guide and foster positive and productive cultures. In establishing the principles for your innovation ecosystem, we thought that these could give some inspiration.

Backstory

These rules emerged bottom-up from the practices of the developing Burning Man events, from the early days on a Seattle beach - a fascinating story in itself, check it out at your leisure. The enormous scale of the events in the desert requires a deep level of common understanding and also organization, which is not easily achieved when the whole event is focused on freedom of experiment and creative expression.

The nine rules below were created as a 'cultural guide' to try and achieve this paradoxical result. The nine rules weren't much liked and consequently didn't really work that well, until the 10th rule was added by the founder. Then everything fell into place.

Since then, these rules (and lots of special practices we can discuss in our session) have allowed spin-off festivals across the globe that all manage to take part in the fantastic culture of Burning Man.

Burning Man principles

Radical Inclusion

Anyone may be a part of Burning Man. We welcome and respect the stranger. No prerequisites exist for participation in our community.

Gifting

Burning Man is devoted to acts of gift giving. The value of a gift is unconditional. Gifting does not contemplate a return or an exchange for something of equal value.

Decommodification

In order to preserve the spirit of gifting, our community seeks to create social environments that are unmediated by commercial sponsorships, transactions, or advertising. We stand ready to protect our culture from such exploitation. We resist the substitution of consumption for participatory experience.

Radical Self-reliance

Burning Man encourages the individual to discover, exercise and rely on his or her inner resources.

Radical Self-expression

Radical self-expression arises from the unique gifts of the individual. No one other than the individual or a collaborating group can determine its content. It is offered as a gift to others. In this spirit, the giver should respect the rights and liberties of the recipient.

Communal Effort

Our community values creative cooperation and collaboration. We strive to produce, promote and protect social networks, public spaces, works of art, and methods of communication that support such interaction.

Civic Responsibility

We value civil society. Community members who organize events should assume responsibility for public welfare and endeavor to communicate civic responsibilities to participants. They must also assume responsibility for conducting events in accordance with local, state and federal laws.

Leaving No Trace

Our community respects the environment. We are committed to leaving no physical trace of our activities wherever we gather. We clean up after ourselves and endeavor, whenever possible, to leave such places in a better state than when we found them.

Participation

Our community is committed to a radically participatory ethic. We believe that transformative change, whether in the individual or in society, can occur only through the medium of deeply personal participation. We achieve being through doing. Everyone is invited to work. Everyone is invited to play. We make the world real through actions that open the heart.

Immediacy

Immediate experience is, in many ways, the most important touchstone of value in our culture. We seek to overcome barriers that stand between us and a recognition of our inner selves, the reality of those around us, participation in society, and contact with a natural world exceeding human powers. No idea can substitute for this experience.

THE DOGME GOALS & RULES

Backstory

The Dogme 95 movement produced some very raw and disturbing films. The rules were developed by von Trier and Vinterberg as a set of constraints and enablers (see rule 10) to elevate story, acting, and theme in film-making.

To this end, von Trier and Vinterberg produced ten rules to which any Dogme film must conform and are referred to as the "Vow of Chastity".

1. Shooting must be done on location. Props and sets must not be brought in (if a particular prop is necessary for the story, a location must be chosen where this prop is to be found).
2. The sound must never be produced apart from the images or vice versa. (Music must not be used unless it occurs where the scene is being shot)
3. The camera must be hand-held. Any movement or immobility attainable in the hand is permitted.
4. The film must be in color. Special lighting is not acceptable. (If there is too little light for exposure the scene must be cut or a single lamp be attached to the camera.)
5. Optical work and filters are forbidden.
6. The film must not contain superficial action. (Murders, weapons, etc. must not occur.)
7. Temporal and geographical alienation are forbidden. (That is to say that the film takes place here and now.)
8. Genre movies are not acceptable.
9. The film format must be Academy 35mm.
10. The director must not be credited.

BRIAN ENO'S OBLIQUE STRATEGIES

Brian Eno and Peter Schmidt (1975) have developed and used these strategies to insert creativity into situations where people are working together, originally in the context of the recording studio.

These are available at enoshop.co.uk

THE BOOK OF FIVE RINGS

Miomoto Musashi, the Book of Five Rings (1645)

"This is the way for men who want to learn my strategy."

1. Do not think dishonestly.
2. The Way is in training.
3. Become acquainted with every art.
4. Know the ways of all professions.
5. Distinguish between gain and loss in worldly matters.
6. Develop intuitive judgment and understanding for everything.
7. Perceive those things which cannot be seen.
8. Pay attention even to trifles
9. Do nothing which is of no use.

RICHARD STRAUSS' TEN GOLDEN RULES FOR THE ALBUM OF A YOUNG CONDUCTOR

1. Remember that you are making music not to amuse yourself, but to delight your audience.
2. You should not perspire when conducting. Only the audience should get warm.
3. Conduct Salome and Elektra as if they were by Mendelssohn: Fairy music.
4. Never look encouragingly at the brass, except with a brief glance to give an important cue.
5. But never let the horns and woodwinds out of your sight. If you can hear them at all, they are still too strong.
6. If you think that the brass is now blowing hard enough, tone it down another shade or two.
7. It is not enough that you yourself should hear every word the soloist sings. You should know it by heart anyway. The audience must be able to follow without effort. If they do not understand the words, they will go to sleep.
8. Always accompany the singer in such a way that he can sing without effort.
9. When you think you have reached the limits of prestissimo, double the pace.
10. If you follow these rules carefully, you will, with your fine gifts and your great accomplishments, always be the darling of your listeners.

INNOVATION AS A COMPLEX SOCIAL PRACTICE

(Inspired by Hwang & Horowitt, 2012)

1. **It's Not Just the Ingredients–It's the Interaction**
   Innovation ecosystems don't emerge by simply assembling talent, capital, and ideas. Like a rain forest, they depend on the interplay between these elements. It's not a matter of inputs, but of context and relationships that enable serendipity and novelty.

2. **Plantations Are Efficient. Rain forests Are Generative.**
   The "plantation" model–linear, managed, efficient–is good for scaling known solutions. But innovation lives in complexity and diversity. The "rain forest" model supports the wild growth of ideas, especially those that don't fit established patterns. It requires environments that embrace ambiguity, failure, and emergence.

3. **Markets Don't Automatically Enable Innovation**
   Markets distribute known value efficiently–but they don't create it. Innovation needs something more: a system that lowers invisible barriers (like mistrust, distance, or social silos) and deliberately connects unlikely collaborators.

4. **Human Nature Works Against Innovation–Unless We Design for It**
   We default to familiarity and tribalism. That's a problem, because breakthrough value often arises between people with different worldviews. Innovation ecosystems must actively counteract these biases by fostering long-term, trust-based exchange over short-term, self-serving transactions.

5. **Keystone Actors Enable the System**
   Certain people and institutions serve as connectors, trust brokers, and culture-setters. They bridge divides, facilitate collaboration, and embody the values the ecosystem needs. Without them, the social "plumbing" of innovation clogs.

6. **Culture Eats Capital for Breakfast**
   Capital is not just financial. It's social. It flows through relationships. In high-functioning ecosystems, investors and entrepreneurs see each other as co-creators, not adversaries. The best systems align incentives for mutual, sustained benefit–across stages, from seed to scale.

7. **You Can't Measure What Matters Directly–But You Must Try**
   Traditional metrics fail to capture the subtle dynamics that drive innovation. What matters is flow: the movement of people, ideas, and trust. Proxy indicators–collaboration frequency, deal speed, network density–can signal ecosystem health.

8. **The Work Is Cultural, Not Just Structural**
   Innovation requires re-engineering human behavior. That means cultivating cultures of openness, experimentation, fairness, and generosity. The future lies in "active capitalism": intentionally designing ecosystems that generate the conditions for serendipitous collaboration to occur.

APPENDIX 3 - NEXT GENERATION STRATEGIC INNOVATOR

STEWARD OF THE FUTURE

Are you ready to be guide of the future where in a world that's complex and anything but straightforward? We're seeking a fearless navigator of change who can transform people and organizations with seemingly intractable challenges into breakthrough spaces.

Your Mission (should you choose to accept it)

YES!

~~NO!~~

Dive into the deep end of innovation where your imagination becomes the compass for organizational transformation. As our Strategic Innovator, you'll see "what's next," turning abstract challenges into concrete strategies that nobody else saw coming.

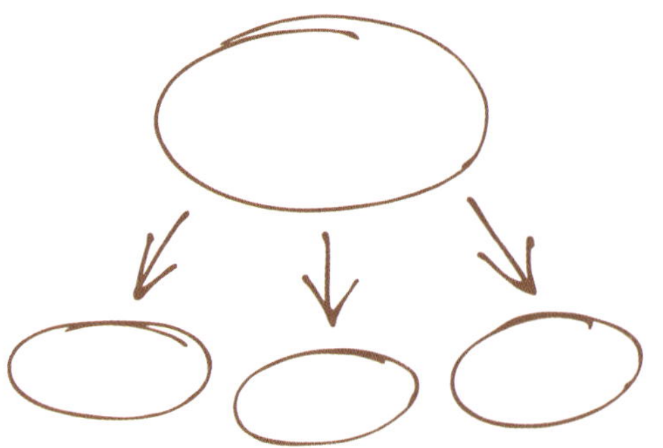

What You'll Actually Do

- Transform traditional thinking into quantum leaps of innovation, using creativity as your superpower to tackle complex challenges that make others run for cover
- Orchestrate diverse teams and minds, turning potential chaos into integrated collaboration
- Lead change initiatives that don't just adapt to the future but actively shape it, using your workspace as a living laboratory for innovation
- Navigate through complexity with the grace of a tightrope walker and the strategic mind of a chess grandmaster

Your Superpowers Should Include

- The ability to see around corners, identify blind spots and spot opportunities where others see obstacles
- A mind that metabolizes new information like a creative powerhouse, turning data into insights and insights into action
- The finesse to build bridges between different disciplines and communities creating symphonies of collaboration where others hear noise
- A natural talent for making the complex simple and the impossible achievable

What Makes You Perfect for This Role

- You're allergic to "we've always done it this way" thinking
- Your idea of fun is dismantling complex problems and rebuilding them into innovative opportunities
- You've got a track record of inspiring teams through transformative change (bonus points if you did it while everyone was smiling)
- You're comfortable in the trenches of practical execution and the stratosphere of strategic thinking

What We Offer

- A playground for your imagination where "thinking outside the box" is just the beginning
- The chance to work with independent, passionate minds who make the future their daily responsibility
- A platform to be part of a network of change-makers who are actively reshaping industries
- The opportunity to turn your work challenges into real-world transformations.

The Fine Print

This isn't just another job - it's an invitation to be part of a movement that's redefining how organizations tackle complexity. We're not looking for someone to maintain the status quo; we're seeking a masters of change who can turn creativity into collaborative benefits. Your journey to a creative legacy you can be at peace with, starts here.

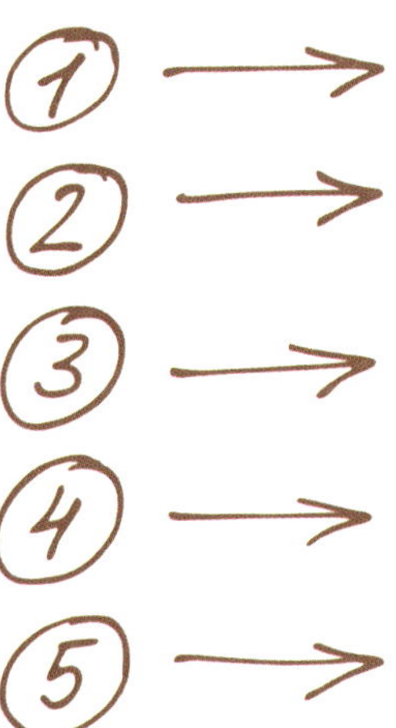

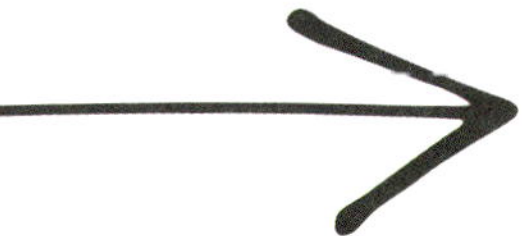

AUTHOR BIOGRAPHIES

Kees Dorst is Professor at Princeton University's Keller Center and at the University of Technology Sydney. He is considered one of the lead thinkers developing the field of design, valued for his ability to connect a philosophical understanding of the logic of design with hands-on practice. He has developed a set of methodologies to tackle today's complex organizational and societal challenges.

Rodger Watson is an innovator and educator committed to the common good. Drawing on his expertise in design, innovation, psychology, and criminology he advises public, private, and nonprofit organizations on innovation strategy. He is a Research Fellow at Central Saint Martins, University of the Arts London and Adjunct Fellow at the University of Technology Sydney.

Dr Barbara Doran directs Creative Intelligence and Strategic Innovation at the University of Technology, Sydney. She brings deep expertise in creativity as a catalyst for change, helping people and organizations expand how they think, collaborate, and lead. Barbara drives national and international projects that activate wellbeing, unlock creative capacity, and deliver transformative impact across sectors.

ACKNOWLEDGMENTS

This book is somewhat of a life's work. It brings together thinking and doing (the theory and the practices) developed over a period of more than 15 years. And not just by us, the main authors: as you have seen, there are more than 30 contributors to this book. You have put great trust in us, and committed considerable effort to making the world a better place. We would like to thank each and every one of you for doing so, and for being on the journey with us.

Around us there are hundreds of people we have all worked (and lived) with along the way, the people who over the years have helped to create the professional and lifeworld conditions where this body of work could happen - it is impossible to name you all in person here, but please know that we thank you deeply. Good things don't happen by accident.

Kees Dorst

Rodger Watson

Barbara Doran

REFERENCES

Alexander, C. (1979). *The timeless way of building (Vol. 1)*. New york: Oxford university press.

Antle, M. C., & Silver, R. (2005). Orchestrating time: Arrangements of the brain circadian clock. *Trends in Neurosciences*, 28(3), 145-151.

Argyris, C. (2000). *Flawed advice and the management trap: How managers can know when they're getting good advice and when they're not. Oxford University Press.*

Beccaria, C. (1764). *On crimes and punishments.* (Original Italian: Dei delitti e delle pene). Massé.

Berger, W. (2019). *The book of beautiful questions: The powerful questions that will help you decide, create, connect, and lead.* Bloomsbury.

Bernard, T. J., Snipes, J. B., & Gerould, A. L. (2010). Vold's theoretical criminology (7th ed.). Oxford University Press.

van der Bijl-Brouwer, M., & Dorst, K. (2017). Advancing the strategic impact of human-centred design. *Design Studies*, 53, 1-23.

Blake, W. (1790). *The Marriage of Heaven and Hell.*

Brown, S. (2009). *Play: How it shapes the brain, opens the imagination, and invigorates the soul.* Penguin.

Bourdieu, P., Accardo, A., & Balazs, G. (1999). *The weight of the world: Social suffering in contemporary society.*

Bower, D. J., Crabtree, E., & Keogh, W. (1997). Rhetorics and realities in new product development in the subsea oil industry. *International Journal of Project Management*, 15(6), 345-350.

Byrne, D. (2017). *How music works*. Crown.

Campbell, J. (2003). *The hero's journey: Joseph Campbell on his life and work* (Vol. 7). New World Library.

Camus, A. (1955). *The Myth of Sisyphus.* 1942. *Translated by Justin O'Brien.*

Candy, S., & Kornet, K. (2019). Turning Foresight Inside Out: An Introduction to Ethnographic Experiential Futures. *Journal of Futures Studies, 23(3).*

Cave, N. (2022). Is it better to keep quiet, or to speak one's mind? *The Red Hand Files (Issue #212).*

Chambliss, W. J. (2001). Making law: The state, the law, and structural stratification. *Parliamentary Affairs, 54*(3), 528-541.

Cleese, J. (1991). And now for something completely different. *Management Review*, 80(5), 50.

Cohen, J. J. (2015). *Stone: An ecology of the inhuman.* University of Minnesota Press.

Cohen, L. E., & Felson, M. (2010). Social change and crime rate trends: A routine activity approach (1979). *In Classics in environmental criminology* (pp. 203-232). Routledge.

Cottam, H. (2018). *Radical help: How we can remake the relationships between us and revolutionise the welfare state.* Hachette UK.

Coupland, J. (2014). *Small talk.* Routledge.

Cross, N. (2006). *Designerly Ways of Knowing.* London: Springer.

Dewey, J. (1910). *How we think.* D.C. Heath & Co.

Dewey, J. (1925). *Experience and nature.* Open Court Publishing.

Dewey, J. (1933). *How we think: A restatement of the relation of reflective thinking to the educative process.* D.C. Heath & Co.

Diller, S., Shedroff, N., & Rhea, D. (2005). *Making meaning: How successful businesses deliver meaningful customer experiences.* New Riders.

Doran, B. (2025). *Creative practice and embodied narratives: Transdisciplinary inquiry through the body, story, and system.* Palgrave Macmillan. (Palgrave Advances in Possibility Studies).

Doran, B., & Watson, R. (2021). *Creative Reboot.* BIS Publishers, Amsterdam.

Dorst, K. (2008). *Design expertise: What it is and how to pursue it.* BIS Publishers.

Dorst, K. (2015). *Frame innovation: Create new thinking by design.* MIT press.

Dorst, K., Kaldor, L., Klippan, L., & Watson, R. (2016). *Designing for the common good.* BIS Publishers.

Dorst, K. (2017). *Notes on design.* BIS Publishers.

Dorst, K. (2018). "Mixing Practices to Create Transdisciplinary Innovation: A Design-Based Approach." *Technology Innovation Management Review* 8: 60-65.

Dorst, K., & Watson, R. (2023). "There is no such thing as strategic design." *Design Studies*, 86, Article 101185.

Dorst, K., & Schaminée, A. (2024). Designing for hypercomplexity: A case study. In Proceedings of the Design Thinking Research Symposium 14 (DTRS14) (Vol. 14, pp. 107-134).

Dorst, K. (2025). *Deep Change: Creating Space for Meaningful Transformation.* MIT Press.

Dylan, B. (1963). *The times they are a-changin'* [Song]. On The times they are a-changin'. Columbia Records.

Dylan, B. (1963). *Last thoughts on Woody Guthrie* [Spoken word recording]. Columbia Records.

Eno, B., & Schmidt, P. (1975). *Oblique strategies: Over one hundred worthwhile dilemmas* [Originally published as a set of cards].

Epp, F. A., Moesgen, T., Salovaara, A., Pouta, E., & Gaziulusoy, İ. (2022, June). Reinventing the wheel: The future ripples method for activating anticipatory capacities in innovation teams. *In Proceedings of the 2022 ACM designing interactive systems conference* (pp. 387-399).

Felson, M., & Clarke, R. V. (1998). Opportunity makes the thief. *Police research series, paper,* 98(1-36), 10.

Ford, D. (2007). *The search for meaning: A short history.* Univ of California Press.

Fournier, S., Lee, L. (2009). Getting brand communities right. Harvard Business Review, 87(4), 105-111.

Gardner, H. (2006). *Changing minds: The art and science of changing our own and other peoples minds.* Harvard Business Review Press.

Gidley, J. (2017). *The future: A new model for futures studies.* Routledge.

Glaser, B. G., & Strauss, A. L. (1967). *The discovery of grounded theory: Strategies for qualitative research.* Routledge.

Gould, S. J. (1996). *Mismeasure of man.* WW Norton & company.

Hassan, I. (2015). *The cultural politics of emotion.* Routledge.

Heifetz, R. A., Grashow, A., & Linsky, M. (2009). *The practice of adaptive leadership: Tools and tactics for changing your organization and the world.* Harvard Business Press.

Hill, D. (2022). *Designing missions: Mission-oriented innovation in Sweden - A practice guide.* Vinnova.

Hwang, V. W., & Horowitt, G. (2012). *The rainforest: The secret to building the next Silicon Valley.* Regenwald

Johnson, M. (2015). Embodied understanding. *Frontiers in Psychology, 6, 875.*

Kemmis, S. (2019). *Praxis, place, and participatory education: An introduction.* Springer.

King James Bible. (1769/2017). *The Holy Bible: King James Version.* Thomas Nelson. (Original work published 1769)

Koskinen, I., & Hush, J. (2016). *Design research through practice: From the lab, field, and showroom.* Morgan Kaufmann.

Kuhn, T. S. (1997). *The structure of scientific revolutions* (Vol. 962). Chicago: University of Chicago press.

Lake, D., & Whipps, J. (2023). Feminist pragmatist design: Evolutionary systems change. *Design Issues*, 39(4), 21-34. https://doi.org/10.1162/desi_a_00735

Lakoff, G., & Johnson, M. (1980). The metaphorical structure of the human conceptual system. *Cognitive science*, 4(2), 195-208.

Leadbeater, C. (2008). *We-think: Mass innovation, not mass production.* Profile Books.

Max-Neef, M. A. 2005. Foundations of Transdisciplinarity. *Ecological Economics*, 53(1): 5-16.

McChrystal, S., Collins, T., Silverman, D., & Fussell, C. (2015). Team of teams: New rules of engagement for a complex world. Penguin.

McGilchrist, I. (2019). *The master and his emissary: The divided brain and the making of the Western world* (2nd ed.). Yale University Press.

Musashi, M. (1993). The book of five rings (T. Cleary, Trans.). Shambhala. (Original work published 1645)

Nagji, B., & Tuff, G. (2012). Managing your innovation portfolio. Harvard Business Review, 90(5), 66-74.

Parks, N. (2014). *Narratives of social change.* Palgrave Macmillan.

Perowne, C. (1986). *Roman Mythology,* Newnes Books.

Pierce, C. S. (1931-1958). *Collected papers of Charles Sanders Peirce* (Vols. 1-8). Harvard University Press.

Pine, B. J., & Gilmore, J. H. (2013). The experience economy: past, present and future. *In Handbook on the experience economy* (pp. 21-44). Edward Elgar Publishing.

Powers, R. (2018). The overstory. W. W. Norton & Company.

Schaminée, A. (2018). *Designing with-in public organizations: Building bridges between public sector innovators and designers*, BIS Publishers.

Schön, D. A. (1992). *The reflective practitioner: How professionals think in action.* Routledge.

Slessor, K. (1933). *Five Bells.* Faber and Faber.

Soros, G. (2013). *The age of fallibility: Consequences of the war on terror.* PublicAffairs.

Stacey, R. D., Griffin, D., & Shaw, P. (2002). Complexity and management: Fad or radical challenge to systems thinking? Routledge.

Taylor, C. (1989). *Sources of the self: The making of the modern identity.* Harvard University Press.

Thinkplace. (2024). *Walgett community design report.* Thinkplace Publications.

Thomson, B. (2018). *Leadership and innovation in public services.* Routledge.

VandenBos, G. R. (Ed.). (2015). *APA dictionary of psychology* (2nd ed.). American Psychological Association.

Van Manen, M. (1990). *Researching lived experience: Human science for an action sensitive pedagogy.* State University of New York Press.

Vermaak, H., & de Caluwé, L. (2018). The colors of change revisited: Situating and describing the theory and its practical applications. *In R. Shani & D. Noumair (Eds.), Research in Organizational Change and Development* (Vol. 26, pp. 167-216). Emerald Publishing Limited.

Yunkaporta, T., & McGinty, S. (2009). Reclaiming aboriginal knowledge at the cultural interface. Aust. Educ. Res. 36, 55-72.

Yunkaporta, T. (2019). *Sand talk: How Indigenous thinking can save the world.* Text Publishing.

NOTES AND SKETCHES

SPARKS AND IDEAS

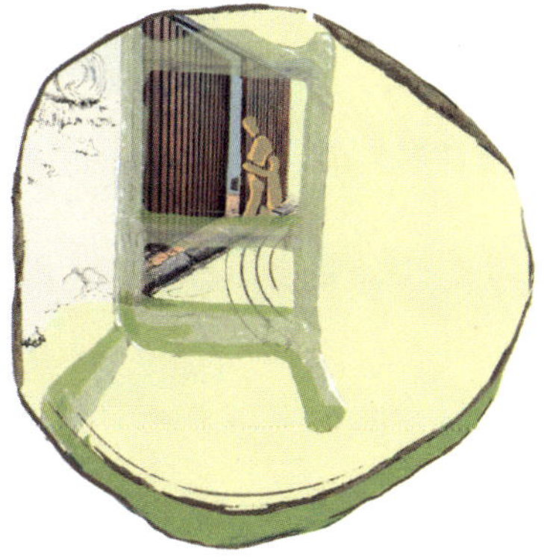